A SACRED TRUST

Stories Of Jewish Heritage & History

Rabbi Eugene Labovitz
Annette Labovitz

Volume One

Jewish Cultural Literacy Series

Isaac Nathan Publishing Co., Inc.
Los Angeles

Stories Copyright © 1994 by Annette Labovitz and Eugene Labovitz.

Maps and Time Lines Copyright © by Isaac Nathan Publishing Co., Inc.

10 9 8 7 6 5 4 3 2 1

Library of Congress Cataloging-in-Publication Data

Rabbi Eugene Labovitz, Annette Labovitz.

A Sacred Trust: Stories of Jewish Heritage & History

Volume One

ISBN 0-914615-12-2

Library of Congress Catalog Card Number: 94-068316

Manufactured in the United States of America,
Isaac Nathan Publishing Co., Inc.
22711 Cass Avenue, Woodland Hills, CA 91364

Contents

Part Three

The Sephardic Experience

Location Maps with Modern Borders

The Middle East, 12; Eretz Yisrael, Yerushalayim and Yavneh, 14; The Roman Empire versus Eretz Yisrael, 1st and 2nd century, 20 & 44; Jewish communities on the Tigris and Euphrates Rivers in Babylonia, 50; The Western Relocation of the Four Rabbinic Scholars, 76; Constantinople in the Middle Ages, 86; Mainz on Rhine, the Bamberg Monastary and Rome, 102; The Rhine River Valley, 112, 144 & 188; Medieval cities from *Tales of Rashi*; 118; German Crusade Route, 130; The Massacre at York, 136; Cracow and Rome, 172; Prague, 182; Prague & Amsterdam, 198; Northern German cities, 214; Spain & the Kingdom of Khazaria, 228; Granada, Spain, 233; Barcelona, Spain, 240; Spain to Eretz Yisrael, 250; Spain & Portugal at the time of the Expulsion, 260; Lisbon to Constantinople, 266; Spain, the Canary Islands & the New World, 276; Safed & Yerushalyaim in Eretz Yisrael, 282.

Acknowledgments

We wish to thank:

Rabbi Shlomo Carlebach, who showed us the effectiveness of authentic Jewish stories, and guided our research; David Epstein, our friend and publisher who believes in breaking rules in order to improve Jewish family education; Rabbi Chaim ben Zvi Asher Gross^ZʟL who taught us that through the pages of Jewish history we can learn to what lofty goals a Jew can aspire; Bertha (Bryna) Kwalwasser, my mother, of blessed memory, who was my wonderful role model in providing me with beautiful Jewish memories; Isadore (Yitzchak Elchanan) Kwalwasser, my father, of blessed memory, who inspired me, by his example, to know that the study of Torah is as precious as life itself; my brother Hy Labovitz and my late brother Joe Labovitz^ZʟL who physically sustained me through my yeshiva years; our devoted and loyal friends Rabbi Chaim and Devera Richter who were patient sounding boards for many of the ideas in these stories; and the congregants of Ner Tamid in Miami Beach, who listened to stories instead of sermons, and thereby helped up prove that stories are one of the most effective methods to attain Jewish cultural literacy.

Finally, our thanks to the rabbis, educators and Jewish professionals who contributed their thoughts and knowledge to the story introductions, thus bringing to life the Jewish values that sustained our people and brought us to today.

Rabbi Eugene Labovitz
Annette Labovitz

Preface

Our previous books have all had esoteric titles, but specific purposes. *In Time For My Soul*, we hoped that our readers would be inspired to set aside time to sanctify and nourish their souls by understanding the observances and rituals of our holy days. In *A Touch of Heaven* we explored how altruism, unlimited acts of kindness and devotion together create the ladder between man on earth and God in Heaven. The focus of these books was holy stories. We provided a glimpse of a world where man truly walks with God.

The title of these two volumes is, *A Sacred Trust: Stories of Jewish Heritage and History*. We chose these words because we believe that our magnificent heritage and history should be known to every Jew.

Ke le-kach tov na-ta-te la-chem, To-ra-te al ta-a-zo-vu.
"For I have given you a sacred trust,
abandon not my Torah."

Mishlei, Proverbs 4:2

A Sacred Trust is being published at a time when the Jewish community finds itself in the midst of a struggle over issues of identity and continuity. Communal leaders speculate whether we will be here tomorrow. We say "yes" for God promised that Jewish life will never be extinguished. To us, and many others, the real unknown is the quality of this Jewish life. To make it rich and meaningful we all need to gain basic knowledge. We need to expand our fundamental Jewish literacy level., so that we will know and understand how to live as Jews.

We have to make the decision whether we want to be ethnic Jews, often called lox-and-bagel Jews, or whether we want to be *Jewish* Jews; part of a dynamic Jewish culture.

The stories in this series of books cover the period from the destruction of our Second Holy Temple in the year 70 C.E. to modern times. Far too many people think that Jews, dressed in desert clothing, left the historical scene with the Roman conquest and dispersion 1,800 years ago, only to re-appear in Polish landlord garb in eastern Europe during the eighteenth century. Nothing could be further than the truth.

During this almost 2,000 year period, we survived, remained Jews, and, in many cases, were the glue that held together civilizations. Our values kept our people alive while other civilizations rose, fell and disappeared. These values run throughout the stories in *A Sacred Trust*.

We hope that both readers and users of these volumes will explore our precious and unique heritage with the goal of understanding what proceeded our generation, for the books include stories that every man, woman and child should know to be Jewishly culturally literate. By understanding the experiences and values of our ancestors we will be able to build meaningful Jewish bridges into the future.

Rabbi Eugene Labovitz
Annette Labovitz
January, 1995
Shevat, 5755

PART ONE
THE TALMUDIC AND POST-TALMUDIC PERIOD

Part One Time Period

| 70 c.e. | 600 c.e. | 1000 c.e. | 1400 c.e. | 1600 c.e. | 1800 c.e. | 2000 c.e. |

— Location: Ancient Israel and Babylonia/Persia —

INTRODUCTION

Our story begins in *Eretz Yisrael,* [the Holy Land], the ancestral homeland of the Jewish people. The country is small, triangular in shape, and it links three continents, Asia, Africa, and Europe. From time immemorial, it has been a coveted jewel, not for building, settlement, and development, but as a strategic crossroad. The ancient Egyptians, Assyrians, Babylonians, Greek/Syrians preceded the Romans In their conquest of the Holy Land.

The Romans lay siege to *Yerushalyaim* (Jerusalem) in 67 C.E., attempting to force the Jewish people to succumb to their rule by destroying the second Holy Temple, the symbol of Jewish nationalism. But Rabban Yochanan ben Zakkai understood that Jewish survival depended upon Torah, not upon buildings, so he risked his life, carefully planned his escape from the besieged city, sought out the Roman general, and beseeched him to permit the Sanhedrin, (the Jewish supreme court), to move to Yavneh, a sleepy village near the Mediterranean, away from the turmoil that seethed in *Yerushalyaim,* (Jerusalem). He prepared the Jewish people for the long, arduous exile which followed the Roman conquest. (*Rabban Yochanan ben Zakkai Saves Torah,* Chapter One.)

In Eretz Yisrael, other great leaders impacted Jewish history by their decisive accomplishments. Until the oppressive Roman restrictions prohibiting the study of Torah, scholars learned and transmitted Torah orally. Rabbi Akiva was apprehensive that the Jewish people would forget Torah, primarily because they feared gathering in study halls to learn. He began the process of writing down Jewish law which, upon the completion of the process by Rabbi Yehuda HaNasi some seventy years later, became known as the *Mishna.* Unsuccessful in his attempts to relieve his people from harsh Roman decrees, Rabbi Akiva became one of the revolutionaries that led the rebellion for Jewish independence against Rome. (*Rachel and Akiva,* Chapter Two; *The Ten Martyrs,* Chapter Four.)

Although the Talmud does not mention many women by name, those who were recorded for posterity are synonymous with learning and courage. Beruriah was one of those women. (*Beruriah: An Inspiring Lady*, Chapter Three.)

Because the mothers of Rabbi Yehuda HaNasi and Antoninus were friends, the boys grew up respecting each other's differences. Both became leaders. Rabbi Yehuda HaNasi became president of the Sanhedrin. Antoninus became Emperor Marcus Aurelius Antoninus. Roman oppression was eased allowing the Jewish people to live peacefully in their own land. Scholars were permitted to circulate throughout the country and to travel to the Babylonian/Persian Jewish community, modern day Iraq. (*Yehuda and Antoninus,* Chapter Five.)

After the destruction of the first Holy Temple by the Babylonians some six centuries before, Jews were taken into captivity and settled in Babylonia. There they planted seeds of a dynamic Jewish community. Even when allowed to return to Eretz Yisrael, most Jews chose to remain in Babylonia, where life was easier. As an increasing number of scholars traveled between the two countries, Babylonian Jewish life blossomed into a resplendent, scholarly community where the *Talmud Bavli* (the Talmud written in Babylonia) was developed. (*Rav, The Teacher's Teacher,* Chapter Six.)

The Jewish people lived in cities such as Sura, Pumpedita, Machoza, and Neherdea, located along the banks of the Tigris and Euphrates Rivers. The Sassanid rulers were cordial to the Jews who lived in their midst, and permitted them to live under their own autonomous system of government. In gratitude, Shmuel, one of the leading Babylonian scholars formulated a Talmudic dictum: *"Dena d'malchuta, dena:* the civil law of the land is the law by which we abide unless it contradicts Judaism)."[1]

The *Resh Galuta,* the Exilarch, descended from King David, was empowered with well defined political duties. He was the civil leader of the Jewish people and their representative to the throne. (*Bustenai,* Chapter Seven.)

The *Roshei Yeshivot,* heads of the Jewish academies, were honored as if they were kings: *"Man malki? Rabanan!* Who are kings? The scholars!"[2] They had the power to judge cases of both civil and religious law, always trying to avoid secular courts. (*The Wheel of Fortune,* Chapter Eight.)

As time rushed forward, Jewish communities stretched from Babylonia/Persia to the Franco/Germanic lands in Western Europe. When these European trail blazers had questions about religious life they could not answer, they sent these questions in the mail pouches of traveling merchants, to the heads of the Babylonian academies. Towards the end of the tenth century, when the *yeshivot* (academies) in Babylonia were beginning to lose their prominence, scholars settled in Western Europe where new centers of Jewish life were born. (*The Journey of the Four Captive Rabbis,* Chapter Nine.)

∽

These are the stories of our ancestors of Talmudic times.

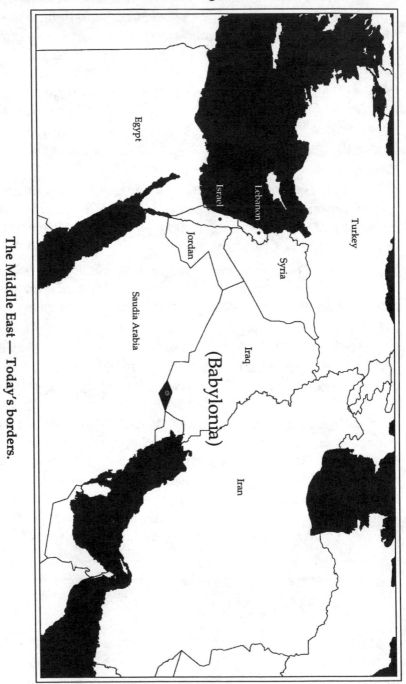

The Middle East — Today's borders.

A Sacred Trust
— Commentary —
Rabban Yochanan ben Zakkai

❧

The Jewish people have two great gifts which were given to us from Heaven: the Torah and *Eretz Yisrael*.

We must ask ourselves the question: can we live without either gift? Truthfully, the answer is no. If we have *Eretz Yisrael* without the Torah, we will lose *Eretz Yisrael* in no time. If we have the Torah, sooner or later we will return to *Eretz Yisrael* because the study of Torah guarantees it.

When we really learn Torah, every word connects us to *Eretz Yisrael*; studying every letter connects us to *Yerushalayim*; studying every dot connects us to the Holy Temple above.

What does exile mean? The Chozeh of Lublin, Rebbe Yaakov. Yitzchak Halyave Horwitz, said in the name of the prophet Elyahu: *"When God opens gates, we are permitted to make the gates wider."*

Rabban Yochanan ben Zakkai saw the gates opening, but he feared to make them open wider. He asked only for Yavneh and the scholars. He could have asked for *Eretz Yisrael*.

The true meaning of being in exile is the fear of opening the gates wider.

—Rabbi Shlomo Carlebach,
The Carlebach Shul,
Scholar, Teller of Holy Stories, and Creator of
Inspirational Song. Author of "Shlomo's Stories."

❧

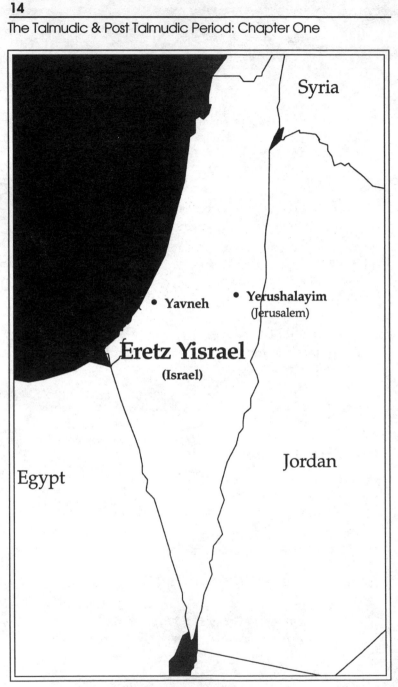

**Yerushalayim and Yavneh,
within today's borders**

Chapter One
RABBAN YOCHANAN BEN ZAKKAI SAVES TORAH

Time Line

70 c.e.	600 c.e.	1000 c.e.	1400 c.e.	1600 c.e.	1800 c.e.	2000 c.e.

— **Location:** *Yerushalayim*—

The three year Roman seige of *Yerushalayim* portended doom for Jewish nationalism. The inhabitants of the Holy City were divided; some were wearied from the hopelessness of the situation; others, although refusing to surrender, fought among themselves. Hunger and disease were rampant. Rabban Yochanan ben Zakkai was among those leaders who determined to do something about the impending destruction of *Yerushalyim.*

"The Jewish people are fighting among themselves," he reasoned. "There are so many different political parties, so many different opinions how to deal with the enemy; the *Sicarii*, or *Biryonim*, as they sometimes call themselves, are clandestine killers. Anyone they see speaking to a Roman finds his life endangered and becomes a target for their foul play. The *Zealots* want to fight the mighty enemy and restore Jewish independence; they think the situation is the same as it was in the days of the *Maccabbees.*

[**Ed.** Approximately two hundred years prior to the Roman seige, the Jewish people rebelled against pagan Greek/Syrian domination and overcame them. Mattathias and his five sons (one was named Judah, and was called *Maccabbee*) organized the rebellion. The holiday of Chanukah is celebrated to commemorate the victory over paganism and the restoration of Jewish life.]

"I, and the rest of the *Pharisees* only want to live peacefully, so we can study and transmit Torah. The *Saducees* want to become allied with the Romans. And the Romans? what do they do? They enforce the seige and wait patiently while brothers destroy brothers. Woe unto us! If the Holy Temple is destroyed, it will be because my people did not want to live together in peace. It will be because we hated each other for no reason. We are one people, but we act so differently. There are four political parties, each with its own agenda.

[**Ed.** Why was the Second Holy Temple destroyed? Because needless hatred prevailed. *Talmud Bavli Yoma 9b*]

"I must do something, something spectacular, something that will save the Torah way of life. The Jewish people will be able to survive without the Holy Temple, but they will not survive without Torah. Hmm ... Maybe my plan will work. But, perhaps my nephew, Abba Sikra, will conceive an even better plan."

The next morning, he called his nephew, who was the leader of the *Biryonim:*

"How long will you continue to kill your brothers?"

"What can I do to stop them? I am their leader, but they do what they want. If I reprimand them, they will think that I have joined with you and the *Pharisees,* and they will kill me too.

"Listen, I have to escape from *Yerushalayim* in order to try to save the Torah way of life." He explained his plan. "What do you think of it? Is it possible for me to succeed?"

"Let's do it this way, uncle. I believe it will have a better chance. No one must know what we are planning except you and your two most loyal disciples, Rabbi Eliezer and Rabbi Yehoshua.

"I want you to pretend that you are gravely ill. We will announce throughout *Yerushalayim* that Rabban Yochanan ben Zakkai is dying. People will come to pay their respects. You will pretend to grow weaker and weaker. Finally, you will feign death. I will find some decayed flesh, that has a terrible odor, and I will place it on your bier. You must practice lying perfectly still, not moving a muscle, not even an eyelid. Eliezer, Yehoshua, and I will carry the bier to the gates of the city. We will demand that the guards let us pass, in order to bury you outside the walls.

"What will you do once you are outside the walls?"

"Make sure that I get out of the city safely, and you will see!"

It did not take many days for Rabbi Eliezer and Rabbi Yehoshua to announce the death of their revered teacher, Rabban Yochanan ben Zakkai. A great procession followed the bier until the gates of *Yerushalyim*, where it was halted by the Jewish guards posted inside the gates.

"Let us through," Rabbi Eliezer, Rabbi Yehoshua and Abba Sikra demanded. "The cemetery is outside the walls and we must bury our teacher with dignity."

"We must check that you are not tricking us; that he is actually dead," they insisted. One of the guards lifted his sword, preparing to stab the body.

"How can you do that?" they clamored. "The Romans will say that the guards at the gates violated a body and thereby disgraced their revered master."

"Then we will just shove the body a little," they continued stubbornly.

"Then all the Jews inside the city will also condemn you for not having respect for the dead."

Ashamed, they opened the gates and allowed Rabbi Eliezer, Rabbi Yehoshua and Abba Sikra to walk through with the bier.

As soon as they reached a safe distance, out of sight of the gates of *Yerushalyim*, Rabban Yochanan ben Zakki jumped off the bier, bid farewell to his students, and ran toward the Roman camp. Once there he demanded that the guards escort him to General Vespasian's tent. Stunned to find a Jew among them, they pointed to the place where Vespasian sat in war council with his lieutenants.

"Peace to you, your majesty, King of Rome," pronounced Rabban Yochanan, as he lowered his head respectfully.

"You deserve to die twice," ranted Vespasian. "First, you have pronounced me 'king,' while I am but a general; second, if I am the king, why haven't you come sooner to pay your respects?"

"I will answer your second question first, your majesty," whispered Rabban Yochanan. "You see, my people are sorely divided. Some among them would surely have put me to death, had they found that I tried to contact you. As it is, my escape from *Yerushalyim* on a bier is nothing short of miraculous."

At that exact moment, a messenger from Rome arrived.

"Your majesty," the messenger called out. There was a stunned silence all around. "Nero has died. The Senate has sent me to inform you that they have proclaimed you emperor!"

Rabban Yochanan no longer had to answer the first question.

"You are so wise," continued Vespasian. "Before I return to Rome, and leave the seige of your holy city in the hands of Titus, my son, I will grant you any request."

"Grant me, your majesty, permission to move the *Sanhedrin* (the Jewish court) and its scholars from the beseiged city of *Yerushalyim* to Yavneh, a small town near the Mediterranean coast; allow the family of Rabban Gamliel, descendants of the Davidic dynasty to live; and send a doctor to cure Rabbi Zadok who has fasted so long for *Yerushalyim* to be saved that it is almost impossible for him to digest food."

Rabban Yochanan ben Zakkai's requests were granted. Yavneh became a major center of Torah learning, the first of such cities where Torah was the focus of Jewish life. There Jewish spiritual leaders prepared for a long and arduous exile that was to begin three years later when the Holy Temple lay in ruins. The precedent of moving the Torah center from *Yerushalyim* to Yavneh, and then to other cities in the *diaspora* (lands outside of *Eretz Israel*) sustained the Jewish people in the centuries that followed.

[**Ed.** As the (first) Holy Temple was burning, a group of young priests went to the roof. Their leader carried the keys in his hand. He prayed: Master of the Universe! We were not worthy keepers of Your House. Therefore, please take back your keys. In the presence of the other young priests, he threw the keys heavenward. Immediately, a Heavenly Hand emerged and grasped the keys. *Talmud Bavli, Taanit 29a]*

A Sacred Trust
— Commentary —
Rachel and Akiva

All of us have dreams. To the extent that we can encourage those we love to pursue their dreams, we share in their heaven. There is no greater pleasure than seeing a loved one fulfill a life-long dream following years of support and confidence in his/her ultimate success.

We speak of *Yerushalayim L'mata* and *Yerushalayim L'mala*, the earthly and the heavenly Jerusalem, the real and the ideal. Rachel could see the *Yerushalayim L'mala* in Akiva's dreams. What did she do for him? She made it possible for him to study and thereby fulfill his dream, What did he do for her? He fulfilled the potential she had seen in him all along. Why was the golden crown significant? Because it symbolically united the dream with the real, the heavenly with the earthly, *Yerushalayim L'mala* with *Yerushalayim L'mata*.

Today it is not just the wives who encourage and support their husbands' studies. Countless husbands presently are encouraging their wives to not only seek out study but to continue it as well, often necessitating a complete restructuring of the management of the household! What strength and courage it takes, what love and unfaltering belief, to see the potential and be an enabler of dreams.

Julie Auerbach,
Director of Jewish Family Enrichment, Temple Emanu El,
Cleveland, OH and Numbers 2000 Project Coordinator
at the Jewish Education Center of Cleveland.

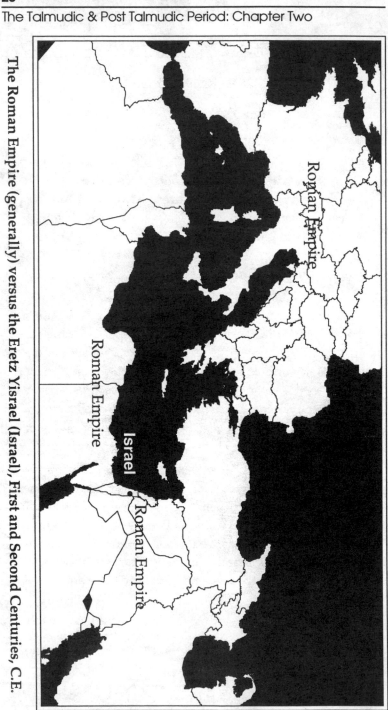

The Roman Empire (generally) versus the Eretz Yisrael (Israel), First and Second Centuries, C.E.

Chapter Two
RACHEL AND AKIVA:
A LOVE STORY

Time Line

70 c.e.	600 c.e.	1000 c.e.	1400 c.e.	1600 c.e.	1800 c.e.	2000 c.e.

— Location: *Eretz Yisrael* under Roman Rule —

"You ask me what kind of man Akiva is," mused Rachel. People crowded around her. It is comforting to reminisce about the past. I don't know what gave me the strength to go on alone for twenty four years while he studied. But the years flew by, just like they flew by for our patriarch Jacob when he worked for his Rachel.

> [**Ed.** Jacob worked for Rachel for seven years. After the agreed time, he wanted to marry his beloved, but her father Laban substituted Leah, her older sister. Jacob married Rachel a week later, but was obligated to work for an additional seven years. *B'rayshit, Genesis 29:21-30*]

If you have time to listen, I will tell you the whole story, how we met, how we loved each other.

~

My father, Kalba Savua, brought me many young suitors. I refused all of them.

> [**Ed.** Kalba Savua literally means a "satisfied dog." He was one of the richest men in *Yerushalayim,* and he generously fed the poorest people at his own table; they entered his house starving like dogs, but emerged satisfied.]

I was looking for a husband who was not interested in my wealth. I told my father over and over: "what good is wealth, if the person who owns it is wicked? I would rather have a poor husband who is good and kind!"

Once, my father challenged me, "You must have some one in mind," he insisted, otherwise you would at least consider the young men that I propose for you."

"You are right, father. I do have some one in mind. I love Akiva, and I want to marry him."

"Akiva!" he exploded, "Akiva, that ignorant, poor shepherd. He doesn't know the difference between an *alef* and *bayt*! (Hebrew for A and B; the ABC's) I am one of the most respected people in *Yerushalayim*. My daughter should marry a scholar!"

I protested my father's hasty judgment. "I know that if Akiva is given a chance, he will become a great scholar. When we talk about different things, when I explain ideas to him, he always remembers everything that I say. He has such a good mind. He is kind and gentle. Instead of opposing him as your future son-in-law, why don't you help him with his education, so we can be married?"

"You will not marry an ignorant shepherd! If you disobey me, I will disinherit you. I swear it! This is my final word!"

I married him anyway. We were forced to live in a tent outside the city. We ate only dry bread, we drank only water, and we slept on straw.

My father's friends ridiculed me. I used to hear them taunting me:

"That Rachel, the stubborn daughter of Kalba Savua. Imagine what she gave up to marry Akiva, the poor, ignorant shepherd. She could have married any man her father chose for her, and be living in a beautiful house, with servants and all kinds of luxury. Instead, she supports herself cleaning other peoples houses. She even sells her hair!"[1]

Once, a man stood at the opening of our tent. He pleaded. "Please, my wife is so ill, and I can't even provide her with a pillow."

I gave the man some of my straw for his wife. I didn't know that there were people who were poorer than us. We, at least, had bread to eat. Afterwards, when I told Akiva what had happened, he said, as he picked slivers of straw out of my hair:

"Doing that *mitzvah* must have made you very happy. You

know, I've been thinking about something, and I want your opinion. As I shepherd my flocks each day, I notice that the stones in the nearby brook become smoother and smoother from the flowing water. Didn't you once tell me that Torah is compared to water? Now, if the stones in the brook become smooth from the water, doesn't it stand to reason that if I study Torah I can also become smooth (a great scholar)?

"Akiva, I am so happy that you have come to that conclusion on your own. Nothing will make me happier than you giving up shepherding your flocks and going to study with two of our greatest teachers, Rabbi Eliezer ben Hyrcanos and Rabbi Yehoshua ben Chananya in Lod."

Do you know what Akiva then told me?

"One day, I will buy you a golden crown. It will be engraved with the words, *Yerushalayim*, the Holy City, and I will set it upon your head."

He was forty years old when he left for Lod. He was so motivated, that he mastered the *aleph bayt*, rudimentary prayers, and script in five days. He wrote to me occasionally of his progress. Sometimes, he sent me a few dinars that he earned by cutting trees and selling it for kindling.

∽

Akiva studied day and night; weeks became months, and months turned into years—twelve years. His teachers agreed that he deserved to be ordained, to be called Rabbi Akiva.

It was then that he sent a message to me. He wrote, "We have been apart for twelve years. I really want to be with you. I am very lonely. I will return home soon."

Accompanied by many students, he came to *Yerushalayim*. As he neared our tent, he heard a woman taunting me; I paid her no attention, for I was used to people's ridicule.

"You are so silly! You are waiting for his return, and I tell you, he will never return," she smirked. "Had you listened to your father, you would not be living in such poverty!"

This time I could not contain myself, "My husband is learning Torah. One day he will be a great scholar. I am so proud of him. I would wait another twelve years for his return."

Akiva overheard what I said. Without seeing me, he returned to his *yeshiva*. He did not come back to *Yerushalayim* for another twelve years. This time he was accompanied by 24,000 students.[2]

One of my friends said, I will lend you my Shabbat dress, so that you will look nicer when you greet your husband."

I refused her offer. "Even though I appreciate your kind offer, my husband thinks that a person's deeds are more important than his clothing."

Hundreds of people thronged the streets to honor him. I had to push my way through the crowds. Most people didn't recognize me; they thought I was a beggar. But when Akiva saw me, he shouted, "Let her pass. All the honor that you bestow upon me belongs to her. All the Torah that I learned, that I teach you, everything is because of her self sacrifice. She was the one that sent me to study, while she lived in poverty. She is the one that made all this happen!"

Even my father, who hadn't spoken to me in all these years, was among the crowd. I was standing nearby when he pushed his way forward. He did not know that this Rabbi Akiva was the same shepherd who had worked for him so many years ago. I overheard his question.

He said, "Many years ago I made a vow that I very much regret. How can I nullify it?"

"What was your vow?" Akiva asked gently.

"I vowed that I would disown my daughter if she married an ignorant shepherd."

"Had you known that your daughter would marry a scholar, would you have made that vow?"

"No," whispered Kalba Savua, "if I would have forseen that her husband knew one chapter, one law, one sentence, I would never have made that vow."

"In that case," Rabbi Akiva responded, "it is possible to have your vow annulled."

When he realized that Rabbi Akiva was his son-in-law, he reinstated me and divided his wealth with us.

It was then that Akiva fulfilled the promise he made to me. He bought me the golden crown with the words "*Yerushalayim*, the Holy City" engraved on it."[3]

A Sacred Trust
— Commentary —
Beruriah

&

The heroes and stories of any people not only reflect the values of that community, but help to mold the values of the next generation.

In these excerpts about Beruriah, we can learn many things: that study is an ongoing, lifelong enterprise; that we judge people by their actions; that we respect wisdom and learning in both men and women; that we correct people gently; that the universe belongs to God and because of His love and kindness we are privileged to share it temporarily.

On the other hand, Beruriah and Rabbi Chalafta probably embarrassed Rabbi Yossi HaGalili and Rabbi Shimon, Beruriah's brother, respectively. (See Baba Metzia 58b about verbal wrongs.) Beruriah does not support the intellectual abilities of other women when *"some men taunted women..."* and she jokingly responded, *"All, except Beruriah."*

Jewish heroes, whether in the Bible or the Talmud, are accessible models for us because they are human beings, capable of greatness yet imperfect because of their humanity.

—Marlynn Dorff,
Curriculum and Instruction Consultant,
Bureau of Jewish Education, Los Angeles, CA.

BERURIAH:
AN INSPIRING WOMAN

Time Line

70 c.e.	600 c.e.	1000 c.e.	1400 c.e.	1600 c.e.	1800 c.e.	2000 c.e.

— Location: *Eretz Yisrael* under Roman Rule —

Beruriah! Her name is synonomous with learning and courage. Who was this woman who was one of the few mentioned in the entire body of Talmudic literature, whose views on *halachic* (Jewish law) matters were seriously reckoned with by her contemporaries?

Beruriah was the daughter of Rabbi Chaninah ben Teradyon and the wife of Rabbi Mayer. Both Rabbis were among the greatest scholars in *Eretz Yisrael* during the fearsome Hadrianic persecutions, the second century of the common era. They inspired her to love learning. Because it was unusual for a woman to be involved in the Talmudic process, the many quotes attributed to her in its pages reflect her great knowledge.

In the following Talmudic source, she is compared to a prominent male contemporary:

∼

Rabbi Simlai asked Rabbi Yochanan to teach him the laws of genealogy in three months. He replied, "If Beruriah, who studied 300 laws from 300 teachers in one day [metaphor for three years] could not master them adequately, how do you propose to master these same laws in three months?"[1]

[**Ed.** It is interesting to note that a woman is cited as a role model of scholarship, thus proving that the Rabbis of that period were not averse to women studying, as has been commonly supposed. The anecdotes that are recorded in the pages of the Talmud about Beruriah tell us much about what a Jewish woman could achieve.]

Once, some unruly neighbors angered Rabbi Mayer so much that he prayed that they die. Beruriah overheard his prayer and reprimanded him, "Why do you pray for their death," she demanded. "You know, as well as I, that the passage in *Tehillim* (Psalms) reads *"Let wrongdoing perish from the earth."*[2] It does not read: "Let wrongdoers perish from the earth."

"If you prayed appropriately, then wrongdoing would perish from the earth. Instead of what you are praying, pray that God have compassion upon our neighbors, that they repent their evil ways."

Rabbi Mayer changed his prayer. His neighbors repented.[3]

∽

Once, she met Rabbi Yossi HaGalili walking along the road. He stopped her to ask for directions. "By what road do we go to Lod?," he queried.

"Foolish Galilean," she quipped, "did not our sages teach that it is improper to speak too much with women?[4] You should rephrase your question: By what to Lod?"[5]

∽

Another time she discovered a student who was mumbling as he studied. She was very gentle with him. She said, "It is written 'organize (the learning of Torah) and it will be sure,' otherwise, it will not be sure."[6]

This means that you will remember what you learn better if you repeat the words out loud."[7]

∽

Some Rabbis and Beruriah were discussing the process of making an oven *kosher*. Rabbi Chalafta turned to Rabbi Shimon, the son of Rabbi Chaninah ben Teradyon (Beruriaha's brother) and asked, "How would you *kasher* (make kosher) an oven?"

After Rabbi Shimon responded, Rabbi Chalafta turned to Beruriah and asked, "How would you *kasher* an oven?"

After Beruriah responded to the question, Rabbi Chalafta turned to Rabbi Yehuda ben Bava and exclaimed, "His daughter understands the issues that are involved much better than his son."[8]

⁓

Some men taunted women by saying that they had limited ability to understand intricate *halachic* [legal] discussions. "*Nashim, daatan kalot,*—women have less understanding (then men)," they teased.

Beruriah quipped back, "All, except Beruriah."[9]

⁓

One of the most poignant stories about Beruriah shows her unusual courage:

Beruriah and Rabbi Mayer were the parents of twin sons. One Shabbat, after Rabbi Mayer had returned to the synagogue for afternoon prayers, Beruriah noticed that her boys were feverish. Wrapping them in blankets, she sat down in her rocking chair, cradling a child in each arm, rocking them gently. The children coughed, sputtered deliriously, and shivered. She held them until their breathing ceased. Then she placed each child on his own bed, covered the body, and returned to her rocking chair to await Rabbi Mayer's return. She decided not to tell her husband until after Shabbat had ended.

"Where are my boys?" he asked, as soon as he entered the house. "They always meet me for prayers. They did not come to the synagogue this afternoon."

"I gave them permission to go to the other synagogue with their friends," she said, trying to control her voice. "I'm certain that they will return shortly. They will probably hear *havdalah* at their friends, so don't wait."

[**Ed.** *Havdalah*, meaning to separate, is the ceremony which bids farewell to Shabbat.]

She handed Mayer a cup of wine, a double wicked candle, and a spice box for the *Havdalah* ceremony, then she served him some food. By the time he had finished eating, the boys had still not returned. Guiding the discussion away from his expression of worry, she said, "Mayer, I have to ask you a very important question. A while ago, a merchant left a package of precious stones in my trust. Today, he came and demanded that I return his possessions. Must I?"

Rabbi Mayer was taken aback at Beruriah's question, for he knew the level of her scholarship. Without hesitating, he replied, "Of course, you must return his possessions. What the merchant left with you for safekeeping belongs to him. Now that he demands it, you must return it."

She grasped his hands and led him gently to the room where the dead children lay. Slowly, she uncovered their faces. He cried out in bitter anguish.

Beruriah whispered, "Mayer, didn't you just tell me that one must return precious possessions to their owner. God has given and God has taken; may the name of God be blessed."[10]

When Rabbi Chaninah heard the way his daughter handled the tragedy, how she comforted her husband, he uttered, "A valiant woman, who can find, her value is far beyond pearls, her husband's heart relies upon her."[11]

A Sacred Trust
— Commentary —
The Ten Martyrs

જ

In reading the painful yet deeply inspiring accounts of *The Ten Martyrs* you may notice common ideals held by these rabbis. Each knowingly gave their life to teach love of God, love of Torah, and love of Israel to the Jewish people. Through the way they lived and died, they continue to teach us what it means to be a Jew.

In our world, where preoccupation with the self is all too common, we learn from these brave ancestors that there is something that transcends the self. These rabbis believed that living a Jewish life and the transmition of Jewish values were ideals worth dying for.

Let us be reminded that despite our painful history contemporary Jews are very fortunate. Most Jews can celebrate their Judaism with profound joy. And, in our lifetime, we witnessed the fulfillment of a two thousand year dream of the re-birth of the Jewish State of Israel.

With a few exceptions around the globe, it is the best time in the history of the world to be a Jew—a beautiful distinction and privilege for this generation. Perhaps thousands of years after these martyrs gave their lives for the love of God, this is one way that God shows love for the Jewish people.

Rabbi David Woznica, Director
Bronfman Center for Jewish Life
92nd Street Y, New York City. NY

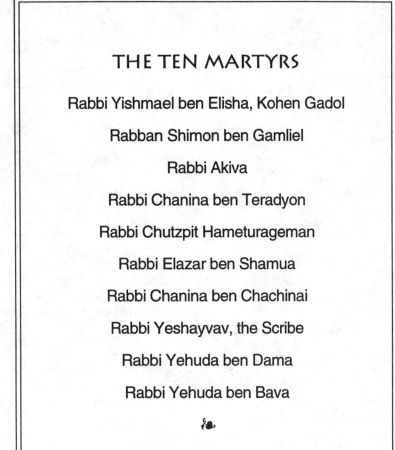

THE TEN MARTYRS

Rabbi Yishmael ben Elisha, Kohen Gadol

Rabban Shimon ben Gamliel

Rabbi Akiva

Rabbi Chanina ben Teradyon

Rabbi Chutzpit Hameturageman

Rabbi Elazar ben Shamua

Rabbi Chanina ben Chachinai

Rabbi Yeshayvav, the Scribe

Rabbi Yehuda ben Dama

Rabbi Yehuda ben Bava

Chapter Four

THE TEN MARTYRS:
THESE I REMEMBER

Time Line

70 c.e.	600 c.e.	1000 c.e.	1400 c.e.	1600 c.e.	1800 c.e.	2000 c.e.

— Location: *Eretz Yisrael* under Roman Rule —

[Ed. The Roman Emperor Hadrian[1] was determined to rebuild Yerushalayim, not as a city holy to the Jewish people, but rather as a pagan city named Aeolina Capitalina. He re-issued the harsh decrees that Antiochus, the Syrian/Greek had imposed approximately two hundred years before, hoping to extinguish both the Jewish religion and the yearning of the Jewish people for independence from the oppressive Roman yoke. The old decrees prohibited the study of Torah, kashrut, [Kosher laws] circumcision, the observance of the Sabbath, and the celebration of Rosh Chodesh (the new moon, which regulated the celebration of the holidays), and he added the prohibition to ordain rabbis. Ignoring Roman law was punishable by death; and many Jews willingly sacrificed their lives, for they believed that if they could not live as Jews, their lives were not worth living. [2]]

[Ed. The liturgical poem about the *Asarah Harugay Malchut*, (ten illustrious sages who died to sanctify God's Holy Name) is read twice each year, and can be found in the *Machzor* [prayer book] of Yom Kippur, with the words beginning *Ayleh Ezkerah*, and in the *Kinnot* of Tisha B'Av beginning with the words *Arzay Halevanon*. The poem describes the martyrdom of ten sages who lived under Roman oppression from the period of the destruction of the second Holy Temple in 70 C.E. until the fall of Betar 65 years later even though it seems from the poetry that all the sages were murdered at one time.]

∾

Emperor Hadrian (or, according to Midrashic sources, a Roman governor[3]), called together a council of the ten leading Jewish sages. He was looking for a pretext to murder them. The sages did not know Hadrian's evil intention.

"I want you to try a case for me," he commanded. "According to your Torah, what is the punishment for kidnapping?"

"Our Torah teaches, they said in unison, *"he who kidnaps a person and holds him for ransom shall surely be put to death."* [4]

"If that is the law," he thundered, "I decree that all of you be put to death. According to my recollection, no Jew has ever been punished for the brothers selling Joseph into slavery. Therefore, I sentence you to death for that crime, as is commanded by your Torah."

$\backsim$

Rabbi Yishmael ben Elisha Kohen Gadol & Rabban Shimon ben Gamliel

The Roman emperor insisted that lots be cast to decide who should be brutally tortured and murdered first, Rabbi Yishmael ben Elisha Kohen Gadol or Rabban Shimon ben Gamliel. The lot fell on Rabban Shimon ben Gamliel. The Roman ordered that he be immediately decapitated.

Rabbi Yishmael picked up the severed head of his friend and colleague and bitterly cried out: "Is this the reward for the one whose tongue so skillfully transmitted the beautiful words of Torah, and now it licks the dust?"

The emperor's daughter watched the execution. She asked her father to spare Rabbi Yishmael, for he was an exceedingly handsome man.

"Lift your face that I might look at it," she called out, "and I will spare your life."

"No," he replied, "I will not forfeit my reward in the world to come for any pleasure that you might have from gazing at me."

Incensed with his refusal, she commanded the executioner to tear the skin from his face while he was still alive.

$\backsim$

Rabbi Akiva

Rabbi Akiva was condemned for teaching Torah and for treason, because he was one of the leaders guiding the Jewish uprising against tyrannical Roman rule. His sentence was carried out in Caesaria. The morning of his execution, he rose early, so that he might say *Sh'ma* one last time. As the Roman executioners flayed his flesh with iron combs, he continued his recitation, "*Sh'ma Yisrael, Adonay Elohaynu, Adonoy Echad.* Here O Israel, the Lord our God, the Lord is One."

His students asked him, "Master and teacher, how is it possible for you to stand the pain and yet have a smile upon your face?"

"All my life," he replied, "I have sought to understand the meaning of '*and you shall love the Lord your God with all your heart, with all your soul, and with all your might.*' "[5]

"I have interpreted '*with all your soul*' to mean even if He takes your soul. I always wondered when I would have the opportunity to fulfill this commandment. Now, I am able to do it. Shall I not fulfill it with joy?" He prolonged the word *E-chad* (One), until the sound was no longer audible.[6]

Rabbi Akiva's students carried his body across the Galilee and buried him on one of the highest hills in Tiberias overlooking the Kinneret Sea. (Sea of Galilee)

❧

Rabbi Chanina ben Teradyon

Rabbi Chanina ben Teradyon was studying Torah publicly with many disciples. The Roman bailiffs arrested him, for the study of Torah was prohibited. They wrapped him in the Torah scroll that he had been studying, placed bundles of branches around him, and set them on fire. The bailiff inserted wet woolen sponges over his heart, so that he would suffer longer. As the flames crept upward, his wife and daughter Beruriah wept. "Why are you weeping," he asked Beruriah?

She replied, "Because I have to watch you suffer."

His disciples asked, "What do you see?"

He responded, "I see the parchment consumed with the flames, but the letters of the Torah are returning to their source in Heaven.[7]

Rabbi Chutzpit Hameturageman

Rabbi Chutzpit Hameturageman[8] used to translate and interpret the lecture of the head of the yeshiva. His students pleaded with the Roman emperor to have mercy on him when he was sentenced to death. He inquired, "How old are you? Why do you want to live longer?"

"I am one hundred and thirty years old," the sage responded, and I want to live one more day so that I might recite *Sh'ma Yisrael* one more evening and one more morning in order to declare that God is my King."

"Hah!" laughed the emperor. "How long will the Jewish people cling to a God that does not help them? If your God is omniscient and omnipresent, why doesn't He save you from my death decree?"

Rabbi Chutzpit rent his garment and cried in anguish: "You blaspheme the Lord! What will you do when He punishes you and your mighty empire?"

"As punishment for your audacity, you shall be slain, stoned and hanged!" roared the emperor.

Rabbi Elazar ben Shamua

Rabbi Elazar ben Shamua was one of Rabbi Akiva's primary students. He was murdered on Yom Kippur, the holiest day in the Jewish calendar year. He was a humble and gentle man who never quarreled with his colleagues even though they sometimes disagreed with his opinions. He never occupied himself with useless matters. His students pleaded with him to reveal what he saw as his life's breath was being squeezed from him:

"I see," he whispered, "the soul of every righteous man being purified in the waters of the Shiloah pools, preparing them to enter the gates of Heaven. There Rabbi Akiva is already sitting upon a golden throne, teaching Torah to those who enter."[9]

Rabbi Chanina ben Chachinai

Rabbi Chanina ben Chachinai was taken to the place of execution on Friday afternoon just as he finished his preparations for Shabbat. He wanted to usher in Shabbat with prayer and song, just as he had done every week of his life, so he began chanting: *"L'chu N'ranenah,*[10] (Come, let us praise!)

The executioner was enchanted with his intense devotion and the rhythm of the melody, so he waited. He waited and waited, and then decided he could not wait anymore. As Rabbi Chanina chanted the words of the kiddush: *"And God blessed the seventh day and sanctified it . . ."*[11] he acted. Rabbi Chanina never finished the remainder of the verse: *"for on that day, God rested from all His work which He had created."*

Rabbi Yeshayvav, the Scribe

Rabbi Yeshayvav, the Scribe, a colleague of Rabbi Akiva, was so generous that he had to restrain him from giving too much charity. Being shoved toward the place of execution when he was arrested on a Monday, the day of the week on which he usually fasted, he implored his students to follow so that he might instruct them in one last lesson:

"Remain loving and devoted to one another," he urged. "Love peace and justice, and pray for the redemption of the Jewish people from this oppressive enemy."

As he was being torn to death by wild dogs, a voice called out: "Blessed be Rabbi Yeshayvav the Scribe who never for an instant deviated from the law of Moses."

∾

Rabbi Yehuda ben Dama

Rabbi Yehuda ben Dama was arrested the day before Sukkot. He pleaded with the emperor to allow him to live one more day so that he might be privileged to perform the mitzvah of sitting in the *sukkah* and blessing the *etrog* and *lulav* (citron and palm branch.)

"What reward will you receive for your insistence in observing these commandments?" the emperor mocked.

Rabbi Yehudah replied quietly, "Oh, how abundant is Your goodness which You have stored for them that fear You."[12]

The emperor raged, "You are a fool if you believe in life after death, in some sort of eternal reward."

"There are no fools greater than those who deny a living God," argued Rabbi Yehuda.

Incensed, the emperor ordered that Rabbi Yehuda be tied by his hair to a horse's tail and dragged through the streets.

∾

Rabbi Yehuda ben Bava

Rabbi Yehuda ben Bava courageously defied the Romans by teaching Torah publicly. He understood that if the Romans succeeded in carrying out their edict prohibiting the study of Torah and the ordination of Rabbis, the Jewish people would not survive. The Roman edict stated that whoever ordained a Rabbi would be punished by death, whoever was ordained would be put to death, and the city where the ordination was performed would be razed.

The aging, seventy year old Rabbi Yehuda ben Bava took five of the most promising young leaders to the uninhabited valley between the Galilean cities of Usha and Shefaram. He did not want innocent people to suffer what he was about to do. In the secluded valley he ordained Rabbi Mayer, Rabbi Yehuda, Rabbi Shimon, Rabbi Yossi and Rabbi Elazar ben Shamua. He placed upon their shoulders the responsibility for the continuation of Jewish life.

A Roman patrol, roaming through the surrounding hills, saw them in the valley and turned to investigate.

Rabbi Yehuda ben Bava noticed the soldiers closing in and pleaded, "Run for your lives!"

"But, what will become of you?" they implored. "We can not leave you here."

"I have lived my life fully." he said. "I will slow down your chance to escape if you wait for me. You must live and teach because I will die soon anyway."

The Roman soldiers caught and tortured Rabbi Yehuda ben Bava to death by piercing his body with three hundred iron spearheads.[13]

The five young Rabbis escaped and became the leading sages of the next generation.

ॐ

A Sacred Trust
— Commentary —
Yehuda and Antoninus

❧

"And the Almighty spoke to him saying: As for Me, My part in the Covenant will be that you will become the father of a multitude of nations. And your name will no longer be Abram, but Abraham, for I will make you the father of a multitude of nations . . .

And the Almighty said to Abraham: But for your part, you shall keep my Covenant, you, and your descendants after you, throughout their generations. This is My Covenant which you shall keep, between Me and you, and your descendants after you, throughout their generations. This is My Covenant which you shall keep, between Me and you, and your descendants after you. Every male among you shall be circumcised. You shall circumcise the flesh of your foreskin. And this will be a token of a Covenant between Me and you, and a perpetual reminder to walk in My ways. He among you, who is eight days old must be circumcised . . ."

B'rayshit, Genesis 17:4-5, 9-12

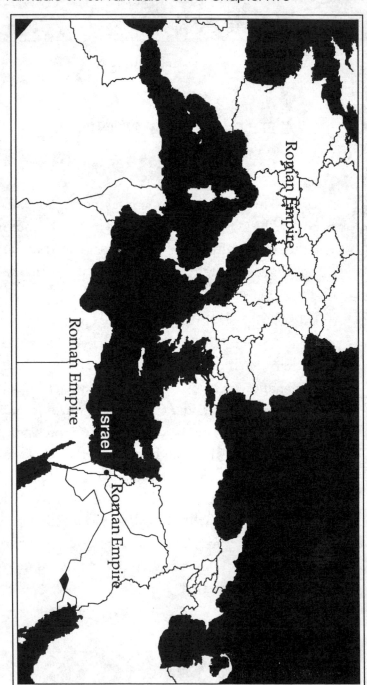

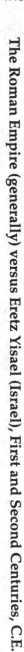

The Roman Empire (generally) versus Eretz Yisael (Israel), First and Second Centuries, C.E.

Chapter Five

YEHUDA AND ANTONINUS
(RABBI YEHUDA HANASI
AND EMPEROR MARCUS AURELIUS ANTONINUS)

Time Line

70 c.e.	600 c.e.	1000 c.e.	1400 c.e.	1600 c.e.	1800 c.e.	2000 c.e.

— Location: *Eretz Yisrael* under Roman Rule —

[Ed. The Romans, in their quest for world supremacy, marched through *Eretz Yisrael* to engage the Parthians (Babylonians/Persians) in battle. The majority of the conquered people on their route accepted Roman rule; only the Jewish people revolted. In retaliation, Emperor Hadrian and his Roman soldiers continued to suppress every expression of national and religious Jewish life.]

[Ed. When Rabbi Akiva died, Rabbi Yehuda HaNsai was born; when Rabbi Yehuda HaNasi died, Raba was born. This teaches us that a righteous man does not depart from the world until another righteous man like himself is created, as it is said *"the sun rises and the suns sets."*[1]]

There was great rejoicing in the house of Rabban Shimon ben Gamliel and his wife on the night that their son was born. But the next day they had to cope with the problem of subverting Emperor Hadrian's edict. The death penalty was inflicted upon Jewish parents convicted of circumcising their sons.

The eighth day approached, the day of circumcision for a new born male, and anguish slowly replaced their joy. The mother wept, pitifully, realizing the perilous situation.

"Whose law will we obey," whispered Rabban Shimon gently, "the law of God or the law of man? We have been commanded to circumcise our male children on the eighth day after birth, and we will do what we have to do."

Rabban Shimon stooped over his son. After the circumcision, he stood upright and announced, "Our son will be called Yehuda Hakadosh (the holy), for we have risked

danger, we have defied Roman law, to fulfill the commandments of our Creator."

[**Ed.** When he became the leader of the Jewish people, he was described
as "Rabaynu Hakadosh," our holy teacher, and everyone knew to
whom the adjective referred.[2]

It was also said of him, "He was supremely great in both Torah and
worldly affairs."[3]

It did not take long for a Roman spy to inform the governor
that there had been some sort of celebration in the house of
Rabban Shimon. "I suspect that a newborn baby had been
circumcised," he reported.

Enforcing the law was the governor's job, so he confronted
Rabban Shimon, "Why did you break the law of the land?"

"I chose the law of my Creator."

"I have great respect for you, yet I can't neglect my
obligation to my emperor. Therefore, I insist that you send
the baby and his mother to the emperor, who is vacationing
in Caeseria, and he will decide what should be done."

Mother and child set out. Towards evening, they were still
far from their destination. The Mother thought, "I have
recently given birth, I am very tired, and I don't have to
appear before the emperor until tomorrow afternoon. I will
rest for the night at the home of my friend Gilda, the wife of
Senator Paul. We have shared each other's joys and sorrows
for such a long time This visit will afford me the opportunity
to properly congratulate her upon the birth of her son last
week. I've been so wrapped up with my own baby, that I have
not communicated with her."

The two friends embraced warmly.

"You must have a very important reason for travelling
with your baby so soon after birth," Gilda queried.

"Yes, I have to appear before Emperor Hadrian tomorrow.
You know that law that he enforces prohibiting circumcision.

Well, we defied that law, because that is what our Torah commands. I fear the worst."

"I have an idea," said Gilda, excitedly. "My baby Antoninus is just a week older than yours. He is not circumcised. I will exchange babies with you, and you will show my baby to the emperor. He will never know the difference. I will feed your child, and you will feed mine. The emperor will not be able to accuse you of defying his law. Everything will work out well. When you return here, we will exchange again. Only the two of us will know the secret."

Yehuda's mother was taken aback with such a gracious offer. She slept more peacefully that night than she had since the birth of her son.

The following day she was ushered into the presence of Emperor Hadrian.

"Remove the child's swaddling cloth," he demanded. "I have to see for myself if this child is circumcised."

An officer removed the swaddling cloth. The emperor's face turned ashen.

"I certainly thought that the child of Rabban Shimon would be circumcised," he shouted, "but it is clear to me that this is not the case. It seems that their God performs miracles to make circumcised children uncircumcised. I can not compete with a God who performs such miracles. I will no longer enforce a law contrary to the wishes of your Creator. Therefore, I am easing the prohibition against circumcision. From now on, you, and your people may do what you are commanded. And my dear mother of a newborn son, you may depart for your home in peace."

∾

Yehuda and Antoninus were raised by their own mothers. The boys grew up together, always respecting both their differences and common beliefs.

Yehuda became Rabbi Yehuda HaNasi, leader of the Jewish people, president of the *Sanhedrin*, (Jewish court), and he completed the codification of the *Mishna*, the oral law that Rabbi Akiva began to arrange the generation before.

Antoninus became Emperor Marcus Aurelius Antoninus.[4] He legislated care for the poor, leniency to political criminals, and less brutality at the gladitorial circuses.

Because of their relationship, Roman repression against the Jewish people was eased during their lifetimes, and scholars were permitted to circulate throughout *Eretz Yisrael* and the Babylonian Jewish community.

᪵

A Sacred Trust
— Commentary —
Rav

ൿ

Rabbi Chaim Vital, (sixteenth century kabbalist), observed that the purpose of the *Mitzvot* (commandments) are to bring us to *Middot*—the highest level of ethical living. The *Mizvot* are like a road map of life, but the *Middot* are the highways toward a more complete, more perfect ethical existence.

In contrast, the protagonists in these stories lived by the "letter of the law" and observed the *Mitzvot* but lacked the understanding of their purpose. Rabbah lacked compassion and Natan was haughty.

The litigants appealed to Rav, for he was known for his understanding of the "spirit of the law." His decisions were based upon the *Middot*.

Rav personified the virtues of a Jewish judge: wisdom, humility, fear of God, destain of profit, love of truth, love of fellow-men, and a good name. (*Rambam, Maimonides, twelfth century codifier of Jewish law*)

Authors

ൿ

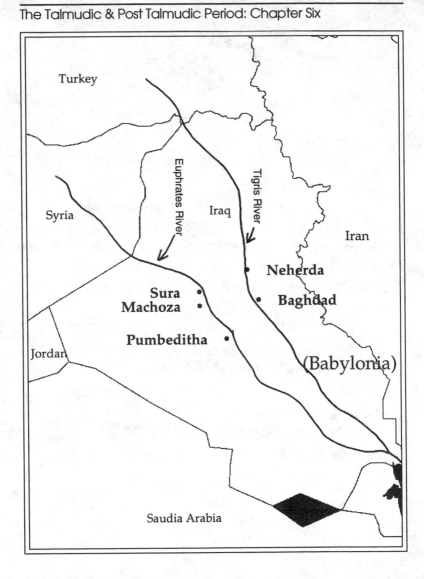

General location of mentioned Jewish communities on the Tigris and Euphrates Rivers in Babylonia, currently in central Iraq.

Map uses modern borders for reference.

Chapter Six
RAV:
THE TEACHER'S TEACHER

Time Line

70 c.e.	600 c.e.	1000 c.e.	1400 c.e.	1600 c.e.	1800 c.e.	2000 c.e.

— Location: *Eretz Yisrael* and Babylon [Iraq] —

His name was Rav Abba Aricha. Aricha means tall. Rav was the tallest man in his generation.[1] But he is remembered as "Rav." How did he achieve such stature? How did it happen that when people talked about "Rav," everyone knew to whom they were referring?

[**Ed.** Just as Rabbi Yehuda Hanasi was known as "Rabi" in Eretz Yisrael, so Rav Abba Aricha was known as "Rav" in Babylonia.[2]]

Let's rewind the video tape to the last decades of the second century of the common era. A group of scholars were studying with "Rabi, the recognized leader of the Jewish people. One of his disciples named Rabbi Yochanan said, "I remember when I was sitting seventeen rows behind Rav who was sitting before Rabi and sparks of fire were leaping from the mouth of Rabi to the mouth of Rav and from the mouth of Rav into the mouth of Rabi, and I could not understand what they were discussing. Even though I could not understand the words, I could feel the transmission of Torah from one generation to the next."[3]

∽

A few years later, Rav left Eretz Yisrael to settle in Neherda, Babylonia. From there he moved to Sura, and worked to help make it a major center of Jewish life. He trained another generation of young scholars, for they came from far and near to study Torah with him in a peaceful and protected environment. He was often called upon as a decisor of Jewish law and his study hall was considered a miniature Holy Temple.[4]

It happened that a colleague, Rabbah bar Chana, hired two porters to move some barrels of wine from his vineyard to his house. "Please be very careful with these clay barrels. This wine has aged a long time, and I have been saving it for a very special occasion," he cautioned them.

"We have been porters for a long time," they assured him. "We guarantee to deliver your barrels in good condition."

As they trudged along with their heavy load, they stumbled into a pothole in the street. Losing their balance, they dropped the barrels. The barrels shattered and the wine spilled all over the street. Passers-by gazed silently at the plight of the porters, but they could do nothing to help them, so they continued with their own business.

Despairing and embarrassed, they proceeded to Rabbah's house to tell him what had happened.

Angrily, he shouted, "You were careless with my barrels. I trusted you to bring them here intact. You have to pay me the value of the barrels and the wine that was in them!"

"But, we earn our living as porters. We have no extra money to repay you what you demand."

"In that case, I will keep your shirts and jackets as security, until you have the money to pay me what you owe."

The porters were distressed with the harsh judgment of Rabbah. "What can we do?" they moaned.

The younger porter exclaimed, "The garments that he took from us as security are the only garments that we own. We use them for blankets at night. Let's go to the court of Rav and appeal for justice."

Rav listened patiently to the facts of the case. When the porters had finished describing in full detail what had happened, he instructed Rabbah to return their garments.

Rabbah demanded an explanation, for he had not understood the law in the manner in which Rav interpreted it.

"Why can't I hold their garments as security, when the facts show that they were clearly negligent?"

"You can not hold their garments, because it is written, "That you may walk in the way of good men, and keep the paths of the righteous."[5]

"This means that you should treat your fellow man graciously and help him unconditionally, even though you think he may not be deserving. When you perform unconditional acts of kindness, you are considered righteous."

The porters pressed forward with their demand to be cleared of negligence. The older one continued, "We appreciate that Rabbah will return our garments, but he also demands that we pay him the value of the barrels and the wine. We have worked this day without earning any money. Our families will be hungry tonight."

Rav turned to Rabbah, "You must also pay them the wages that you promised."

"Is that really the law? Is it not enough that so much damage was caused to my property? I can not keep their garments as security, and, in addition, I must still pay them for their labor?"

"Yes," answered Rav. "Even, if according to the letter of the law you are not responsible to pay them, nevertheless you are not exempt from having compassion upon them. They are poor, and they worked hard for the money that they thought they would earn. How can you send them to their homes empty handed? We must act beyond the requirements of the law, for this is the intent of our Torah when we are instructed to, 'Do what is right and good in the eyes of God.' "[6]

∾

Another time, a very poor man named Chama had a complaint against Natan, one of the wealthiest men in Sura. He hesitated to take him to court. "He is so powerful, so wealthy, so respected; he will laugh at me, for I am so poor."

Chama thought a long time about his grievance, and then he decided to file his complaint anyway. Our Torah teaches, he reasoned:

> Do not pervert justice in your courts.
>
> Do not be partial to the poor litigant, by sympathizing with him,
>
> Nor show excessive honor to the influential person,
>
> Judge your fellowman truthfully.[7]

I will go to the court of Rav. Being such a great scholar, he will be able to settle my grievance, and I will abide by his judgment.

Chama waited patiently in the long hall where other litigants sat, waiting his turn to be called before Rav. When his name was called, he walked meekly into the courtroom.

In a very gentle voice, Rav asked him to present the details of his complaint.

"I have a grievance against Natan, but I hesitated to file this complaint."

"I do not want you to worry. I am ordering my bailiff to serve him with a warrant to appear in court tomorrow morning. His money and power do not exempt him from not treating you fairly. Please return tomorrow morning also."

The bailiff was not welcomed at Natan's house. He laughed when he saw the warrant.

"How dare Chama challenge me! There are not enough camels in the Arabian desert to carry my wealth, and that poor nothing files a complaint with the court of Rav. I will not submit to his or anyone else's judgment!"

The bailiff returned to Rav and told him of his encounter with Natan.

"I don't understand how Natan could be so arrogant. After all, his wealth is only a gift from Heaven. It was given to him to use wisely, but it can also be taken from him with the blink of an eye," said Rav.

Meanwhile, Natan went hurriedly to the marketplace. He gathered a group of his friends around him. He told them the story of how the bailiff served him with a summons. He laughed raucously, and his friends joined him in laughter. People rushed toward the group, curious to find out the reason for the hilarity.

Suddenly, all the snickering and ridicule ceased when King Artaban IV's magistrate, accompanied by four officers, marched directly toward Natan.[8]

Natan trembled apprehensively, fearing the worst possible accusation. Since a harmonious relationship between the Jewish people and the government existed, he wondered what he could possibly have done to anger the king to such an extent that the magistrate was about to arrest him.

"What have I done to incur the king's wrath?" he stammered.

"I will read the accusation." The magistrate unfurled the papyrus scroll, cleared his throat and announced, "You are accused of haughty, insolent and brash behavior. You live as if the whole world is your property. You think that you do not have to pay the required taxes to the king's treasury. King Artaban is infuriated with your arrogance. Therefore, he has commanded that all your movable property be confiscated into his treasury, and that you be required to work for him as an indentured servant!"

"What can I do to reinstate myself in the eyes of the king?" pleaded Natan.

"There is nothing you can do. The king has been very patient with you; you have no idea how long he has been observing you. His decree is final!"

Natan knew he had only one recourse before his punishment was imposed. "Please," he cried humbly, "give me the opportunity to do one thing before I accompany you."

"Under the circumstances," the magistrate said, "you can have one hour to arrange your affairs."

Natan ran to the court of Rav and did not wait for the bailiff to announce him.

"Help me atone for my arrogance. I have scoffed and ridiculed. I have not respected my fellow man. King Artaban has confiscated my property and sentenced me to indentured servitude for the remainder of my life! I recognize why this misfortune has befallen on me. If only I could revoke his judgment, I would gladly stand facing the poor man who has a grievance against me." He stopped confessing, breathlessly.

Rav questioned him. He wanted to ascertain if Natan truly regretted his behavior, if he had learned his lesson.

After what seemd to him a very long time, Rav rose, put his arm around Natan and whispered, "Return to your home as you promised the magistrate. I am confident that your desperate situation will be somewhat improved."

When Natan arrived home, the four officers were not present; only the magistrate waited for him.

"King Artaban, because he is considerate of all his subjects, and wants to retain the friendship and loyalty of the Jewish people, has decided to give you another chance. He warns you to remember that this second chance is your last. He will be watching for much improvement. He wanted me to tell you that at any time, his original sentence can be carried out if you revert to your previous behavior."

Natan was guided by this verse for the rest of his life:

> *God makes poor and rich*
> *He humbles and lifts up.*[9]

Rav lived a very long life. He saw his grandson, Rav Simi the son of Rav Chiya follow in his footsteps.

∽

[**Ed.** Rav was such an exemplary leader that parents blessed their children:

May you be like Rav.[10]

When Rav concluded his prayer,[11] he added:

May it be Your Will, O Lord Our God, to grant us a long life, a life of peace, a life of good, a life of blessing, a life of subtenance, a life of bodily vigor, a life in which there is fear of sin, a life free from shame and confusion, a life of riches and honor, a life in which we may be filled with the love of Torah and the fear of Heaven, a life in which You will fulfill all the desires of our heart, for good."

About 200 years ago, these words were added to *Birkat HaChodesh*, the blessing of the new month. Declaring the arrival of the new month was one of the functions of the *Bayt Din*, a Jewish court that met in the courtyard of the Holy Temple.

He ordained the inclusion of part of the *malcheyot*, the section of the *musaf* on Rosh Hashana describing the process of the King of the World judging His subjects.[12]

He also is remembered for many pithy maxims that reflect Jewish life.

It is known that a person who has compassion on others must certainly be of the descendants of our father Abraham.[13]

Rav advises matchmakers;

A man may not bethroth a woman until he see her.[14]]

∽

A Sacred Trust
— Commentary —
Bustenai

From generation to generation, the Jewish people have woven their fate into the lives of people from many different cultures. These stories contain new names and new situations, but the themes remain much the same. They speak of our love of family and our respect for the traditions and values which guide our encounters with the rest of the world.

The beauty of this story flows from weaving together themes that find their origins in the Biblical narrative. The House of King David is the source of our dream and the foundation of our belief that we are a nation among the peoples of the earth. Generations that followed David longed to return to his land. They dreamed of the great day when his spirit would draw us back.

Bustenai is an example of how this tradition has become such a central feature of our literature. Building on the belief that our roots are contained in the lives of our forbears, we are able to demonstrate the survival of our people who move within the cultures of diverse, and often hostile, nations. By utilizing our wisdom and understanding of the human condition and the ability that results from a life filled with study and learning, we have been able to manage our interactions with those more powerful and influential. All the while, we have maintained a clear vision of who we are and what we stand for as Jews, even living outside of our own land.

Paul A. Flexner,
Director of Human Resources Development,
Jewish Education Service of North America, Inc.
(JESNA)

Chapter Seven
BUSTENAI: The Exilarch

Time Line

70 c.e.	600 c.e.	1000 c.e.	1400 c.e.	1600 c.e.	1800 c.e.	2000 c.e.

— Location: Babylonia [Iraq] —

[**Ed.** The Exilarch, the leader of all the Jewish people living in the Babylonian exile, traced his ancestry as far back as David, King of ancient Israel. He was invested with authority over all the congregation of Israel at the hands of the caliphs, and was honored by them as the representative of the Jews. His duties included the collection of taxes, the supervision of businesses, and the jurisdiction over court cases. Concerning the Exilarch, Mohammed had commanded: "grant him a seal of office over all the congregations that dwell under his rule, and everyone, whether Mohammedan or Jew, or any other nation, must rise up before the Exilarch and salute him." "When the Exilarch left his palace to visit the Caliph, he rode on a horse, attired in silk, embroidered robes, a large turban adorned his head, and from the turban a long white cloth was suspended with a charm upon which the cipher of Mohammed was engraved. He appeared before the Caliph and kissed his hand, and the Caliph rose and placed him on the throne which Mohammed had ordered made for him. He was seated on the throne opposite the Caliph.[1]"]

∽

The Exilarach, Mar Chanina escorted his son Mar Huna to the wedding canopy which had been erected near the banks of the Euphrates River, facing the city of Machoza. The young groom stood next to Yaleta, daughter of Rabbi Chofni, one of the rabbinic authorities of Sura, as their marriage was solemnized. Thoughts about their future together obsessed him: "I am a descendant of the House of King David. My bride is the daughter of one of the leading scholars of this generation. One of our children might be the redeemer, scion of the House of David, who will lead our people out of this land of exile back to the Holy Land."

The wedding guests danced joyously and sang happily with the bride and groom; Mar Huna dreamed his dream.

But his dream was short lived. The political situation was filled with turbulence and upheaval. The power struggle between the Persians and the Byzantine Romans resulted in the shedding of much innocent blood as they fought for control of the Middle East. To add to the unrest, the Persian King Korzoi II, believed that his life was threatened, so he unmercifully eliminated any person whose loyalty he suspected.

Tragically, many Jews, among them Mar Chanina and Mar Huna, were the innocent victims of his vengeance. Hearing the devestating news, Yaleta fled to her father's home. When Rabbi Chofni heard of the circumstances of the death of his son-in-law and his father, he quickly sent his pregnant daughter, along with a trusted friend to hide with a family far from Sura until the king's wrath subsided.

One morning when King Korzoi awoke, he felt a burning sensation across his forehead. Raising his hand, he stroked the painful, moist area and lowered his hand covered with fresh blood. Shaken, he remembered his awesome dream and immediately called his court advisors for their interpretation.

"This is what I dreamed," he proceeded, but the advisors were puzzled. None of them could explain the dream, the open wound, or the blood on his forehead. Word spread quickly that the king was searching for someone to interpret his dream.

Rabbi Chofni thought: "I will go to the king, for if I can interpret his dream, he might always remember that I helped him. He will be indebted to me and to my people."

King Korzoi was about to begin repeating the dream, but Rabbi Chofni said respectfully: "Please, your majesty, let me tell you your dream before I interpret it.

"You were walking along the banks of the Euphrates River on the first night of the new moon. Suddenly, you saw a garden filled with the most wondrous trees, more beautiful and lush than any in your own palace garden. This made you very angry, for the law of your land clearly states that no one is entitled to anything better than the king's. You grabbed an ax, and started to slash at the tree trunks. You hacked at the gashes until you felled one tree after another. When the branches snapped, you tore the leaves one by one, and crunched them with your bare hands. Only one slender, young sapling remained upright in the garden. The sapling had recently been planted; it had little foliage. Flowering tassels dangled from skinny twigs. You were about to strike the sapling, when a curly red haired man, dressed in a flowing white linen robe, girdled with a leather sash, appeared to you and shouted: 'Don't chop down that tree!' "

King Korzoi stared in disbelief as Rabbi Chofni recounted his dream. Agitatedly, he whined: "Let me continue telling you the rest, for it is the end of the dream that frightened me the most. The man grabbed the ax from my hand, and swung it at my forehead; I saw my blood trickle down and form a puddle around my feet."

"You will die for destroying my garden," he roared.

I threw myself at his feet and pleaded for mercy. "I will do anything you demand, but please, I beg you, spare my life."

He seemed to ignore my pleas. "My garden was much more beautiful than any of yours. You had no reason to destroy it."

"Please, forgive me, forgive me. If you spare my life, I swear that I will personally care for the remaining sapling, and as its flowers bud, I will give them to you, so that you may replant your garden." The man seemed appeased and lowered his ax.

King Korzoi panted, short of breath. "Now, I can interpret your dream," said Rabbi Chofni. "You see, the old man was

King David. He was enraged that you destroyed his garden, for symbolically that means that you destroyed his house, his descendants. He only recanted his determination for revenge because you swore that you would personally care for the one remaining sapling. You must know that when you ordered the murder of Mar Chanina and Mar Huna, you almost succeeded in wiping out the house of King David. Yet, there is one sapling that survived your crazed massacre; Yaleta, the young widow of Mar Huna is pregnant with his child."

"Where is Yaleta?"

"I sent her to live with family friends in a village far from Sura."

"You must go and bring her back to this city, so that she may live in comfort for the remainder of her pregnancy. I swear that no harm will befall her; I will personally see that she is protected. When her child is born, if it is a boy, please name him Bustenai, for he will always remind me that his life was saved because of the incident in the garden."

[**Ed.** Bustan is the Persian word for garden]

༺

Bustenai was raised under the watchful eyes of his grandfather Rabbi Chofni. For twenty years, the two studied together, side by side. Bustenai amazed his grandfather by his quick comprehension of both Torah texts and worldly concerns.

When he was twenty years old, King Korzoi insisted that Bustenai live in the palace. He appointed him Exilarch, with all the honors that this position demanded. The Jewish people were satisfied that a scion of the House of David had achieved such honor in a land of exile, but their satisfaction was short lived.

King Korzoi decided that Bustenai was a threat to his rule, so instead of protecting him as he promised, he sentenced him to death. Most people assumed that the sentence had been carried out, but, Bustenai escaped. He found himself trapped between the warring Byzantine Christians and the Persians who battled each other for supremacy. Meanwhile Arabs, under the leadership of Mohammed, roared out of the Arabian peninsula on their way toward world conquest attempting to convert the peoples of the countries between Spain and Persia to Islam.

The legal status of the Jews under this new religion was infinitely better than under the Byzantine Christians; their legal status was more favorable, and they enjoyed increased economic success. Bustenai decided to seek the favor of Mohammed, hoping that the common tenets of both their religions would become the basis for mutual co-existence. He sought out Ibrahim, Mohammed's closest advisor in Medina.

"You must arrange an audience for me with Mohammed," he pleaded. "Tell him," Bustenai said, "that we have much in common. We need to talk over our situations, to the benefit of both of us."

It did not take long for Bustenai to find himself standing before Mohammed.

"I have heard," began Bustenai, "that your religion espouses monotheism, the belief in one God, creator of the world and designer of human destiny; Who is just and merciful, before Whom all His creations are personally responsible; that you are respectful of learned men; that you hold scholars in high esteem. I have also heard that you believe that we share common ancestors, Noah and Abraham. I beseech you to treat my people with kindness; we have suffered so much under the rule of tyrants.

"I propose an alliance between my people and yours, to help you in your wars of conquest, to eradicate all forms of idolatry. We are a large and flourishing Jewish community, with our main cities located on the banks of the Tigris and Euphrates Rivers. I want you to know that I am a grandson of King David. The pagan king, Korzoi, tried to destroy all traces of my family, but I managed to survive. I pledge to you and your followers our loyalty in exchange for the freedom to worship our God in peace."

Bustenai became an advisor to Mohammed, and in that position was able to protect the Jewish people from the exploitation of the combatting armies.

Caliph Omar, successor to Mohammed, reconfirmed Bustenai's position as Exilarch and some peaceful years followed.

∾

A Sacred Trust
— Commentary —
The Wheel of Fortune

❧

This tale about the vicissitudes of the life of Saadya Gaon, rabbinic authority and head of the Yeshiva in Sura, teaches us about the nature of the life God fashions for us. We meet a humble, faithful teacher who accepts the turns in life's journey without leaving the path or deserting his work, the writing of an important philosophical treatise.

The story creatively conveys a perception of life: that the good things like power, glory, and honor do not last nor does misfortune, be it strife, illness or exile. Man must accept his fate and live in a way that responds to life's changes. One must do one's best in times of misfortune and celebrate and build in times of blessing. All this done while remaining a kind, productive human being, constantly faithful to God.

—*Dr. Betsy Dolgin Katz,*
North American Director,
Florence Melton Adult Mini-School, Chicago, IL

TITLES AND HONORS

In reading Jewish works one comes across
a number of titles and honors given as
part of a person's name.

— RAV —

Title of scholars who lived in Babylonia.
Mar Rav and HaRav HaGaon were additional
titles for special teachers.

— RABBI —

Title of scholar who lived in *Eretz Israel.*
It became the basic title for Jewish spiritual leaders.

— RABBAN —

Title of the head of the Sanhedrin.
(The Jewish Supreme Court)

— RABAYNU —

"Highly honored teacher"
Given to Moshe (Moses), Yeduda Hanasi, and
Gershom, among many others.

— RABAYNU HAKADOSH —

"Our Holy Teacher"

— REBBE —

A beloved teacher, oftentimes referring to a
Chassidic master.

— R. —

Literary abbreviation for "Rabbi."

— GAON —

Title originally given to head of
Babylonian Jewish academies. Later
became a title given to a person with
great knowledge of Torah.

Chapter Eight
THE WHEEL OF FORTUNE

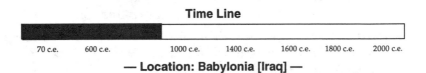

Time Line

70 c.e.   600 c.e.   1000 c.e.   1400 c.e.   1600 c.e.   1800 c.e.   2000 c.e.

— **Location: Babylonia [Iraq]** —

Rabbi Saadya dwelt in a splendid villa replete with luxurious furnishings and attentive servants, befitting the acknowledged leader of world Jewry.

The entire household was in a frenzy that beautiful spring day. Maids polished silver and washed dishes; servants moved furniture, swept floors and washed windows. The corners of every room were carefully inspected, so that no *chametz* (leaven bread) would be seen or found during the coming festival of *Pesach* (Passover). Acha, administrator of Rav Saadya's estate personally packed the new ceramic dishes, the pottery serving pieces and a crystal wine bottle and tray into a box, lifted them gently into the back of a wagon, hitched up a horse, and pointed it in the direction of the Euphrates River. His special job was to immerse these new pieces into the river, to purify them for use at the Seder.

> [Ed. "If one purchases cooking utensils, those which are customarily cleansed by water must be immersed (before they can be used)..." *Talmud Bavli, Avodah Zarah 75b, Mishna*]

Just as gently, he unloaded the box from the wagon, and placed the objects to be immersed alongside the edge of the river. As he immersed each piece, he placed it on a slope of higher ground directly in back of him. Relieved that he was almost finished without mishap, he recoiled as a sudden furious wave crashed the shoreline. The surge carried away the last item, the crystal tray, into the depth of the river.

Acha was horrified. He sat down on the sand to think.

"How can I be held responsible for such an unfortunate mishap?" he pondered. "I was extremely careful with my master's possessions. The weather is so beautiful today, the water was so calm; there is no logical explanation for that sudden surge. My master will never miss that one crystal tray that was carried away; he has so many others. Rather than tell him what happened, I will keep the mishap secret. No one except me will ever know."

He rose, returned the rest of the objects to the box, lifted it to the wagon, jumped up to the driver's ledge at the front and pointed the horses toward Rav Saadya's villa.

He continued working; his expressionless face did not reveal the secret he concealed.

~

The year rushed by, and Acha found himself stooping along the river's edge once again, immersing different new vessels. This time he was more careful; he placed everything on the slope, climbed up each time to retrieve the piece he was going to immerse, and replaced it before picking up the next piece. Immersing each piece, he paused, scanning the surface of the water. He squinted from the bright sunlight that sparkled with long rays across the surface of the water. Unexpectedly, he noticed a shiny clear object riding the crest of a wave. As it languidly washed ashore, he picked up the object; it was the crystal tray that had washed away the year before.

Acha could not believe his eyes. He rubbed them hard, for he thought that the sun's rays were playing games with his perception. He picked up the tray, turned it over and over, walked up the slope, sat down, and pondered:

"This is the exact tray that was washed out to sea last year. No one will ever believe this. It's like a fairy tale. I've been told that the waters of the world are all connected and they have no end. This tray must have been carried over the waves all through the world, and now has been returned to its proper owner. Now, as soon as I return to the villa, I will reveal to Rav Saadya the secret that I have concealed all year. He will be so happy with the news that his tray was returned."

Contrary to his belief, Rav Saadya was not happy when Acha revealed his secret. He sighed painfully, groaned pitifully, deeply anguished, as if evil were lurking all around him, evil that he was powerless to control. Acha was puzzled, but decided not to press the issue further.

After *Pesach*, Rav Saadya became more and more involved in controversy with the Exilarach David ben Zakkai, who controlled the administration of the Jewish community. Rav Saadya stood his ground in the dispute; finally he resigned his position as leading rabbinic authority and head of the *yeshiva*, and went to live in Baghdad, relinquishing his right to communal support. Financially, he lived on a much lower standard than he had been accustomed to.

Acha debated his future. "Before I go to work for someone else," he thought, "I think I would like to attempt investing in my own business. After all, I successfully administered Rav Saadya's estate for many years, which provided me with much experience."

So Acha moved north, to a city along the banks of the Tigris River. He sought opportunities to supply people with silk fabric, and when he had acquired many customers, he added household articles to his stock of commodities. With the profits, he bought farmland and vineyards. During the next few years, Acha became a very wealthy man. He settled in a villa, similar to the one he had administered for Rav Saadya.

Meantime, Rav Saadya was peacefully working on his important philosophic work, without being interrupted with communal matters.

[**Ed.** *Emunot V'Dayot:* Beliefs and Opinions]

From time to time, he halted his writing, and went to visit Jewish communities in other cities.

Once, he arrived in a city without making previous arrangements where he would stay. He hoped that one of his supporters would offer him home hospitality.

Acha happened to be in the marketplace, arranging some business deals and saw him. Embracing his former master warmly, he said: "You must be my house guest for the duration of your stay here. I have become very comfortable, and I live in a large villa. You shall have your own quarters, peace and quiet to study as you wish, and every convenience that I can possibly provide for you. I see that you are not carrying too many personal belongings. I will see to it that you have a new tunic appropriate for the leader of all Jewry."

Rav Saadya was overwhelmed by Acha's offer of hospitality. Together they walked to the villa. Conversing softly as they walked, Rav Saadya and Acha shared the events of the seven years that they had been separated.

Two days after Rav Saadya arrived, he became very ill. As lovingly as Acha had cared for his master previously, he now did everything he could to find the best doctors to cure him, but to no avail. It seemed that Rav Saadya hung perilously close to death. Finally, a friend of Acha's recommended another doctor who lived a distance away. Acha sent for him immediately.

Arriving in Acha's house, the doctor spoke gently to Rav Saadya to determine what hurt him. "I am going to prescribe a medicine for you that I think will cure you."

Turning to Acha, he said: "I want your cook to prepare a chicken soup from two fat chickens whose broth has evaporated to one tablespoon. The nourishment in this medicine will help him recover."

The cook carefully prepared the soup, mixed it tenderly as it simmered, placed the required tablespoon of broth into a cup many hours later, and served it to Rav Saadya. As he raised his head from the pillow to sip the broth, a spider landed in the cup. The broth was inedible.

A small smile played around the corners of Rav Saadya's lips.

Somehow, a flashback ... Acha remembered hearing that anguished sigh, that pitiful groan when he told Rav Saadya about the crystal tray that had been carried away by the waves and had floated up on the shore a year later. He should have been very happy. He was more puzzled now than he had been seven years before.

"I don't understand, my master," whispered Acha, "the connection between your smiling now and your groaning seven years ago. I thought that when I found the tray, you would be very happy, and you would groan and sigh when the medicine that was cooked for you was rendered inedible. You reacted the opposite of the way I thought. Please explain."

"I want you to know, Acha, that when a person attains power and glory, when he has the respect of the entire Jewish community, it does not mean that it will necessarily last forever. When you told me about the tray that floated back to shore, I somehow understood that it was a sign that I had reached the climax of my power and influence. I sighed because I feared my fate. These past seven years have not been easy. True, I almost completed writing the book which has been a most important part of my life, but I certainly did not live in the comfort to which I had become accustomed. I believe that a person's misfortune only lasts for a prescribed time. When the spider fell into that broth, that medicine which the doctor thought would cure me, I perceived that the years of my misfortune were past. Now, I am confident that I will recover soon. As soon as I am strong enough, I shall return to Sura to heal the breach between me and the Exilarach David. We have been divided in our opinions long enough. It is not good that our people are forced to take sides. For God is judge; He puts one down, and lifts another up."[1]

[**Ed.** The Midrash explains that this world is comparable to a rotating wheel placed over a well in a beautiful garden; the upper portion of the wheel, with buckets attached to it, is lowered into the well to draw water and is raised with full buckets. This process empties the buckets on the lower level. Every rotation of the wheel either empties the full buckets or fills the empty buckets. So it is that anyone who is rich one day may not be rich the next day; and anyone who is poor one day may not be poor the next, for the world is a rotating wheel.

Midrash Sh'mot Rabbah, Mishpatim, 31:14]

Rav Saadya returned to Sura shortly athereafter. He resumed his role as Rabbinic authority and head of the *yeshiva*.

∾

A Sacred Trust
— Commentary —
The Journey of the Rabbis

❧

Mitzvah Gor-ret Mitzvah . . . one noble act can set the tone of a religious environment and impact entire communities.

Journey of the Four Captive Rabbis illustrates *Pidyom Sh-vuyim,* one of the highest obligations for a Jew. Early in the morning and during the *Amidah,* the most important prayer focus, we refer to the Maker as a liberator of captives.

To win back, even at great sacrifice, the freedom of a Jew, became a priority on the Jewish agenda.

First, the ethics of the issue — human dignity — demand it.

Second, the act itself brings rewards . . . in this case, whole communities and institutions receive new life from the impact of the *Mitzvah.*

The spiritual spiral continues even in the next generation, as the diary account at the close, reveals.

—*Rabbi Gerald B. Zelermeyer*
Emanuel Synagogue
West Hartford, Connecticut

❧

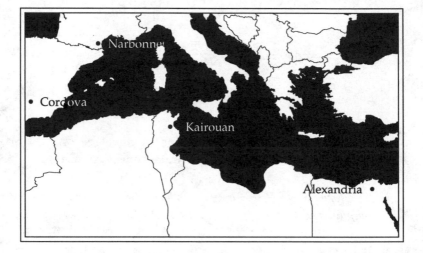

The Western Relocation of the
Four Rabbinic Scholars

Rabbi Shemaryah ben Elchanan to Alexandria, Egypt

Rabbi Chushiel ben Elchanan to Kairouan, Tunisia

Rabbi Moshe ben Chanoch to Cordova, Spain

The fourth rabbi is said to have been ransomed
to Narbonne, France

Chapter Nine
THE JOURNEY OF THE FOUR CAPTIVE RABBIS

Time Line

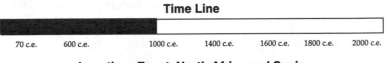

70 c.e. 600 c.e. 1000 c.e. 1400 c.e. 1600 c.e. 1800 c.e. 2000 c.e.

— **Location: Egypt, North Africa and Spain** —

[Ed. *Gaon*, plural *geonim*, is the title of rabbinic leaders begining around the seventh century. The period of the Babylonian *Geonim* ended in the eleventh century.]

"I never cease to be amazed at the survival of the Jewish people, at their patterns of migration, at the shifting focus of Jewish life from one part of the world to the other," thought Rabbi Abraham ben David Halayvi ibn Daud. "To me, this phenomenon proves that there is a Guardian of Israel. Let me give you an example . . .

During the last hundred years of the period of the *Geonim* in Babylonia, an amazing event occurred which effectively shifted the center of Jewish life from the eastern to the western world. The following is what I have found out about it in the course of my research. It seems that four esteemed rabbis sailed from Bari, Italy, in 974, to collect money to be used either as dowries for poor brides or to sustain the *yeshivot* in Babylonia, which were operating under tremendous stress.

At that time, the seas were controlled by pirates employed by the princes and kings of Spain and Italy. The booty that they accumulated and the prisoners that they ransomed, were good sources of income for their masters' treasuries. The Caliph of Spain, Avad al Damchan Alnatzar had commissioned the pirate, Ibn Demachin (or Ibn Rumahis) as commander of his flotilla with the responsibility of capturing as many vessels as possible from the king of Italy. Ibn

Demachin sailed along the southern coasts of the Mediterranean Sea watching for his prey.

Sighting potential success, he sailed alongside a large schooner, three square-rigged masts fluttering in the wind, and demanded that the captain surrender. He boarded, found four men huddled on deck and recognized them to be Jews by their distinctive dress.

"Jews always redeem their brethren," he must have thought. "I do not have to kill them. I will earn a tremendous reward from my master from their redemption money. And I won't dispose of them in the same city, for each Jewish community has limited funds to redeem captives."

He bound the four Jews, ordered that they be transferred to his vessel, and permitted the schooner to proceed. He sailed for Alexandria, and auctioned Rabbi Shemaryah ben Elchanan as a slave. Apparently he did not know his true worth, but he was satisfied with the money he received. It did not take long for the Jewish community of Alexandria to recognize the scholar that they had ransomed. They invited him to become the head of the Talmudic Academy in Fostat (Cairo).

◯

Rabbi Chushiel ben Rabbi Elchanan was auctioned in Kairouan, Tunisia. When the Jewish community discovered his identity, they persuaded him to accept the position of head of the community. He developed it into a major center of Torah life in North Africa.

◯

Rabbi Moshe ben Chanoch was auctioned in Cordova, Spain. He was a very unassuming man, so for many weeks, he sat in the back of the Knesset Hamidrash Synagogue where people studied after prayers. Sometimes, the leader of the Jewish community, *Dayan* (Judge and Arbitrator) Natan lectured. Once, he was discussing a very obscure point of Jewish law, and he could not clarify the main issue to the participants.

Rabbi Moshe rose from his seat in the back and said softly:

"Allow me to explain." People turned their heads toward him, and only when he helped them understand, did they realize the capabilities of the man who they had recently redeemed from the hands of pirates. They invited him to become the head of the *yeshiva*. His leadership marked the beginning of independent Jewish scholarship in Spain, coinciding with The Golden Age.

[**Ed.** See Part Three for stories about The Golden Age.]

◯

Very little is known about the fourth captive, but I have heard that he was ransomed in Narbonne, France.

These four redeemed captives made a tremendous impact on the development of Jewish life in Europe, for they established centers of Torah learning in their new homes.

◯

Years later, I came across this diary entry. It was dated the first half of the eleventh century, and it was written by the Jewish community of Alexandria (Egypt), addressed to Rabbi Ephraim ben Rabbi Shemaryah (son of one of the four ransomed captives) and the Elders of the Palestinian Jewish community who resided in Fostat (Cairo, Egypt).

". . . You are the supporters of the poor and aid men in need. You study diligently, you rouse the good against the evil impulse. You walk in the right way and practice justice. For this, may God grant you peace and security.

"We turn to you today on behalf of a captive woman who has been brought here from Byzantium. We ransomed her for 24 dinares, beside the government tax.

[**Ed.** 33 dinares was about 16 pounds of gold]

You sent us 12 dinares; we have paid the remainder. Soon afterwards, sailors brought two other prisoners, one of them a fine young man possessing knowledge of Torah, the other a boy of about ten. When we saw them in the hands of the pirates, how they beat and frightened them before our own eyes, we had pity on them and guaranteed their ransom.

"We had hardly settled this, when another ship arrived carrying many prisoners; among them were a physician and his wife. Thus we are again in difficulties and distress. And our strength is over-strained, as the taxes are heavy and the times critical . . ."

∽

Medieval Europe,
The Middle Ages and the Renaissance

Part Two Time Period

| 70 c.e. | 600 c.e. | 1000 c.e. | 1400 c.e. | 1600 c.e. | 1800 c.e. | 2000 c.e. |

— Location: Germany, France, England, Poland —

Introduction

The early part of the Middle Ages, from the fall of Rome in 476 of the common era to the first Crusade in 1096, was referred to by many historians as the "Dark Ages," because there was little learning. It was not until much after the two hundred years of the Crusades that the course of Western Civilization advanced, inspired by the Renaissance, beginning in the 1500s.

During the period of the destruction of the second Holy Temple (70 C.E.), Jews, some taken into captivity, and others following the Roman conquerors northward and westward across the European continent, established small communities, usually along the river banks. Depending on the whim of the ruler of the Holy Roman Empire, they lived in relative security, for they were a very inconspicuous minority and the Church was in its infancy.

For hundreds of years, the Jews were welcome residents in the towns and villages of the Franco/Germanic lands (France and Germany). Some owned land and pursued agriculture. Many earned their livelihood as merchants. A network of trade routes developed, not only throughout the area of the Germanic lands, but also throughout the lands bordering the eastern shores of the Mediterranean Sea, effectively linking East and West. The study of Torah was an intregal part of life.

Therefore, this early part of the Middle Ages for the Jews, was in contrast to the non-Jewish world, actually a period of "Light Ages," marked by economic and intellectual achievement. (*A*

Tale of Two Wives, Chapter Ten; *Tales of Rashi,* Chapter Thirteen; *We Are The Custodians of the Divine Dream,* Chapter Fourteen.)

In 1095, Pope Urban II called for a Crusade to free the Holy Land from the Moslem infidels. Nine times, Crusaders marched eastward during the next two hundred years (1096-1299), none of them successfully establishing Christian dominion over the Holy Land for any length of time. The leaders of the Crusades, searching for power, promised salvation to sinners, freedom to prisoners, trade routes to merchants. They reasoned: "Why travel 2,000 miles to find infidels in the Holy Land when they are living in our midst?" In the wake of the Crusades, Jewish blood flowed through the streets of the towns along the Rhine River, the route that the Crusaders used to travel eastward. Darkness extinguished the "Light Ages." (*The Massacre at York,* Chapter Fifteen.)

The allegation of "Deicide" (killing of the Christian god) resulted in forced conversions, blood libels, and massacres of untold numbers of Jewish communities. The Jews were powerless to defend themselves against the atrocities inflicted upon them, and preferred martyrdom, *"al kiddush hashem,* for the sanctification of His Name." *(I Will Die a Jew,* Chapter Twelve; *The Blood Libel,* Chapter Seventeen; *The Golem Comes to Prague,* Chapter Twenty Two.)

Prominent Jewish leaders, scholars or merchants, lived in constant fear of being kidnapped for ransom. The ransom was used to fill the coffers of priests to cover their extravagant styles of living, or nobles to finance their battles. Generally, Jewish communities were pathetically poor, but occasionally an individual was able to raise the required exorbitant sum. (*The Jewish Pope,* Chapter Eleven; *Rabbi Mayer's Letter,* Chapter Sixteen.)

The Black Plague (1348) was imported to Europe from Asia by sailors carrying the disease. Within three years, one-third of Europe's population succumbed. Medieval people, lacking an understanding of the spread of disease, and being extremely superstitious, searched for a scapegoat on whom to blame the deaths of their loved ones. They accused the Jews of poisoning the wells and rivers. Violence against Jews included confiscation or burning property, expulsion, and murder. (*The Majesty of the Number Seven,* Chapter Eighteen.)

Depending on the toleration of some Popes during the height of the Renaissance and their leanings toward cultural interests, Jews that lived in Italy were more accepted than in the rest of Western Europe. (*The Mitzvah of Netilat Yadayim,* Chapter Nineteen.)

Generally, the Jewish people lived separately from their non-Jewish neighbors benefiting from cohesive communities, but they were officially forced into ghettos at the beginning of the sixteenth century. (*Shimon the Silent,* Chapter 20)

When Martin Luther (1483-1546) criticized the Church for its harsh treatment of the Jews, they were relieved, for they sought some respite from the previous centuries of degradation and violence. However, his attitude changed when the Jews refused to convert. Among his proposals in his book, *Against the Jews and Their Lies,* he recommended burning synagogues, homes, books, and abolishing safe conduct. (*Joselman, Luther and the Emperor,* Chapter Twenty One.)

As modern times crept after the footsteps of the Renaissance, some of the more enlightened rulers of Europe broke the stranglehold of the trade guilds, which had excluded Jews for centuries, in the hope of rebuilding the economies of their countries after the Thirty Years' War, 1618-1648. Although living conditions were still restricted by ghetto regulations, Jewish merchants stepped forward cautiously to engage in commerce and repeat what their ancestors had done for the Franco/Germanic lands during the early part of the Middle Ages. (*Diary of a Lady: Out of the Ghettos,* Chapter Twenty Three.)

These are the stories of our medieval Ashkenazic ancestors.

∽

A Sacred Trust

— Commentary —

Rabaynu Gershom

Why have Jews survived? Because we value life above all else, The tale of Rabaynu Gershom illustrates the value of life in Judaism — the value of giving life and of saving a life.

Jews have been called the people of the book, but we are just as surely *the people of the family*. In traditional Judaism, having children is not only a religious obligation—*be fruitful and multiply*—but the crowning fulfillment of a marriage. The story of Rabaynu Gershom unfolds precisely because of pursuit of the Jewish value of raising a family! When, like the matriarch Sarah, his wife Devorah is unable to bear children, she too resorts to the desperate measure of acquiring a second wife for her husband. Surely, her actions and the ensuing tale will arouse emphaty and support for those who expend great emotional, physical and financial resources to pursue this value,

Saving lives is at the core of this story. Not only does Rabaynu Gershom save the life of Princess Theodora (thereby saving the entire Jewish population of Constantinople), but his ever-faithful wife Devorah devises an elaborate scheme to free him from imprisonment and save his life.

We learn from Leviticus 18:5, *"You shall therefore keep my statutes ... which if a [person] does... he/she shall live, by them [the commandments)"* that the preservation of human life takes precedence over all other commandments. Not all of us have the opportunity to hold life and death in our hands as dramatically as Rabaynu Gershom; but each of us has the potential and opportunity to be a life-saver. By contributing to feed the hungry, clothe the naked, redeem the captive and speaking out for those who are oppressed, we too can pursue the value of *pikuach nefesh* — of saving a life.

—Dr. Leora W. Isaacs, Ph.D.
Director, Research and Evaluation,
Family Education Programing, JESNA,
Co-Author: "A Jewish Grandparent's Gift of Memories"

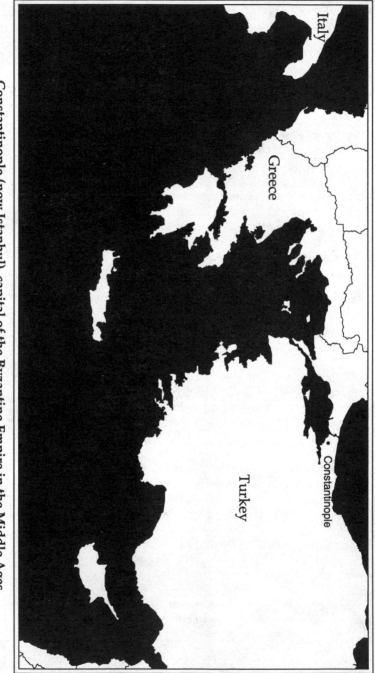

Constantinople (now Istanbul), capital of the Byzantine Empire in the Middle Ages.

CHAPTER TEN
RABAYNU GERSHOM: A TALE OF TWO WIVES

Time Line

70 c.e.	600 c.e.	1000 c.e.	1400 c.e.	1600 c.e.	1800 c.e.	2000 c.e.

— Location: Constantinople, Turkey —

Constantinople was one of the largest and most splendid cities during the middle ages. It was not only the capital of the Byzantine Empire, but one of the commercial links between East and West. It was here that Rabaynu Gershom decided to live after his marriage to Devorah, daughter of his teacher, Rabbi Yehuda ben Mayer HaKohen Leontyne of Mainz.

The young couple settled there because they thought that his skills as an artisan, metallurgist, gold and silversmith would enable him to earn a comfortable living in this thriving metropolis. Gershom could work part time and devote the remainder of his day pursuing his Talmudic studies. On the surface, the couple seemed contented, but they shared the grief of childlessness. One night, Devorah passed the open door of her husband's study, and heard him pleading in prayer:

"Our patriarch Abraham asked God what possible earthly reward could He give him, if he died childless. I am asking the same question. What good is all this comfort, all this wealth that I have accumulated, if I have not been blessed with children to carry on after me? Children are our eternity."

His prayer turned into uncontrolled sobbing.

She could not contain herself. She tiptoed into the room, walked over to his desk, stood facing her husband, and whispered gently: "Gershom, I am the one who has been unable to conceive. It is not right, that because of me, you should not have children. Let us follow the example of our patriarch Abraham and our matriarch Sarah. After they had been married for ten years, and Sarah remained childless, she proposed to Abraham that he marry another woman for the purpose of having children with her. Remember, how she said to him: 'God has withheld children from me. Perhaps He intended that His promise that you become the father of a great nation be fulfilled through another woman. Marry my maid servant (Hagar) so that I might build a family through her.'[1] I want you to take another wife who will be able to bear children for you."

At first, Gershom adamantly refused to listen to Devorah. He acquiesced only when she promised that she would chose his second wife.

Devorah was acquainted with a pious and prosperous merchant named Menachem. He had raised his only daughter by himself after the tragic loss of his wife, and he indulged her every whim. Mileta was very beautiful, but unknown to Devorah, she was also self-indulgent and selfish. She spent money extravagantly, purchased the most expensive gowns, and spent much of her day primping in front of her mirror. Mileta was also in love with Michael, nephew of Johann, King Basil's prime minister.

When Johann found out that his nephew was courting a Jewish girl, he forced him to swear that he would never see her again. Johann, envious of Jewish business success, fearing the Jews a threat to his position at court, had long ago promised himself that he would find a way to destroy them. The appropriate time had not arrived yet to plot a plan, for King Basil was a just and honest monarch.

Mileta did not know why Michael suddenly disappeared. Heartbroken, after waiting for him for many months, she finally agreed to the match between herself and Gershom.

[**Ed.** At the time when Gershom married Mileta, a Jew was permitted to have more than one wife.]

Devorah had no way of knowing Mileta's true character until after she had married Gershom. By that time, it was too late. Yet, she kept her peace, for she was the one who had chosen her husband's second wife.

One night, a fire broke out in one of the best neighborhoods of Constantinople. The blaze destroyed many homes. People lost their lives trying to find refuge; others found themselves homeless after the blaze had burned itself out. Thieves plundered, ravaging what the fire had spared. Johann, waiting for an opportunity to devise a plot to incriminate the Jews, realized that he could concoct a pretext for their expulsion by blaming them for having set the fire.

The next morning, at his daily meeting with the king, he accused: "The Frenchman, the goldsmith, their leader, the one the Jews call Rabaynu Gershom is guilty of arson. He is responsible for the loss of property, the looting, and the general state of anarchy that followed. If you expel him, and all his people, I promise to enrich your treasury with all the confiscated Jewish property."

Even though the king was reputed to be honorable and just, he could not ignore Johann's promise of a great deal of wealth, so he signed a decree of expulsion, permitting the Jews only three months to settle their affairs.

In the meantime, a mysterious disease followed in the footsteps of the fire. Sickness spread rapidly through the population. Rabaynu Gershom devoted his nights and days to saving life, a skill that he had learned in Pumpedita at the same time he was studying Talmud

[**Ed.** Pumpedita, situated on the banks of the Euphrates River, (Iraq) was a center of Torah study beginning with the period of the Second Holy Temple, a century before the common era, and grew steadily until the eleventh century. Leading Talmudic scholars such as Abaye (326-338) and Rava (338-352) lived there, and guided its yeshiva and Rabbinic court. By the tenth century, Pumpedita had reached the peak of its achievement under the leadership of Sherira Gaon (968-998) and his son Hai Gaon (998-1038). They maintained communications with

Jewish communities in North Africa and Spain, and students came from other countries to study with them.]

His heart ached at the fate that had befallen his people. "I can return to Mainz or Metz, but what of them?" he wondered. "They have lived here all their lives, they have homes, businesses, schools. Where can they possibly go? Which country will permit them settlement, without the money to pay the entrance taxes? How can they rearrange their lives in three months?"

While he was agonizing how to help his people, an opportunity presented itself. Rabaynu Gershom found out that the niece of the bachelor King Basil, the Princess Theodora, had also been stricken with the disease. No doctor had been able to find a cure. The princess was the apple of his eye; he lavished attention on her; he laughed with her, and glowed over her every accomplishment, as she grew from an infant to a beautiful young woman. Now, a pallor hung over the royal household in anticipation of her imminent death.

Running to his friend Roman Arniropolis, a confidant of the king, he blurted out: "You must go to the palace at once and propose to King Basil that you know a Jewish doctor who could cure the Princess Theodora!"

"I understand your good intentions, Gershom. I also am aware of your tremendous medical skill, but the king has given up all hope."

"That is all the more reason that you must go to him. At least, I should be given the opportunity to try to save her life."

Roman Arniropolis set out immediately for the palace. Soon the king summoned Rabaynu Gershom. Johann sat next to the king as he spoke.

"You must know," he began, "that all of our doctors have given up. I am resigned to the fact that Princess Theodora will die.

"Let me at least attempt to save her life," pleaded Rabaynu

Gershom. "While I was studying in Pumpedita, I learned some amazing cures."

Johann interrupted haughtily: "I know what method he will use! He will use witchcraft!"

"Your Majesty," argued Rabaynu Gershom, "I swear to you that I will not use witchcraft. Our Torah forbids it."[2]

King Basil deliberated. He had to balance between his hateful Prime Minister and Rabaynu Gershom.

"I'll give you the opportunity to use your medical skills," he said at last, "but only on one condition. If you succeed in curing the princess, you shall have the reward of your choice. But, if she dies, you will pay with your life!"

Rabaynu Gershom left the throne room. Servants directed him to the bedchambers of Princess Theodora, where she lay listless. She looked pale, gaunt, lethargic. Her eyes were closed. He touched her feverish head, and held her shaking shoulders as she coughed unrelentingly, interrupting her anguished sleep.

Rabaynu Gershom turned his eyes heavenward and prayed. "Only a miracle will restore the princess to health," he murmured. "Almighty God, heal the princess, not for my sake, but for the sake of Your people who are in terrible danger."

He beckoned to a servant and instructed him to stand guard over the princess. "Do not let anyone into this room. I must run home for some medicine. I will return shortly."

Rabaynu Gershom ran as quickly as he could. Once home, he mixed a rich broth with a tincture of opium and camphor, and carried it back to the palace. Inside the princess' room, he wrapped her tightly in extra blankets, then gently slipped a few drops of the broth mixture under her tongue. He waited for an hour to pass, then repeated the treatment. Patiently, every hour for three days, he repeated the treatment, gently rehydrating the ill girl. He never left her side. He never closed his eyes. At the end of the third day, he noticed that she had fallen into a peaceful sleep. The fever had subsided, and the cough slackened. He watched over her an entire week, continuing to feed her the nourishing broth. On the eighth day, he instructed the servant to inform her parents that she was on the road to recovery. He permitted them to visit her.

"Theodora, Theodora," they called to her gently as they stooped to kiss her brow. She opened her eyes and smiled. They were overjoyed. Their daughter was recovering.

During the second week of care, Rabaynu Gershom stopped the medicine, but continued the broth. Slowly, she regained her strength, a little more every day, until she was able to smile at him. She pulled herself up in her bed and whispered: "Where am I? What happened to me?"

"You were very ill, but you have almost fully recovered. Tomorrow, you may walk around this room a bit, and the next day, you may be strong enough to walk down the corridor of the palace to visit with your uncle, King Basil. Since I feel satisfied that you are better, I will leave your bedside for a while, but tomorrow, I shall return to examine you and see if you are able to resume normal activity."

Word of Princess Theodora's miraculous recovery quickly spread throughout Constantinople. King Basil summoned Rabaynu Gershom immediately after he saw his niece. Johann was sitting on the right side of the throne.

"Gershom, I am eternally grateful to you for restoring her to life. As a reward, I am giving you 50,000 golden ducats."

"Your Majesty," interrupted Gershom, "Remember, when I pleaded with you for a chance to treat the princess? You agreed that I should have the reward of my choice, if I could restore her health. Know, that I will take no money. I only wish as my reward that you rescind the decree of expulsion that was promulgated against my people."

Johann scowled. Seething in anger he thought: "This did not turn out the way I expected. He has ingratiated himself with King Basil. Soon he will be offered my job. He will be the prime minister. I must find a way to rid myself of him and his people. I must have patience. The opportune moment will yet present itself."

"Are you certain, Gershom, that this is all the reward you want?"

"Yes, your Majesty!"

"In that case, I officially rescind the decree of expulsion against the Jewish people. Further, I give to you, Gershom, this signet ring, as a symbol of my affection for you. If, at any time in the future, you are in need of help, show me this signet ring. It will symbolize our pact of friendship and I will do my utmost to help you in your trouble, just as you helped me now."

❧

Rabaynu Gershom was welcomed to the palace any time he chose to visit. He watched the Princess Theodora closely, and often times stopped to chat with King Basil.

Once, he made an unusual request: "Did the Jews have a king named Solomon?"

"Why, yes, we did. It was many years ago. He lived in *Yerushalayim* and he was instrumental in building our first Holy Temple."

"I am interested in Solomon's throne. Can you describe it to me?"

"Of course, your majesty. Solomon's throne was constructed out of ivory and gold. Precious stones decorated it. It had a base upon which twelve golden lions stood. The lions faced twelve golden eagles. There were six steps that led up to the throne which was placed on the seventh step. Different golden shaped animals adorned the steps on either side; a lion faced a calf on the bottom step, then a wolf and a lamb faced each other, a tiger faced a camel on the third step, while an eagle faced a peacock on the next level; a cat faced a rooster on the fifth step, and a hawk and a dove lay on the sixth step. As King Solomon ascended his throne, the animals would growl, bray, whistle, call, in the lanuguage that was peculiar to each of them. As he ascended, a mechansim moved his feet from one level to the next, until he reached his throne."

"Gershom, I know you to be a skilled goldsmith. I want to know if you would consider undertaking the job of building me a throne exactly as the one you described?"

"I could consider it, but two problems need to be solved. First, I would suggest that the major part of the throne, the animals and the steps be built from silver rather than gold. Second, if I consent to this project, how will it be possible for me to control the workers from pilfering your majesty's silver? I never want to be accused of stealing."

King Basil considered the problems for a few minutes. He yearned to have a throne exactly as King Solomon's. He had never met so skilled a craftsman as Rabaynu Gershom who had the ability to execute such a project.

"I agree with you that the throne should be constructed from silver. Your other concern, that of pilfering; I trust that you will do your best to control the workers. If, at any time, you feel a problem exists, you need only use the ring I gave you not too long ago, in order to summon my help."

The work proceeded slowly on the throne. Rabaynu Gershom was totally immersed in its design and production. Every so often, King Basil passed the construction site, stopped to chat with Rabyanu Gershom, and continued happily with his other duties, anticipating the planned celebration for the throne's dedication.

Courtiers applauded, diplomats cheered, ambassadors heaped lavish praise and sent messengers back to their homeland with news of the wondrous throne. Rabaynu Gershom was appointed as the king's most trusted advisor.

Through all the honor showered upon her husband, Mileta was unforgiving that he had rejected the monetary reward she had planned to spend on new gowns and expensive jewelry.

Johann seethed with uncontrollable anger and jealousy at the king's recognition of his arch enemy. After the festivities had subsided, he called Michael to his side.

"Do you remember that Jewish woman that I forbid you to see? She has become the wife of this Gershom person, and I hear that she is very unhappy. Have her meet you in the tea and spice shop in her neighborhood. Tell her that she is the most beautiful woman you have ever seen. Bring her this jewelled bracelet as a gift. Explain to her that the reason she hasn't seen you for such a long time, is that you have been fighting in a distant land for your king. When she sees the bracelet, she will believe anything you tell her. You must gain her trust. When you have done this, you will return to me, and I will instruct you what to do next."

Michael followed his uncle's instructions. It did not take long for him to gain Mileta's trust. He promised that he would meet her again in a few days. Johann was setting up a plan to implicate Rabaynu Gershom for stealing silver from the king's treasury for personal gain, while Gershom had been constructing the throne. Johann needed the signet ring, so that his arch enemy, Gershom would not have a means of protection.

At their next meeting, Michael, after proclaiming his ardent love for Mileta and promising to marry her, asked her to do him a favor. "Do you know where Gershom keeps the signet ring that King Basil gave him?"

"Of course," responded Mileta. "He wears it always."

"Does he ever remove it from his finger?"

"He removes the ring only when he washes his hands before a meal."

"Then, this is what you must do. Pretend to be a caring wife. Start attending to his needs at mealtime. After a few days, he will take your presence at the table for granted, and he will not be suspicious of you. When the opportune moment arrives, when he removes the ring to wash his hands, you must take it and bring it to me."

It was not difficult for Mileta to fulfill Michael's request. Rabaynu Gershom was very troubled that he had lost the ring. After thoroughly searching for it, he despaired ever finding it again.

Johann laid the ground work for his plan to implicate Rabaynu Gershom in the theft of king's silver. Cunningly, he suggested to the king: "Have you instructed your servants to weigh the silver used in your new throne against the amount that this Gershom person said that he used? After all, he pretends to be honest, he has even gained your trust, but what if he has been fooling you? Remember when he said those words, 'I never want to be accused of stealing?' Maybe he was using those words as a ploy?"

King Basil was troubled by Johann's accusation.

Devorah noticed that every day around the same time, Mileta disappeared. She decided to follow her. Mileta led Devorah to a small tea and spice shop. Unbeknown to Mileta, Devorah knew the inside of that shop well, for she was friendly with the proprietor, and often purchased spices there. Devorah knew that a curtain separated the front of the shop from the back. When Mileta didn't come out in a reasonable time, she walked around to the back, hoping she would find a clue for Mileta's strange behavior.

To her horror, Mileta was speaking to a man whose voice sounded strange to Devorah.

"Michael, I love you so much. I stole his ring and I will do anything else that you ask of me."

"You must know that the king has searched for an artisan who can devise a method to weigh the amount of silver used in his throne without dismanatling it. None have a plan. Only Gershom can possibly devise a method, since he designed and constructed it . Use any means in your power to find out the method to weigh the throne."

Mileta knew that finding the secret of weighing the throne would be much more difficult than stealing the ring. She became very attentive to Rabaynu Gershom's every need. She sat with him during mealtime, and pretended to be interested in his studies, asking him to explain various points of law to her.

"Maybe Devorah's idea of me taking another wife was not so bad after all," he thought. He did not know what Devorah knew about Mileta. Devorah held her tongue, lest her husband think that she was gossiping.

One night, Mileta cleverly guided the conversation with her husband to the issue of trust. "Gershom, do you trust me?" she schemed subtley. "Why don't you involve me in some of your business decisions?"

"Of course, I trust you Mileta, but I never knew that you were interested in my work."

"For example, I'd really like to know the method that you used to construct King Basil's throne. After all, you were honored when it was dedicated. I was not even part of the celebration festivities. I would feel better if you described some of the details to me."

He described to her, slowly, carefully, and in great detail, the construction of the throne. She listened patiently, waiting for an opportunity to find out what she really wanted to know.

When he paused, she pounced on him. "Now tell me, how is it possible to weigh the throne without dismantling it?"

"Why is it so important for you to know?"

"But," sputtered, Mileta, "you just told me that you trusted me. If you are really sincere, then you will tell me." Mileta feigned tears. She sobbed, whimpered, groaned and then accused: "If you really love me, if you really trust me, you will tell me. As proof of my sincerity, I will not eat again until you have told me the secret. "

[**Ed.** Delilah used a similar method to extract from Samson the secret of his strength. Asking him how he could say he loved her if he did not divulge his secret, she nagged him until he gave in. She immediately revealed to his Phillistine enemies that his strength was in his hair. When he fell asleep, she arranged for someone to cut his hair. Weakened, he was taken captive by the Phillistines. *Shoftim, Judges 16*]

Rabaynu Gershom was deeply touched by her words. Slowly, carefully, he spelled out the method for weighing the throne without dismantling it.

The next afternoon, Mileta revealed the secret to Michael.

Johann followed the instructions and demonstrated how twenty-three centners of silver were missing between the weight of the throne and the amount left over in the treasury. He floated a small boat upon a pool of water, marked off the water line, had the throne placed on the boat, marked off a second water line, had the throne removed, filled the boat with rocks to the level of the second water line, then weighed the rocks and proved his point. The thought never entered anyone's mind that Johann had stolen twenty-three centners of silver to incriminate Rabbaynu Gershom.

Johann filed charges against Rabaynu Gershom and proceeded rapidly to a secret trial. Gleeful at the success of his plan, and having possession of the signet ring, he condemned Rabbaynu Gershom to death in the Hunger Tower.

Devorah was paralyzed into inaction for a day after Gershom was arrested. Then, coming to her senses, knowing that only the Princess Theodora could be influential in saving her husband, she tried to gain admission to the palace but was turned away by the servants.

She waited outside for the princess to ride by in her carriage for her daily outing. She threw herself in the path of the trotting horses. Frightened, the coachman reined them in. Theodora emerged from the carriage to find out the cause of the unexpected stop. Devorah pulled herself up from the dusty ground and shaking, pleaded: "my husband Gershom saved your life. Now he is in the Hunger Tower, condemned to death. You must do something to save him."

"Why hasn't he used the ring to summon my uncle's help," demanded the princess.

"Your Highness," cried Devorah. "The ring was stolen."

"I will go to him at once." Princess Theodora raced through the corridors of the palace.

"Uncle Basil, you must know that Johann has condemned Gershom to death. Is this the reward for someone who has been so faithful to you, for the man who saved my life, for the man who built you this magnificent throne, that is the envy of every king in the world? Is this the way you reward goodness?"

"If he is innocent, why doesn't he show me the ring?"

King Basil was surprised when Theodora told him that the signet ring had been stolen, for Johann had convinced him that Gershom sold it for profit.

"Sadly, I can do nothing more about his fate, for this is the law of our land," he said. "Once a person is condemned to the Hunger Tower, it is as if he were already dead."

Theodora found Devorah expecting the news of a reprieve. The look on the princess' face shattered her hope.

"The only thing that I can do for you," whispered Theodora, "is to take you to the Hunger Tower. It is a distant from the city limits. When you reach there, you might be able to make Gershom aware of your presence. Maybe, with your help, he will be able to devise a plan to escape."

Meanwhile, Gershom searched for a way out. He combed every inch of wall, hoping to find a secret passage or loose bricks that would lead to a tunnel. He shook the iron grating that served as bars over the window, and suddenly, he heard the tinkling sound of metal falling next to his feet. Bending, he picked up the key that would loosen the lock that barred the window.

Just then, he heard Devorah's voice call him. "Gershom, what must I do to help you escape?"

"I have a plan," he shouted, wanting to make sure that she heard him. "Go back to the city, and bring me two spools of thread, one silk and one flax, some butter, a wood worm, and a beetle. When you return here, you will tie the silk thread to the wood worm, dab it with butter, and place it on the side of the tower. Hopefully, it will climb up to me. If it doesn't, you will let the beetle loose, and it will chase the wood worm up. When I have the silk thread, I will let down one end, and you will send up the flax. You will send me up more threads, and I will braid them to form a strong rope. You will be able to bring me some food. I will be much safer here, than in the city, for Johann expects that I will starve soon. When you return to the city the second time, sell as much of our home furnishings as you can, and purchase two tickets for boat passage to France. This will not cause suspicion, for it is natural for a widow to return to her family. On the day of the sailing, bring me women's clothing as a disguise. We will flee together."

It took Devorah two weeks to settle their affairs. The household goods that she did not sell were crated and she arranged to ship them along with her personal belongings. No one asked her any questions. Every second day, she trekked outside the city limits and brought Rabaynu Gershom a supply of food.

On the day of their sailing, Rabaynu Gershom slid down the braided rope and fled with Devorah to the harbor. They never looked back as Constantinople disappeared from sight.

[Ed. Among the *takkanot* (decrees) enacted by Rabaynu Gershom, and observed by Ashkenazic Jews to this day, is the prohibition against a man having more than one wife at a time. He enacted this decree because of his personal experience.]

∾

A SACRED TRUST
— COMMENTARY —
THE JEWISH POPE

❧

Is it enough to say that this touching story is about *"honoring one's mother and one's father?"* Perhaps, but I think it must stand in apposition to *"Do not separate yourself from the community."* Perhaps the two values are as one. When we think we can forget where we come from, we are in danger of losing the protection of the Jewish community. When we stand within the community of Israel, we are never alone for *"All Israel are responsible for each other."*

Within the story, the most touching moment for me is when Elchanan rescues Rachel from persecution. At the end of the story, we learn that Elchanan died in the sanctification of God's name. I would like to believe that Rachel was rescued twice, first by Elchanan and then by the Almighty. In every generation, their descendents, or even each of us like Elchanan can return to our roots, no matter how far we have roamed, even to the Vatican.

Judith Paull Aronson
Fellow of Brandeis University
Director of Education, Kol Tikvah,
Los Angeles, CA

❧

Mainz on Rhine, the Bamberg Monestary and Rome

Chapter Eleven

THE JEWISH POPE

Time Line

| 70 c.e. | 600 c.e. | 1000 c.e. | 1400 c.e. | 1600 c.e. | 1800 c.e. | 2000 c.e. |

— Location: Rhine River Valley and Rome —

Elchanan, the four year old son of Rabbi Shimon ben Yitzchak Hagadol, crept into his father's study and climbed up on his lap. He had almost recovered from a recent serious illness, and his father held him tightly. The child's eyes scanned the paper upon which his father had been writing, and excitedly pointed to his name.

"Look, father, you have written my name on your paper!"

"Yes, Elchanan, this is a *piyyut* (religious poem) that we will recite in synagogue on Rosh Hashana which is coming soon. It is my way of thanking God for your recovery. Do you know what it says? Let me read it to you. *'El-chanan nachlato benoam lehashpar.'* It means that God has given to the Jewish people a special gift, the gift of His Torah. You can try to learn the words. I would be pleased if you could remember them."

[Ed. The *piyyut* begins *"Melech amon maamorecha"* "O King, validate Your promise (to Adam) who was made to stand for judgment," and is recited during the Shacharit morning service, on the second day of Rosh Hashana.]

Elchanan repeated the words a few times, slid down from his father's lap and ran to play.

Rabbi Shimon and his wife Leah rose early on the first day of Rosh Hashana, dressed quietly, and, left for *shul*, (synagogue). They did not disturb the sleeping Elchanan who was in the care of Margareta, the Christian governess who had worked for them for many years.

Margareta loved Elchanan as much as if he were her own child. During his illness, she had alternated with Leah bathing his feverish body, wrapping him in warm blankets, dribbling bits of liquid into his clenched mouth, holding him tightly as he deliriously muttered garbled words. Frightened that he would die, she had surreptitiously sought the advice of Father Thomas, her priest.

"Elchanan is a brilliant boy," she confided. "If he dies without conversion, he will be damned. I want to save his soul. What shall I do?"

Father Thomas did not have to think too long.

"Wait for the appropriate opportunity. When his parents are away, you will bring the child to me. I will make arrangements to send him to another town. They will never find him. The Church fathers will be responsible for baptizing him, educating him, and raising him as a Christian. You will be doing the child a great favor."

Margareta waited patiently. Having worked for Rabbi Shimon and Leah for many years, she knew that the Rosh Hashana prayers were very lengthy. She knew she would have time to execute the priest's plan. Taking the sleeping child in her arms that morning, she carried him to the church and returned to Rabbi Shimon and Leah's home.

Father Thomas forcibly transported him to the monastery in Bamberg. The Bishop rewarded the priest for having "saved" another Jewish child for Christendom, baptized Elchanan, and bestowed the name of Felix upon him.

When Rabbi Shimon and Leah returned home from *shul* they found Margareta sitting by herself. She refused to answer their questions as to the where-abouts of Elchanan. Since the government and the Church were one, there was no person to turn to for help.

∽

The priests in the monastery found Felix to be bright and curious. They treated him tenderly, rewarding him often. It did not take long to become accustomed to his new living conditions. Gradually, he forgot the little that he knew of his former Jewish life, only mysteriously remembering the one sentence from the *piyyut*. By the time he was seven, he knew Latin and Greek.

His teachers were so amazed at his ability to learn, that they arranged private tutors. Soon, he knew all that the tutors in the monastery in Bamberg were able to teach him. They decided to send him to Rome, to study with the Cardinals who advised the Pope .

The Pope himself heard about this wondrous child, and personally oversaw his education. When Felix reached the age of eighteen, the Pope appointed him as his assistant. At twenty-five, he was appointed Cardinal. He had all the glory, honor, wealth, and power of Rome at his beckoning.

One day, Felix rode in his carriage through the streets of Rome. Hearing screaming from a distance, he commanded the coachman to head in the direction of the commotion. Two men were harassing a teenage girl. He pulled her into his carriage.

"Who are you?" he inquired.

"My name is Rachel. I am the daughter of Meshullam. I was returning from the market when those two attacked me."

Felix reprimanded the two scoundrels.

They glowered back at him. "She is just a Jewish girl. We can do to her whatever we want! "

Felix signalled the coachman, and he returned Rachel to the safety of her father's house. Gratefully, Meshullam, one of the few wealthy Jews who was permitted to own land, invited the young Cardinal to visit him any time he needed respite from the pressures of his duties. He accepted the invitation and returned often.

Felix served the Pope loyally for the next ten years. Before the Pope passed away, he wrote into his will that the Cardinals should elect Felix as his successor.

Felix ascended to the highest post in Christendom, yet he was plagued about his origin.

"Who were my parents? Was I born into this religion? Where did I live as a child?" He found no peace. He was also disillusioned because he realized that the infighting and competition between the Cardinals was based upon materialistic gain.

"These people are not sincerely religious! They crave only power and wealth!"

One day, a servant announced an unexpected visitor seeking the council of the Pope. Felix did not remember Father Thomas.

"I have been following your career with great interest," he began. "I was the parish priest who plotted with Margareta, the governess who was employed by your parents, Rabbi Shimon and Leah, to kidnap you from your home in Mainz. I arranged for you to study in the monastery at Bamberg. Now the Church has bestowed upon you its highest honors as well as its wealth and glory. I came all the way from Mainz so that you might reward me for the favor which I did for you."

Remaining composed, Felix ordered his treasurer to compensate Father Thomas handsomely. He thanked him and dismissed him. Then he went into his private chambers. His anguished heart convulsed with throbbing pain at the realization that he was Jewish.

"I have to find a way to let my parents know that I am alive. I will have no peace until I can stand face to face with them again."

He explored many avenues toward reconciliation. As the Pope , he had unlimited power, yet, he knew, he could just not visit Mainz, a distant town, for no apparent reason. He needed a pretext. Night after night sleep alluded him, until he formulated, what he thought, was a workable plan.

"I will write a decree of expulsion against the Jews of Mainz. I will give them three months to relocate and sell their property. They will probably send a representative to Rome to plead for mercy. The person they will probably send might be my father, who I once remember hearing is the leader of the Jewish community. That way I will be able to see him again."

So saying, he wrote the decree, and sent it to the Archbishop of Mainz to implement.

The Jews of Mainz sent a delegation, with Rabbi Shimon Hagadol as its leader, to Rome to plead with the Pope .

"We simply are trying to live our lives peacefully, striving to earn a livelihood, to care for our families, and to study our Torah. We don't understand the animosity of the Church in expelling us from this town where we have lived for generations."

Pope Felix rescinded the decree. He sent two of the delegates back to Mainz, but detained their leader. He asked Rabbi Shimon to follow him into his private chamber. Pacing back and forth, the Pope asked: "Is your wife living?"

"Why, yes, and I'm certain that she is praying for my safe return to Mainz."

"Do you have children?"

"I had one son. When I first saw you, I was reminded of him."

"Is there any resemblance between him and me?"

"Many years ago, I dreamed that my son sat on a golden throne, robed in royal garments, with a golden cross adorning his chest. People bowed to him, kissed his hands. Your face is similar to the one in my dream."

"What happened to your son?"

"He disappeared when he was four years old. To this day, we have no idea if he is still alive. We suspect that the governess who cared for him was implicated, but we could

never prove anything because she committed suicide shortly
after his disappearance."

"What was his name," gently prodded the Pope .

"Elchanan!"

"Elchanan nachlato benoam lehashpar, father!"

He fell on his father's shoulders and wept.

 ᔅ

Rabbi Shimon Hagadol remained with his son for a few
weeks, teaching him Torah and the history of the Jewish
people.

Finally, he said: "Elchanan, my son, the time has come for
me to return home. Please, come back to Mainz with me. You
were born a Jew, and you are a Jew in your heart."

"But father, while I sit on the throne of Rome, I have the
power to protect the Jewish people from evil decrees, from
expulsions, from all sorts of false accusations that lead to acts
of violence."

"Elchanan, the God of our fathers, Who has protected us
and sustained us through all of our history, will continue to
do His part."

Elchanan struggled with his choices for a while as Rabbi
Shimon sat quietly.

"Should I return to Mainz and to Judaism or remain in
Rome to use the power of the Church to help my people?"
Finally, he whispered: "Please, return now to my mother and
tell her that I will follow you in a few days." He needed time
to plan his departure.

Three days later, in the middle of the night, he dressed in
peasant's clothing, walked silently out of the papal palace,
and headed for the house of Meshullam where he spent the
remainder of the night.

The next day, he married Rachel, and together they set out
for Mainz. In order not to arouse the suspicion of the authori-

ties, they pretended to be distant relatives of Rabbi Shimon and Leah. They lived peacefully for a few years, until Emperor Henry II decreed the expulsion of the Jews of Mainz unless they accepted baptism.

The Jews that refused conversion were herded into the synagogue. The synagogue was set on fire. Elchanan was among the victims. It was the second day of Rosh Hashana.

To this day, in Ashkenazic synagogues, *"El-chanan nachlato benoam lehashpar,"* reminds us of the story of the Jewish Pope.

[**Ed.** See Author's Note in Sources and Footnote section for variations of the ending of this story.]

∽

A SACRED TRUST
— COMMENTARY —
I WILL DIE A JEW

❧

What is it that has insured Jewish survival through the ages? Torah study, religious observance, transmission of the tradition from parent to child - of course. But this story adds one additional dimension, the power of faith and the willingness to die for that faith.

Countless times throughout Jewish history have Jews been called upon to perform the ultimate sacrifice of *Kiddush Hashem*, giving up their lives for the sanctification of the Divine Name. How strong is our faith, how deep is our commitment that we are prepared to accept the responsibility to structure our lives and, God forbid, if necessary, even our deaths - in accordance with it.

—Rabbi Jacob J. Schacter,
The Jewish Center, New York City
Editor,
"Jewish Tradition and the Non-traditional Jew"

The Rhine River Valley using today's boundries, listing general
locations of many cities and towns mentioned in stories.

Chapter Twelve
I WILL DIE A JEW

Time Line

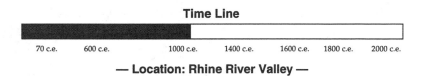

70 c.e.   600 c.e.   1000 c.e.   1400 c.e.   1600 c.e.   1800 c.e.   2000 c.e.

— Location: Rhine River Valley —

Mainz was one of the cities located in the Rhine river valley that had a large Jewish population and a fine *yeshiva*. Rabbi Amnon, a man of wealth and distinguished ancestry, was the religious leader of the Jews of this city in the first third of the eleventh century.

He was friendly with the Bishop of Mainz, which helped further the "relatively secure" relationship between the two religious communities.[1] The two men enjoyed each other's company, and they spent many hours discussing intellectual matters. Usually, as they parted company, the Bishop would say, "Rabbi Amnon, it's time for a man of your intelligence and stature to adopt the true religion. When will you set the example for your people and convert?[2]

Needless to say, Rabbi Amnon always refused to answer.

At one point the Bishop put so much pressure upon Rabbi Amnon that he perceived his request to be more than the habitual closing words of a usually friendly visit.

To put him off, Rabbi Amnon countered, "Give me three days to consider your request!" The Bishop agreed to wait for Rabbi Amnon's answer.

As soon as he left the Bishop's mansion, Rabbi Amnon realized his error. "What did I do?" he cried desperately. "How could I ever utter those words? I could no longer bear the pressure! I only wanted to put him off!" No matter the consequences, I would never consider conversion.

When Rabbi Amnon did not appear on the third day, the Bishop sent soldiers to Amnon's house to remind him of their appointment. Rabbi Amnon refused to return to the mansion with the soldiers.

The Bishop was infuriated. "Return to his house," he ordered, "and drag him here to me."

The soldiers dragged Rabbi Amnon through the streets of Mainz and stood him before the furious Bishop. "For refusing to come as you agreed," thundered the Bishop, "you will suffer an agonizing death."

Rabbi Amnon pleaded, "Allow me one last request: let me decree my own fate. Let the tongue that dared mention conversion be cut from my mouth."

"No," shouted the Bishop. "I will order the legs that did not come to keep their appointment to be cut off. I will order that your fingers be dismembered. I will order salt to be poured onto your wounds to increase your suffering!"

The Bishop's sentence was carried out on Rosh Hashanah. Rabbi Amnon begged his faithful followers to carry him, bleeding and dismembered into the synagogue and on to the *bimah* (pulpit).

He interrupted the *chazan* (cantor) who was chanting the *musaf* prayers, (additional prayer service for Holy Days). Writhing in pain, he affirmed his faith in God with these words:

U'netaneh tokef kedushat hayom,

May our sanctification of Your name ascend,

For You are our God and our King.

Let us observe the holiness of this day.

This is the day Your Kingdom is exalted,

It is established in mercy and truth.

You are the Judge of mankind ...

And You hold each man accountable for his deeds ...

On Rosh Hashanah day man's destiny is inscribed

And on Yom Kippur his fate is sealed...

Who will live and who will die...

But repentance, prayer and charity avert an evil decree ...

And You are Our God, Our Living King.[3]

As Rabbi Amnon uttered these holy words, his soul ascended heavenward. Three days later, Rabbi Kalonymus ben Meshullam dreamed that Rabbi Amnon was teaching him the words of *U'netaneh Tokef.* In the dream, Rabbi Amnon commanded him to travel throughout the Jewish communities and teach the people this prayer.

Rabbi Kalonymus followed the command in the dream and traveled to many Jewish communities, teaching this prayer wherever he went.

[**Ed.** Rabbi Amnon's prayer, *U'netaneh tokef kedushat hayom* is recited today during the Rosh Hashana and Yom Kippur services. It is one of the most solemn prayers of the High Holy Days liturgy.]

A Sacred Trust
— Commentary —
Tales of Rashi

❧

I agree with the authors' view since this particular tale is a legend about Rashi and his son-in-law, who also became an illustrious scholar. It belongs to a genre of legends about the Jewish "heroes" of the Middle Ages who were perforce rabbinic scholars.

Gerson Cohen and others pointed out a long time ago, while the troubadours extolled the great acts of the knights, the Jews told stories about their sages, pointing to the different value systems of the two cultures.

—*Dr. David Lieber*
President Emeritus
University of Judaism, Los Angeles

❧

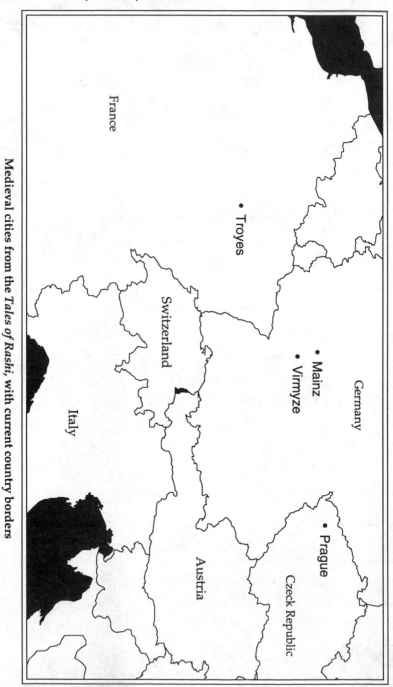

Medieval cities from the *Tales of Rashi*, with current country borders

Chapter Thirteen

TALES OF RASHI

Time Line

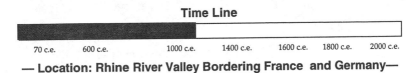

70 c.e. 600 c.e. 1000 c.e. 1400 c.e. 1600 c.e. 1800 c.e. 2000 c.e.

— **Location: Rhine River Valley Bordering France and Germany**—

Rabbi Yitzchak's Diamond

Rabbi Yitzchak, a wealthy merchant, living in Virmyze on the banks of the Rhine River, had inherited an unusually large-sized diamond. He carried it with him at all times, for he dreamed of contributing it towards the rebuilding of the holy temple. The priest heard about it, and decided to buy it to decorate the eye of the statue that stood in the vestry of his church. He proposed to Rabbi Yitzchak: "I will buy your diamond for five thousand marks. You will reap a handsome profit."

But Rabbi Yitzchak refused to sell his diamond to the priest because he knew it would be used for idolatrous purposes. The priest raised his offered sum, but still Rabbi Yitzchak refused to consider his proposition.

Once he had decided on a course of action, the priest was determined to achieve his goal. He plotted to lure Rabbi Yitchak onto a rowboat, hoping that he could convince him to sell the diamond.

The priest rowed far from shore, all the time telling Rabbi Yitzchak how much profit he would reap from the sale of the diamond. His language became coercive; Rabbi Yitzchak was adamant. Finally, he put his hand into his pocket, withdrew the diamond and tossed it into the river.

Defeated and angry, the priest rowed the boat back to shore. As the two men alighted from the boat, they heard a Heavenly voice proclaim: "Since you did not permit the diamond to be used for idoltarous purposes, you will be rewarded with a more precious diamond that will be a sparkling source of light to the Jewish people."

The news of the Heavenly voice quickly spread throughout Virmyze. When the priest realized that Miriam, the wife of Rabbi Yitchak, was pregnant, he attempted to have her murdered, to abort the proclamation of the Heavenly voice.

Once, as Miriam walked through the narrow alleyways of the city on her way to the synagogue, she heard the galloping sounds and screeching wheels of an onrushing carriage heading directly toward her. It was too late to run ahead, so she turned to face the wall, trying to protect her unborn child. Suddenly, she felt the wall heave to accommodate her swollen body. The carriage passed through without harming her. People came running from all over to see what had happened and they chattered incessantly as they pointed to the indentation in the wall. The Jews of Virmyze were grateful for the wondrous deed which God wrought, but some superstitious non-Jews accused Miriam of witchcraft and demanded that she be put to death.

That night Rabbi Yitzchak and Miriam left their home in Virmyze for Troyes. A few weeks later, he dreamed that *Elyahu Hanave* (Elijah the Prophet) appeared to him: "Name your newborn son Shlomo, for he will be blessed with the wisdom of Shlomo Hamelech (King Solomon). He will light up the whole Jewish world with his knowledge of Torah. When the time comes to circumcise him, wait for my appearance before you begin the ritual."

[**Ed.** Rabbi Yitzchak's deceased father had also been named Shlomo.]

On the eighth day after the baby's birth, the Jewish community gathered for his *brit milah* (circumcision). Rabbi Yitzchak delayed the ritual on the pretext that he was awaiting an honored guest. Hours went by, and the people became impatient. One by one, they left Rabbi Yitzchak's house.

"Maybe I am not worthy of the appearance of *Elyahu Hanave*," he wondered. "Maybe my dream had no significance ... but I will still wait a bit." When most of the guests had gone, and Rabbi Yitzchak was despondent, a peasant, dressed in tattered clothes, girdled in a leather belt, entered, appearing on the scene, as if from nowhere. Rabbi Yitzchak joyfully asked him to sit on the " chair of Elyahu," and hold the baby, and the mohel circumcised him. Afterward, the peasant disappeared as mysteriously as he had arrived.

[**Ed.** "He was a hairy man, girdled with leather about his loins. And he said: 'It is Elyahu the Tishbite.' "[1]]

Shlomo's parents realized that they were entrusted with a rare jewel that needed to be cultivated and cultured if he were to develop into the great scholar that they dreamed him to be. They despaired that there was no *yeshiva* in Troyes, so they decided to send young Shlomo to his uncle, Rabbi Shimon Hazaken, who was one of the great rabbinical leaders in Mainz.

Shlomo had an innate thirst for studying Torah, and the older students that learned with him encouraged his curiosity. As he matured, he developed the ability to verbalize the lengthy and complicated commentaries of the Torah and Talmud that had accumulated over the centuries into simple and concise explanations. Soon, he had the reputation of being an *illui* (an intellectual genius). When his knowledge surpassed that of the scholars in Mainz, his family permitted him to travel to *yeshivot* (academies) in other cities. While he travelled, he meticulously recorded the *halachic* (legal) opinions of the scholars he visited.

∽

The Repayment of the Loan

When he was about twenty-five years old, Shlomo decided to return to Troyes to establish his own *yeshiva*. He had already become recognized as a Talmudic authority. He was known as "Rashi," an acronym for Rabbi Shlomo ben Yitzchak.

On his way home, he met Bishop Ullemitz; they shared the same carriage. Sitting side by side, they had plenty of time for discussion during their long journey. But the discussion turned to heated arguments about religious differences. Half way there, the Bishop complained that he felt too ill to continue his journey. Rashi insisted that they stop at a wayside inn. There he cared for him, and nursed him back to health.

"I will reward you," the Bishop said. "You may ask me for anything your heart desires, for you saved my life."

"I only did what the Torah commanded me to do; that is, to come to the aid of any person in need. I will accept no reward; I only implore you that if it ever comes to your attention that a Jew needs help, I hope that you will do for him what I have done for you," replied Rashi.

The Bishop promised; he decided to remain in that inn for a short while, until his strength had completely returned. Rashi continued toward Troyes, and arriving home, he began sifting through the massive accumulation of notes which he gathered during the years he travelled. When he finished writing his concise explanations of the Torah and the prophetic writings he decided to visit other Jewish communities in order to find out if what he had written was actually worthwhile. His reputation preceded him and when he reached Prague, the Jews eagerly welcomed the scholar who had come to visit. Some non-Jews looked for a pretext to make trouble for their Jewish neighbors, and within a few days, their discontented murmurings had reached the attention of Duke Veratislav: "The Jews have an honored guest in their midst. We know that he has wandered from place to place. He has come here for information. He must be a spy. We should stop him from spying on other cities."

The Duke used any pretext to harm his Jewish subjects, so without investigating, he imprisoned Rashi and set the following day for his execution. The Jewish community reacted by praying; terror hung like a heavy cloud over the shul.

That night Bishop Ullemitz reached Prague, for he had been traveling to various communities. Riding through the city, he happened upon anguished wailing and moaning in the Jewish section.

"I have to find out from my friend Duke Veratislav what the problem is," he determined.

"I have imprisoned a Jewish spy," the duke admitted. "Tomorrow he will be hung."

"I insist on seeing your prisoner," demanded the bishop.

Bishop Ullemitz could not believe his eyes. "You are Shlomo, the same Shlomo that saved my life so many years ago! I swear to you, that before dawn you will be a free man."

He ran back to his friend.

"You have imprisoned an innocent man. You must free him immediately. Let me tell you who he is."

Listening to the Bishop tell the tale of how Rashi saved his life, the Duke acceded to his demands. He promised that during his lifetime, the Jews of his city would live harmoniously with their non-Jewish neighbors.

❧

A Marriage Made in Heaven

Rashi had three daughters, Yocheved, Miriam, and Rachel.

Yocheved was known for her wit and her wisdom. Once, when Rashi was ill, he called her and asked her to write the response to a question that he had received.

"I don't have the strength to write a response. I'd like you to do it for me, but first, tell me how you will proceed."

The question dealt with an issue of a prohibited or permitted act, a most difficult area of Jewish law.

[**Ed.** Some of the laws in the category of *eesur* and *heter* [prohibited or permitted] deal with marriage, family law, and Kosher dietary codes.]

He approved her reasoning and understanding of the issue, and permitted her to write the response on her own.

Word spread very rapidly through the entire Jewish community that Yocheved was blessed with a brilliant mind, therefore, few appropriate suitors sought her hand. No man wanted to play second fiddle to her. She did not fit into the mold characterizing the women of the middle ages, who were generally confined to caring for the home and the children. They rarely made public appearances and they almost never were involved with decision making in Jewish law.

In despair, Yocheved's mother and father waited patiently for the proper young man to propose marriage to their daughter. One day, Yocheved's mother was overcome with sadness. She went into her husband's study and cried: "How long will we have to wait for Yocheved to get married? We have two other daughters who are also of marriageble age. We cannot permit the youngest to marry before the eldest. I wonder if we will live long enough to have grandchildren!"

[**Ed.** "It is not done in our place to give the younger in marriage before the older."][2]

Her tears touched Rashi's heart, for he too, was concerned about the welfare of his other two daughters.

Instantaneously, he blurted out: "The first young man who crosses this threshold tomorrow morning will become Yocheved's husband! Pray that this young man will be an appropriate match!"

Neither parent slept that night.

Very early the next morning, a disheveled, bedraggled, dust covered man stood on the threshold of Rashi's study. His lanky height was accentuated by his tipped hat. When Rashi saw him, his heart sank, because he knew that he would not annul the vow that he had made.

"Maybe he is a genius dressed as a peasant," he hoped, trying to comfort himself. "After all, haven't our sages taught us not to judge a book by its cover? As Rabbi Mayer said: "do not look at the bottle, but what is in it."[3]

"What is your name?" he inquired.

The peasant replied that his name was Mayer.

He invited Mayer inside, showed him where to wash his hands and face, and guided him gently to the dining room of his house. After he had satisfied his ravenous hunger, Rashi tried to engage him in conversation. But Mayer shattered Rashi's hope; he seemed totally ignorant.

Rashi was determined to live with the vow he had made, so he decided immediately that he would tutor Mayer himself, privately, and after he had learned some Torah and Talmud, he would make the wedding.

Rashi set aside a few precious hours each day for his new student. As much as he struggled to impart any knowledge, it seemed that Mayer's ears and mind were stuffed. Rashi refused to succumb to despair; he used every skill at his fingertips to motivate Mayer to master basic textual material. He also prayed with deep intent and devotion that God would open his student's mind.

One day, after Rashi had finished teaching Mayer, he retired to a corner of his study to continue writing his commentary on the Talmud. Mayer remained on the far side of the room. Rashi pored over the text , copying his explanations meticulously. He commented on one passage after another, then he reached a verse that he could not explain. The concept eluded him. He sat for hours, trying to understand the meaning of the passage, talking to himself the whole time, as if by reasoning the problem aloud, a solution would become apparent. Finally, he rose, whispered that it was time to pray the afternoon service, and walked away from his writing table, still not understanding the passage.

"I will come back to this problem in the text," he thought, "after I finish my prayers."

While he was gone, Mayer walked over to Rashi's writing table, analyzed the difficult text, and wrote out a clear and concise explanation.

Rashi returned to his writing table a short time later. He noticed that a fresh sheet of paper had been added to his pile of notes. He lifted it and read it carefully. The paper contained an explanation of the problem that had eluded him for so many hours that day.

Happily he ran in search of his wife. "Has anyone been in my study while I was praying," he asked?

"Not that I know of," she replied. "Only Mayer remained there while you were out. "

"In that case," replied Rashi, "You can begin preparations for Yocheved's wedding." Then he proceeded to tell her what had happened.

"Mayer is really a genius. Although he came to us disguised as an ignorant peasant, he is really an equal match for our Yocheved. God's ways are mysterious. I'm glad we trusted Him to chose the right husband for our daughter."

∽

Darkness Descends
Rashi lived through the early years of the Crusades, Pope Urban II's call, in 1095, to conquer the Holy Land and free it from the hands of the Moslem infidels. He wanted to make the Holy Land a province of the Roman Catholic Church.

Godfrey of Bouillon, one of the leaders of the First Crusade, sought Rashi's advise. He wanted to know if he would
be successful in his mission. The two leaders, the spiritual
leader of the Jews and the military leader representing the
church stood face to face.

"In answer to your question," replied Rashi, "I can only tell
you that if you attempt this mission, you will return with
three horses."

Rashi's answer angered Godfrey for he had ships docked
in the harbor, stockpiles of swords, bows and arrows, a vast
army of followers, and much money to replenish his supplies. He had no intention of losing all this, so he yelled:
"Know that if I return with four horses, I will kill you."

Godfrey did not succeed in wresting the Holy Land from
the Moslems. He returned to Troyes, France, with four horses.

"Now I will take revenge on Rashi," he plotted, "for he
forecast my defeat." As he was riding through the gates of the
city, a brick fell from the wall and killed his fourth horse. The
prophecy of Rashi was fulfilled. Godfrey changed his course;
he never saw him again.

Rashi passed away on the 29th day of Tammuz, 1105, soon
after this incident. He did not witness most of the devastation
that the Crusaders were to bring upon his people for a period
of nearly two hundred years.

It is known that toward the end of his life, he transferred
his *yeshiva* to Virmyze, Germany. After World War II, the
yeshiva of Rashi was rebuilt and has become a national
monument.

∽

A Sacred Trust

— Commentary —

Custodians of the Divine Dream

"And God said to Abram: Go from your land, from your birthplace, and from your father's house, to a land that I will show you. And I will make you a great nation, and I will bless you, and make your name great And you shall be a blessing. And Abram went as God commanded him to do.

God said to Abram: Look around now from the place where you are. Look northward, southward, eastward, and westward, All the land which you see, I will give to you and to your children after you, forever And your children will be as the dust of the earth, unable for them to be counted. On that day did God make a Covenant with Abram saying to your children will I give this land, from the river of Egypt, to tile great river, the Euphrates."

B'rayshit, Genesis 12:1-4, 13:14-17, 15:18

"And God appeared to Isaac and said: Live in this land, and I will be with you I will bless you. To you and your children have I given this land. And I will confirm the promise that I made to Abraham, your father And I will multiply your children like the stars of the heaven, and I will give your children all these lands And all thee nations of the earth will be blessed through your children."

B'rayshit, Genesis 26:1-5

"And God said to Jacob I am the God of Abraham (your grandfather) and the God of your father Isaac. The land upon which you lie I will give to you and to your children."

"And your children will be as the dust of the earth, and they will spread westward, eastward, northward, and southward. The families of the earth will be blessed through you and your children."

B'rayshit, Genesis 28:13–14

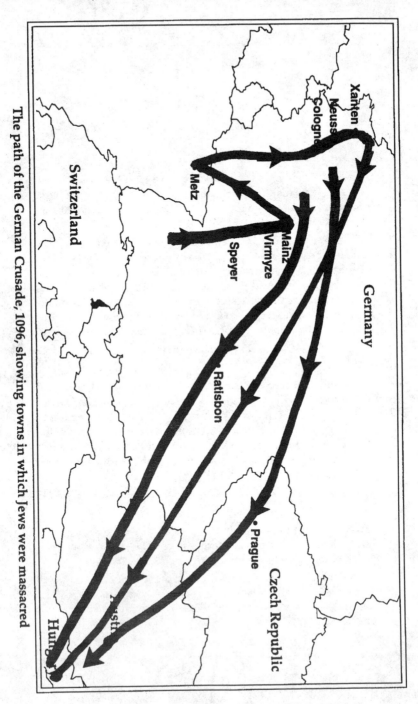

The path of the German Crusade, 1096, showing towns in which Jews were massacred

Chapter Fourteen
CUSTODIANS
OF THE DIVINE DREAM

Time Line

70 c.e.	600 c.e.	1000 c.e.	1400 c.e.	1600 c.e.	1800 c.e.	2000 c.e.

— Location: Europe and Eretz Yisrael —

As the Prince of Coucy was about to lead a Crusade whose purpose was to wrest the Holy Land from the hands of the Moslem infidels, he stopped to see his friend the Rabbi of Coucy.

"Rabbi," asked the Prince, "I am starting out on the most important mission of my life. I have the feeling that I will be successful. If that be so, then I want to return here with a gift for you, as a token of our friendship. Tell me what gift would be most meaningful to you?"

"My dearest friend," responded the rabbi, "our Holy Land has lain desolate for a thousand years. Yet, I have faith that its soil can still be fruitful, that my dispersed people will one day be able to return to their land, that eventually, the Holy City (*Yerushalayim*) will gloriously be rebuilt as the spiritual center of the world. Bring me some sign to show me that the Holy City still has potential for life."

"I promise to bring you such a gift," he said as he slowly backed out of the door of his friend's house.

Many years passed before the Prince of Coucy returned home. He hastened to visit his friend, the Rabbi of Coucy, bearing a wilted flower as his gift.

Handing his friend the wilted flower, the Prince of Coucy whispered softly: "I traveled all over the country. Because of all the fighting during these hundred years, the country is decimated of its population and its fields are desolate. The Holy City lays in ruins. I found this wilted flower on Mount

Zion. I tried to replant it, to revive it in some way, but to no avail. It has no sign of life."

With trembling hands, the rabbi lifted the wilted flower to his nose, feigning to smell its once fragrant scent. Tears dropped from his eyes unto the wilted flower. Miraculously, the petals stretched outward and upward as they absorbed his tears. The flower glistened, as after a soft rain.

The Prince's eyes stared at the amazing sight as he tried to understand the phenomenon of the vitality of the wilted flower.

"I think I understand what happened," he whispered. "You, the representative of the Jewish people, had the power to revitalize the flower. It is only through the Jewish people that the Holy Land will blossom again. Zion awaits the return of her children because only they can rebuild the land."

The Rabbi and the Prince both understood the meaning of the revitalization of the wilted flower.

∽

Another thousand years has passed since the encounter between the Rabbi of Coucy and the Prince of Coucy.

During that time, many other conquerors have attempted to subdue the land, but none has instilled life in her. The small diamond shaped piece of land, strategic bridge between three continents, Europe, Asia, and Africa, has been overrun by Assyrians, Babylonians, Greeks, Romans, Moslems, Christian Crusaders, Turks, and British. They conquered her, but did not possess her. They could not give her life.

Only the Jewish people have given her life.

Only the Jewish people are rebuilding the desolate land.

Only the Jewish people are restoring her to her ancient glory.

Only the Jewish people are redeeming the land flowing with milk and honey.

Only the Jewish people are custodians of the Divine Dream!

∽

A Sacred Trust
— Commentary —
The Massacre at York

ઢ

There are certain genre's of stories. This story echoes the story of
Masada. Among historians, opinions differ whether the Jews
who committed suicide on Masada were heroes or cowards in the
face of Roman tyranny. Had they survived the siege and the
onslaught, they would have been taken captive as prisoners of
war, for Roman sport at the gladiator circus, or sold as slaves.

Choosing to die as free people, their leader Eleazar ben Yair
influenced 960 men, women, and children to mass suicide after
burning the buildings and stores of food. When Roman soldiers
ascended the mountain top, sure of their conquest, they were
greeted with the silence of death. Thus, the heroes of Masada.

The opposing point of view is based upon the Torah's mandate
regarding the sanctity of life. A Jew is expected to live by the laws
of the Torah and not die because of them. We are instructed: *"You
shall live by them, but you shall not die because of them."*

(Vayikra, Leviticus, 18:5, Talmud Bavli, Yoma 85b)

The Jewish court which met in the upper chambers of the
House of Nitza in Lydda resolved by a majority vote that in every
other law of the Torah, if a man is commanded *"transgress and
suffer not death, he may transgress and not suffer death, excepting if he's
forced publicly to idolatry, adultery, or murder."*

(Talmud Bavli, Sanhedrin 74a)

For Israel's youth, Masada is a symbol of courage. On its
summit, recruits of the Israel Armored Corps swear their oath of
allegiance: *"Masada shall not fall again."*

—*Author.*

THE MASSACRE AT YORK

Time Line

70 c.e.	600 c.e.	1000 c.e.	1400 c.e.	1600 c.e.	1800 c.e.	2000 c.e.

— **Location: England** —

The walls of the synagogue echoed with the piercing cries of York's Jews as they agonized over their grim situation. Their leaders tried to calm them.

Baruch Benedict reasoned: "We have lived in this city for two centuries. King Richard (the Lion Hearted) protects us because he depends upon us. When we are prosperous, his treasury is filled with our taxes. Not only have we contributed greatly to the peace of his kingdom, but we have also developed our own religious life. Remember, at his coronation, he quelled the riots and decreed that the Jews of his realm should not be molested. We must try to stay calm!"

Yaakov Josce, the king's treasurer, continued: "Even though King Richard has crossed the channel to join the Third Crusade, we will be safe, for he ordered his sheriffs to protect us. You know that the Jews of Lincoln were saved from the angry mobs through the intervention of his royal agents. We must be patient, and not despair."

Rabbi Yom Tov ben Yitzchak, of Joigny, the *Tosafist* (Talmudic commentator) and *Paytan* (religious poet), rose from his seat on the pulpit and slowly walked down the aisle to the center of the synagogue. He stationed himself near the desk where the Torah was read twice weekly and each Shabbat. The din of the anguished people intensified. He stood, with raised hands, waiting for them to quiet themselves, to gain their undivided attention.

"The situation is different now than it was during the coronation. We are surrounded by nobles who are heavily indebted to us. They might seize the opportunity, created by the king's absence, to rid themselves of their debts by plundering our homes. They could even do worse, for if they destroy both the records of their debt and our property, they will free themselves of the responsibility of repayment of their much overdue loans. I don't think that we can depend upon the good intentions of the sheriffs that King Richard left to preserve the peace of the kingdom. We need to develop some contingency plans to protect ourselves from the mobs who roam this country, who seem to have taken the upper hand since he left.

[**Ed.** The purpose of the Crusades was to free the Holy Land from the hands of the Moslem infidels. Jews were also considered infidels, and for almost two hundred years the Crusaders destroyed Jewish communities in their path eastward.]

Our city is an impressive target for the mobs. We have accumulated wealth. We are living more comfortably than most of our brethren on the European continent."

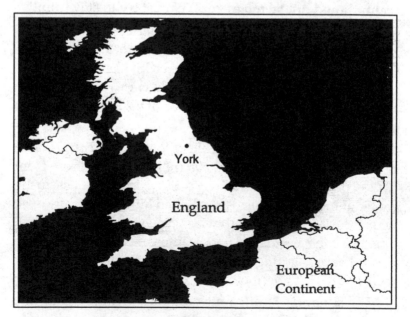

The Massacre at York

He wanted his people to understand that they were in danger. He wanted them to plan one unified action which might save them from annihilation.

A young man stepped forward. "I will volunteer to organize a self-defense group. Who wants to join me? We will patrol our section of the city during the night to protect it from maruaders."

The hands of some twenty young men shot up in the air.

"This is a beginning," proposed Rabbi Yom Tov, "but it will not guarantee our survival. I suggest that we pack our easily movable belongings on wagons, accumulate as much food, water, and warm clothing as possible, and move into the Clifford Tower of the Keep Castle. The warden of the castle is under orders to protect us. If he needs a little encouragement to fulfill his obligations, we might be able to bribe him to shelter us there. Because it is built like a fortress, we will be able to survive, either until the vicious mobs move on or until King Richard returns."

Unanimous voices assented, heads nodded. The people rose in unison, ready to comply with their Rabbi's proposal. Knowing the immensity of the work ahead of them, they emerged quickly from the synagogue, headed toward their homes, and without divulging their plans to outsiders, began the process of packing their belongings.

That night, a mob watched stealthily and waited as the Jewish defenders roamed from house to house making certain the inhabitants were safe. When the defenders were out of sight, they crept closer and closer to Baruch Benedict's elegant mansion. Their goal was to set it ablaze by igniting tar covered rags. As the flames engulfed the house, they gleefully shouted: "One house each night until there are no more Jewish houses left! When those Jews come running out, we will murder them and confiscate whatever wealth remains."

The Jews of York worked feverishly to pack their belongings into heaped high wagons.

Warden Shatogren passed Yaakov Josce's comfortable house. Yaakov was tying bundles together. "What's going on here," he demanded. "What are all these bundles? Why are you packing?"

"We are headed toward the Keep Castle," he replied softly.

"Why are you taking all this garbage over there? The king's castle is not a garbage dump nor a storage place for Jews' merchandise."

"Where the Jewish people go, so goes their belongings. These bundles are our property."

"What do you mean, where the Jewish people go?"

"You are responsible for protecting us, aren't you?"

"Me, protecting you? Ha, Ha!"

"We are the subjects of the king. It is your responsibility to protect us from the raging mobs. Last night, Baruch Benedict's house was burned down. Where were you? You didn't even attempt to control the plundering that ensued. No, we are taking matters into our own hands. For our own safety and protection, we are all moving into the fortress until help arrives from London to rescue us. We can not depend on you. We will not wait until the mob kills us.

"You will not dare to execute such a plan," sputtered Warden Shatogren.

The castle is not an inn, especially not for you Jews."

"Nevertheless, that is our plan. If anything happens to us, it will be your job to explain to King Richard how his loyal subjects were mistreated. Do you hear the noise coming from the fortress? Those sounds are the sounds of Jews who have already emptied their first loads into the safety of the fortress walls. Soon, all the Jews of York will be harbored in the fortress!"

Towards evening, the last caravan of wagons, led by Baruch Benedict, Yaakov Josce, and Rabbi Yom Tov moved slowly towards the fortress. When all the Jews were safely inside, the young defenders raised the lattice bridge and the connection between the city and the fortress was severed.

Inside the fortress, a frenzy of activity ensued. Lanterns shadowed the interior. Stockpiles of food were arranged in one room, salvaged treasures in another. Families were assigned spaces for living quarters. The center hall was turned into a *shul*; the Holy Ark was placed on the eastern wall with the *Sifre Torah* inside; manuscripts of Holy Writings lay on small tables.

Outside, Warden Shatogren raged. "How dare these Jews seek sanctuary in the royal fortress?"

The next morning, he informed Sheriff Richard Malebys, a noble deeply in debt to the Jews, what had occurred.

"Those Jews are all in one place," he sneered. "Even if they have some food supplies, they will not be able to hold out too long. What do you think if we lay seige to the fortress?"

The sheriff was only to happy to comply.

It did not take long for the rabble rousers to gather, ready to comply to the demands of their leaders. Rushing to the edge of the moat, they waited impatiently for their leaders to find a way for them to cross over to the fortress. Exhorting the unruly crowd to action, a white robed monk celebrated mass as he faced the tower of the fortress. Suddenly, a stone was thrown from one of the parpapets, killing him. The crowd was uncontrollable.

Armed reinforcements, trained soldiers, arrived the next day. Rather than restore peace, they plotted the destruction of the innocents sheltered by the fortress walls.

Jewish defenders occasionally walked the parapets, trying to find out their plan of action.

"We are outnumbered," they told Rabbi Yom Tov. "Even if we can hold out for a few days, or a month, they will not give up. The mob will not be happy until our blood flows through the streets of York!

A few days passed. On *Shabbat Hagadol*, the Shabbat preceding *Pesach* (Passover), one of the defenders noticed, from the height of his post, that the attackers were building two wheeled towers, now visible in the distance.

"How long will it take them to complete the towers, to make them tall enough to shoot their arrows down upon us? Soon they will be able to aim the rocks in their slingshots with deadly precision. They must be constructing a portable lattice bridge to lay over the moat also. I have to reveal this information to Rabbi Yom Tov."

He interrupted their prayers with his gruesome news.

"We will not be able to hold out," an old man cried.

"What will happen to our wives, our children? Let us choose now to die *'al kiddush hashem'* (for the sanctification of His Name) rather than be forced to accept baptism."

Rabbi Yom Tov quieted his anguished flock. "We still have a few days. Let us plan to fight in our own defense with all our strength and with all the equipment that we have in this fortress. Let us mete out to the enemy some of what they plan to do to us. Then, if we die, we will have died honorably."

The next morning, they gathered to plan their revenge.

"We will wait until the towers have been moved to the edge of the moat, and the lattice bridges lowered across the water. We will attack them with tarred, flaming rags and we will rain stones down upon their heads."

Wednesday morning was *Taanit Bechorim*.

[**Ed.** *Taanit Bechorim*, the Fast of the First Born, commemorates the slaying of first born Egyptians during the tenth plague and the redemption of first born Jewish males. It is observed on the day before the *Pesach* holiday begins.]

The Jews sheltered in the fortress gathered in their makeshift *shul* to fast and pray.

Yaakov Josce finished repeating the *Sh'mone Esray* (The Eighteen Benedictions), and when he concluded, he raised his hands for everyone's attention. At the top of his voice, he shouted: "Now is the time to act!"

The defenders rushed to their assigned stations on the parpapet. Their elders handed them rocks and tar soaked rags to ignite into fireballs. Having just crossed the lattice bridge, the attackers were totally unprepared as they waited astride their horses. The rocks pelted them, the fireballs burned them alive. But the enemy garrison still proceeded to move the towers forward.

With every toss, the defenders sang out: "Some with chariots, and some with horses, But we, in the Name of God trust."[2]

The mobs clamored: "Kill the Christ-killers! Kill the Jews!"

Yaakov Josce, still standing in the center of the makeshift *shul*, poured out his heart to the Creator of the world to have compassion upon His children. Each emotion filled word he uttered intensified his supplication. Suddenly, a large rock catapulted from the tower, shattered the readers' desk where he had been standing. When the clouds of dust cleared, Yaakov lay dead, blood oozing through the white *tallit* (prayer shawl) in which he had wrapped himself.

Tears streaming down his face, Rabbi Yom Tov whispered: "We have to remove the body from the synagogue."

The day wore on. Dead marauders floated in the moat and murdered Jews lay where arrows picked them off their stations on the parpapet. The women tried to douse the flaming arrows shot by their attackers, but soon the water ran out. Resistance evaporated slowly. Towards dusk, a single attacker succeeded in reaching the parapet. Following a sing-song melody, he found himself in the center of the fortress. Rather than sitting at festive Seder tables, the surviving Jews were totally absorbed in prayer, standing around a smoldering bonfire, and did not take notice of him.

He emerged from the fortress, climbed down to the grassy incline surrounding it, and shrieked: "They are witches! They deserve to die!"

The next morning, silence pervaded the fortress. The mob, led by the single attacker, prepared to slaughter the defenders. Reorganizing their forces, some ascended the incline, moving forward astride their horses; others followed, pushing the movable towers into place for attack. They were so intent on their victory that they didn't question why there was no resistance, no struggle, not even one defender stationed on the parapet.

Stalking through the fortress to determine the fate of those who were sheltered within, the leader of the mob found four dissheveled Jews crouched in a corner. They pleaded with him as he pulled them up: "Have mercy! We will do as you wish, only spare our lives!"

"Where are the others? Why are you the only ones here? Where are they hiding?"

"We will tell you everything, only please, have mercy, we beg you, let us live. We didn't want to die with them, so we hid. There is no living person here. Under the leadership of Rabbi Yom Tov, they all agreed to suicide, to die rather than be forced to convert. They burned their remaining food and clothing. There is nothing, absolutely nothing here."

Enraged, he shrieked: "Kill them. Kill them!"

The marauders impaled the four hapless survivors with the tips of their swords, and then shredded their bodies to pieces.

Victorious, they returned to the city hall. The sheriff burned all the official records of the debts that were owed to the Jews of York.

∽

A Sacred Trust
— Commentary —
Rabbi Mayer

❧

The obligation of a Jew to reach out to follow Jews in difficulty rests on two principles. The first is that being a Jew is more than a matter of affirming certain theological beliefs. It is a matter of being part of a family, part of a community. One cannot be a Jew alone, one can only be a Jew with other Jews. Because of our shared Jewishness, we owe something to those people whether we know them or not, whether we like them or not.

The second principle is the great religious idea that every human being is fashioned in the image of God. How can we show our love of God for all that God has done for us? We love God by loving every one of God's creatures, bearers of God's image.

This sense of responsibility for other Jews does not diminish our feeling of responsibility for non-Jews. Quite the contrary. By practicing on our fellow Jews the art of loving strangers, we learn how to love all of God's children and to help them in their distress.

—Rabbi Harold Kushner,
Author of:
- *When Bad Things Happen to Good People*
- *To Life! A Celebration of Jewish Being & Thinking*
- *When Children Ask About God*
- *Who Needs God*

The Rhine River Valley using today's boundries, listing general
locations of many cities and towns mentioned.

RABBI MAYER'S LETTER

Time Line

| 70 c.e. | 600 c.e. | 1000 c.e. | 1400 c.e. | 1600 c.e. | 1800 c.e. | 2000 c.e. |

— Location: Germany —

[**Ed.** From the cited sources listed in the footnotes, it is possible to reconstruct the general conditions under which Jews lived in medieval Germany and France.]

"My people," thought Rabbi Mayer, "have accepted me as their communal and religious leader. I am head of the *yeshiva* and I personally care for twenty four students who have come to study here from all over the area. I just added that many rooms to my house, and affixed *mezuzot* to the new doorposts. But what good is all this material comfort when the suffering of my people increases daily? I must find a way to ease their pain."

Acts of violence had increased radically in the past few years. He listed the incidences of violence on a piece of parchment, as if he were writing a record for posterity.

"In the past two and a half years there has been numerous blood libels and accompanying massacres.[1] Jews have been murdered in cold blood in Mainz, in Mulrichstadt, and in Munich. Some were burned to death in their own synagogue. Jews were indiscriminately murdered in Boppard and Oberwessel. Emperor Rudolf I has imposed exorbitant taxes on us.[2] He insists that we are his *servi-camerae*, his private property, to treat us as he pleases. He has prohibited us from fleeing to other towns to find safety as we had previously been able to do. My teacher, Rabbi Yechiel set a precedent. He went to live in the Holy Land, together with his family and his students and their families. He believed that it was time to return to our ancestral homeland, that we have lived too long in the diaspora. I remember so clearly when cartloads of holy books were confiscated and burned after he disputed with the apostate Nicolas Donin on June 17, 1242.

The words of the *piyut*, (religious poem), I wrote at that time, *"Shaali Serufa Baesh Lishlom Avaylayich:* O, Law that has been consumed by fire, seek the welfare of those who mourn for you," still pounds in my soul. I know what I have to do. I will prepare my people to follow in his footsteps. We will make preparations to emigrate!"

[**Ed.** This *piyut* is part of the liturgy on Tisha B'Av, the day mourning the destruction of both Holy Temples, the national day of Jewish mourning.]

"The first step is to wait for all of the Jews of this town to gather at *mincha* (the afternoon prayer service), since any special gathering would appear suspicious to the emperor's spies. I am convinced that this is the right thing to do."

That evening, after the services concluded, Rabbi Mayer ascended the *bema* (pulpit), raised his right hand, and waited for attention. A hush fell over the synagogue.

"I have given my words a great deal of thought. I want you to listen to me carefully. Many Jews are emigrating from the German towns of Mainz, Speyer, Virmyze, Oppenheim, and Wetterau. They have left all their property behind. Emperor Rudolf thinks that both the Jews and their property belong to him, so he has appointed the Archbishop of Mainz and Count Eberhard of Katzenellenbogen to manage the confiscated property in lieu of the taxes they will no longer pay him. The Emperor will not be satisfied with what he has confiscated to date; he has an exorbitant appetite, and will continue to extort our last silver coins until we impoverished. In order to maintain our dignity, I propose that we follow are brothers and leave this cursed land."

The people seemed glued to their seats. They were stunned

at their Rabbi's suggestion. They knew that living was becoming increasingly difficult. But emigrating to the Holy Land? It was so far! Without their money, how would they ever be able to start all over again?

The audible rumbling grew louder. Rabbi Mayer pounded the *shtender*, (the reading desk), for silence. "We are all suffering in this town. It is incumbent upon me to help you save your lives."

He walked down from the *bemah*, sat in his chair, satisfied that he had convinced them to think about emigrating.

The next morning, he began to plan his own exit from Rothenberg to the Holy Land.

"I don't want to endanger the lives of my daughters and their husbands, so I need to arrange for their safety," he thought. "And Sarah, my youngest daughter—she seems to be such a perfect match for Rabbi Asher—he is really my best student. In order to allay any suspicion, I will announce their betrothal and set a wedding date for the fifteenth of Elul, a few months from now."

Clandestinely, he sought their consent for a small private wedding in his home, immediately.

After the wedding, he blessed them: "Listen, my children, most of us are going to leave this country. It would be best if this family breaks up and travels individually. I will go to Lombardische Gebirge, and wait there for those of my fellow travelers who want to accompany me, to catch up. From there, we will travel south through the Po River Valley until we reach the western shores of the Mediterranean Sea.

"We will hire passage on a boat and sail to the Holy Land. I know that it has been devastated by the Crusades, but I do not need much in the way of material things. I am an old man; yet this has been my dream for years. Soon my eyes will no longer have to yearn to see our homeland. But, you don't have to come with me. On the contrary, you are both young, and you need to build a comfortable home. I would like to suggest that you rebuild your lives in Spain, a country that welcomes Jews. My very good friend, Rabbi Shlomo ben Aderet lives in Barcelona. I will write a letter to him on your behalf. I'm certain that he will be able to help you resettle."

The Jews who decided to emigrate packed a few of their belongings quietly, while trying to sell some of their household goods in order to have money. They trusted each other.

Knippe was the only person who could have reported their activities to the emperor's guards, so when he left town suddenly, they all breathed a sigh of relief. Knippe was a former student who had been expelled from Rabbi Mayer's *yeshiva*. He had sworn revenge against Rabbi Meyer.

Whether he had been influenced by the forced disputations, by compulsory attendance at Dominican missionary sermons, by censorship and confiscation of Jewish books and the burning of volumes of the Talmud, or just an unworthy, mischievous student, he had become an apostate (one who has turned away from Judaism).

The long, hazardous trip wearied Rabbi Mayer. While awaiting his fellow travelers he had an opportunity to rest in Lombardische Gebirge before proceeding further. One day, as he was returning from a short walk through the town, he was noticed by Knippe, who had been accompanying the bishop of Basel on his way home from Rome.

Knippe wasted no time. He turned to the Bishop and whispered: "Do you see that man rushing away just ahead of us? His name is Rabbi Mayer. He is the leader of the Jews of Rothenberg. I wonder what he is doing here. He is probably running away to avoid paying the taxes which our beloved Emperor Rudolf has assessed. I think you should investigate."

The Bishop, no friend of the Jews, revealed this information to Count Meinhardt of Goerz, the ruler of Lombardische

Gebirge, and he, in turn, passed the information on to Emperor Rudolf.

Rabbi Mayer was arrested on the 4th day of Tammuz 5046 and imprisoned in the tower of Wasserburg.[3]

Emperor Rudolf assessed the sum of twenty three thousand marks for the release of Rabbi Mayer. The Jews tried to raise this sum to ransom their beloved teacher, but Rabbi Mayer discouraged their attempts. He did not want to set a precedent for the imprisonment of other rabbis in order to enrich the treasury of the emperor. He based his decision on the Talmudic principle: "We do not ransom prisoners for more than they are worth."[4]

Finally, the Emperor ordered that he be transferred to the fortress of Ensisheim. He permitted Rabbi Mayer few privileges while incarcerated.

Over and over, Rabbi Mayer repeated to himself: "The Emperor can imprison my body, but he can never imprison my spirit. I have use of my holy books. My students visit me. What more do I need? I will never allow the Jewish community to accede to his demands!"

Rabbi Mordechai ben Hillel, Rabbi Mayer Hakohen, and Rabbi Shimshon ben Tzadok were among a few of Rabbi Mayer's students who visited him. They continued to discuss ritual and legal problems. Outside the prison walls, they recorded his practices and opinions for posterity. These works are part of our *responsa* literature.

[Ed. A *responsum* is a written answer to a legal or religious question. It was often asked because of a problem that the inquirer faced. These inquiries have historical significance because, had the problem not arisen, there would be no reason to ask a speculative question. Therefore, these *responum* provide a description of how our people lived during any given historical period.]

Rabbi Mayer remained in prison for the next seven years, until the day of his death, 19th Iyar 5053.[5] The Emperor refused to release his body for burial until the ransom was paid. Finally, after fourteen years, an individual Jew named Rabbi Alexander ben Shlomo (Susskind) Wimpfen convinced the Emperor to accept his own private funds, which could not be construed as a communal tax. Rabbi Wimpfen offered the money on the condition that when he died, he would be buried at the side of Rabbi Mayer. The graves of both Rabbi Mayer and Rabbi Wimpfen are in Virmyze, Germany.

∾

A Sacred Trust
— Commentary —
The Blood Libel

In many respects, Torah is composed of legal revolutions. From the very beginning, the Torah, departing from the prevailing universal norm, insisted that human life be the paramount value and, through this insistence, removed violation of property from the category of capital crime.

"Man in the image of God" is perhaps the most profound and significant value that Judaism has given the world.

—*Dr. Ronald Brauner*
Publisher of Straight Talk,
the Journal of the Foundation
for Jewish Studies, Inc.

Chapter Seventeen

THE BLOOD LIBEL:
The Endless, Deadly Lie

Time Line

| 70 c.e. | 600 c.e. | 1000 c.e. | 1400 c.e. | 1600 c.e. | 1800 c.e. | 2000 c.e. |

— Location: Germany —

[**Ed.** An imperial decree referring to Cologne, dated 321 C.E. corroborates Jewish settlement in Germany to Roman times. The Jews followed the Rhine River settling in small towns along its banks for commercial purposes. Until the Crusades usurped these trade routes, the Jews were international merchants, bridging East and West.

A side effect of this international trade was the ability for *responsa* literature to move in the merchants mail pouches between the *yeshivot* of Babylonia and Western Europe. As Christianity became more powerful, the Jews were considered alien infidels; their social and legal status was different than the rest of the population and they required special protection to safeguard their existence. The rulers decreed that Jews belonged to their treasury and were private property. The *gezayrot* and *takkanot* (religious decrees) of this period formulated to strengthen Jewish life, reveal how often Jews chose martyrdom rather than convert to save themselves. They also reveal that Jews were forced to be moneylenders to earn a livelihood; that some succeeded as small tradesman, craftsmen, or distributors of agricultural products, but they were generally insecure as one act of violence followed another.]

Leah, mistress of a large house at the edge of the Jewish section in Bachrach, had just finished clearing the table of the Shabbat lunch dishes.[1]

She settled in her large spacious armchair, wondering, daydreaming; her seven year old daughter Sarah played quietly at her feet. She imagined that she was walking with her to the *chuppah* (the wedding canopy).

"I wonder what the world will be like when she marries? How many more blood libels and expulsions will there be until our neighbors learn to live with us in peace? Will she be able to raise my grandchildren in safety?

[Ed. A blood libel is the allegation that Jews murder non-Jews in order to obtain blood with which to bake *matzot* for *Pesach* (Passover). Blood libels led to trials and massacres of Jews during the Middle Ages and continued through recorded history, even into the twentieth century. The first blood libel occurred in Norwich, England, in 1144. It was alleged that the Jews bought a Christian child named William before Easter, tortured him and hung him. Blood libels often coincided with the Jewish holiday of *Pesach* and the Christian holiday of Easter. Motifs for the blood libel varied from the crucifixion, to using Christian blood for baking *matzot* and medicinal purposes, to inciting riots against Jews. Jewish scholars refuted these accusations, citing biblical sources for the prohibition of Jews eating blood, (Vayikra, Leviticus 7:26,27, 17:10,12), to no avail.]

Will she marry a scholar, a merchant, a combination of both? Will she marry a young man who studied Torah in the *yeshiva* of Rabbi Yaakov ben Asher in Toldeo?

[Ed. Toledo, the medieval capital of Spain, became the Jewish spiritual and religious center soon after the Moslem conquest in 711 until the Christian reconquest and succeeding massacres during the fourteenth century. Part Three describes the Jewish experience in Spain.]

Or one who studied in the *yeshiva* of Rabbi Alexander HaKohen Zusselin in Frankfurt-am-Main?

[Ed. Frankfurt-am-Main conjures images of great cliffs, rocky slopes covered with pines, fir, oaks, beeches, and birches, magnificent churches and great cathedrals. Frankfurt was home to an organized, flourishing Jewish community by the twelfth century. It held two semi-annual trade fairs each year, in February and in September. By 1270, the Jewish section had a central synagogue, cemetery, bathhouse, hospital, wedding hall, hospitality house, educational and welfare institutions.

Nevertheless, the Jewish community was subject to numerous massacres and pillage, expulsions, forced baptism. Because the Emperor benefited from Jewish tax money, he tried to protect them, and oftentimes was successful. Around 1347, comets were seen streaking across the heavens following a series of earthquakes which rocked central Europe. Comets were regarded with awe and terror by medieval people who were very superstitious. They interpreted comets as omens of forthcoming unfavorable events. When the Black Plague started ravaging Europe during 1348-1349, the superstitious medieval people believed it to be the fulfillment of the unfavorable event and they looked for an explanation. Rumors spread that the Jews were poisoning the water wells. People reacted irrationally and mob violence multiplied; many Jewish communities were pillaged, and their inhabitants massacred, including illustrious rabbinical leaders, among them Rabbi Alexander HaKohen Zusselin of Frankfort.][2]

Will it be safe for them to build their home in this town ten years from now? Or will they have to wander in search of a secure place to live? Will they have to flee as far away as Toledo or Barcelona? Then I might never see my grandchildren. I hear that the Jews living in Spain are quite comfortable these days!"

The years whirled by, and it was not long before Leah walked behind Sarah as she circled Avraham seven times beneath the *chuppah.*

The young groom, having studied Torah in Toledo for seven years, was invited to accept the rabbinical leadership of Bachrach, so the newlyweds settled in a comfortable house near her parents. Immediately, Sarah set about to make their home into "a gathering place for wise men."[3]

Their door was open to those in need of a meal, to those who needed comfort, to those who needed money, and to those who needed help with the sick. Sarah showed, by her example, that there were no bounds to generous acts of love and kindness.

From the first year of their marriage, they invited all the leaders of the community to their home to celebrate *Pesach* on the first Seder night. Sarah set magnificent tables with sparkling candlesticks, white, embroidered tablecloths, glowing silver *kiddush* cups, a jeweled cup for *Elyahu* (Elijah), a three tiered *matza* platter, a blue pottery bowl filled with salt water, and a glistening brass plate upon which was heaped the symbols of the Seder, the roasted bone and egg, the *charoset,* the bitter herbs, the horseradish head, and bits of greens.

Rabbi Avraham leaned splendidly against the pillow that Sarah had nestled into his arm chair, both of them happily greeting their guests. They sat side by side at the head of the table, she watching her husband with pride as he recited the *kiddush* and waited while all the guests drank the first of the "four cups." Following Avraham's lead, the guests washed their hands, dipped a bit of greens into the salt water, and focused their attention on him as he broke the middle *matza* for the *afikomen*.

Suddenly, a harsh pounding on their locked door interrupted the ritual. Avraham excused himself, rushed to the door to find out who intruded. He opened it a crack.

Two men, a bit disheveled, wrapped in black cloaks, spoke at once: "*Shalom aleichem*, peace to you, we were lost in our travels and found ourselves delayed in Bachrach. We were told that you have many Seder guests, and we hoped that we could join you."

Avraham responded: "*Aleichem shalom*, please come in. Actually, we have just begun our Seder; we were reciting "*kol dichfin yaytay v'yaychol*, all who are hungry come in and eat." He moved aside, opening the door wider to permit the men to enter.

Leading them to the table, he pointed to two places, returned to his arm chair, and continued with the recitation of the *hagadah*. Avraham was totally absorbed in its recitation and explanation. He did not notice that the smile on Sarah's face had become frozen with terror.

When he rose to wash his hands the second time, she beckoned to him to follow her. Hushing his urge to speak, she led him out the side door, practically dragging him toward the side of a neighboring house.

"I don't understand what you are doing," he demanded an explanation. "We are in the middle of our Seder; why am I standing outside?"

Trembling, Sarah whispered: "You did not see what I saw. The two men who intruded are not Jews. They wore those big blacks cloaks to hide the body of a dead child that they succeeding in placing beneath our dining room table. I saw the body. We may still have a little time to escape before it is discovered. I have heard about so many of these plots, these horrible accusations. I waited until you stood up to wash your hands to beckon you outside, so as not to hint to them that we know of their plot. We must flee. Even now, the opportunity to seek shelter grows slimmer and slimmer."

The glowing full moon and the twinkling stars lit their way as they hurried toward the shore of the Rhine River. Sitting on the wharf, Whilhelm, a deaf mute fisherman who Avraham and Sarah befriended and helped care for, understood that they wanted him to row them across the river on his raft.

Toward sunrise, they reached Frankfurt on the opposite shore, and immediately set out for the Jewish section of the city, the ghetto.

[Ed. Although ghetto living was fraught with economic hardship, it inadvertently benefited the Jews by creating strong, cohesive, independent communities within its walls. The origin of the word ghetto is derived from the Italian, *geto*, which means an iron foundry. It was near the iron foundry in Venice that the first ghetto was built in 1516. Ironically, the Hebrew word *get*, means divorce; it was as if the world was divorcing itself from contact with the Jewish people.]

The gatekeeper refused to allow them to enter until he cleared them with the *parnas* (leader) of the city, for the ghetto gates served to protect the Jews inside as well as keep the trouble outside.

The *parnas* came running to the gate himself for he did not understand how it was possible for the Rabbi of Bachrach to sail on a raft on the night of *Pesach*.

Avraham explained agitatedly, breathlessly: "Before I fill in the details, you no doubt know the Talmudic passage which states: saving life supersedes Shabbat.[4] Sarah perceived how dangerous our situation was. She also understood that the two men who intruded into our house wanted to implicate me, the Rabbi of Bachrach; otherwise they would have chosen someone else's house. She perceived that this was a well-drawn plot, and therefore I agreed with her assessment of the situation that we both flee. I also hoped, that if I was the focus of the plot, that the rest of the guests who remained at our table would be able to escape unharmed when they realized that we had fled."

"If they want to implicate you—what if they follow you to this side of the river?" sputtered the *parnas*. "Our city has experienced much hardship, also."

"No one will ever find out how or where we disappeared. Wilhelm, the fisherman who rowed us across the river is our friend, and a deaf mute."

The *parnas* retreated, and welcomed them officially to Frankfurt and the security of his city. "I will be honored to have you stay in my home until the end of the holiday."

Back at the Seder table, the guests wondered what took Avraham and Sarah so long to wash their hands. One of the guests looked into the kitchen, and not finding them, suspected foul play. Nevertheless, they did not know for sure what had happened, so they decided to use time delay tactics to protect them. The two intruders demanded: "What happened to your Rabbi and his wife? We want to continue the Seder!"

One Seder guest countered calmly: "Don' t you know that it is the custom of the Rabbi and his wife to recite the *Shir Hashirim* (Song of Songs) in the *shul* before the Seder meal? Let us sit patiently. They will return soon. "

[**Ed.** It is a custom to recite *Shir Hashirim* on the Shabbat between the first days and the last days of *Pesach*. Sometimes it is recited on the night of the Seder.]

An hour later, the Seder guests, one by one, made varying excuses to leave the house. They wanted to find out what had happened. Finally, the two intruders were alone.

First they rampaged through the kitchen, grabbing and gulping the delicacies that Sarah had prepared for the Seder meal, shoving to the floor all else that did not interest them. Then, they returned to the dining room, dashed the dishes to the floor, gathered the silver candlesticks, the cutlery, and kiddush cups, the jeweled cup of *Elyahu*, the glistening brass Seder plate, four bottles of wine, wrapped them in the embroidered tablecloth, and ran off. They left the body of the dead child underneath the table.

They hid their loot, drank the stolen wine and passed out. When they awoke hours later, they headed for the constable's to inform him that they had found a dead Christian child in a Jewish home.

In the meantime, the Seder guests despairing of finding out what had happened to Avraham and Sarah, returned to the house. To their dismay, they found total wreckage and the body of the dead child. Quietly, they buried the body behind the house, and then reported to the constable that it had been plundered.

The constable wondered: "Is there a connection between the plundered house and the disappearance of the rabbi and his wife? This is the time of the year when people living outside the ghetto try to harm the Jews."

He was busily writing down their testimony, when chaos erupted outdoors. The tumult, the uproar was uncontrolled as the screaming mother of the dead child pushed her way inside. Looking for someone to blame, and recognizing the Seder guests as Jews from their distinctive garb, she pointed an accusing finger at them: "My baby daughter has disappeared. Those Jews need blood for their holiday rituals. They are murderers!"

The constable tried to calm her. "Please describe the clothes that your daughter was wearing when she disappeared," he said.

Just then, the robbers happened on the scene: "We came to report that the house of Avraham and Sarah has been robbed and wrecked. We were hired to help clean after their big Seder last night."

The constable sent two investigators to determine the facts: one was sent to the house of Avraham and Sarah, the other to the house of the robbers.

The first investigator returned from the house of Avraham and Sarah. "The house has been wrecked," he reported. "Broken dishes and food are strewn all over, but if last night was their Seder, what happened to all the cutlery, the *kiddush* cups and the candlesticks that they use?"

The second investigator returned with the embroidered tablecloth and its contents. The robbers paled at the evidence against them. Then one spurted out: "So, we are guilty of robbery, but we did not kill the child!"

"Who said anything about a dead child?" demanded the constable. "Open the tablecloth," he instructed.

Inside the tablecloth he found the bloodied dress of the dead girl, implicating the robbers in the alleged blood libel.

The murderers were hanged. On that day, no Jews ventured forth from the safety of their houses within the confines of the ghetto, for they feared the revenge of those who hated them.

When the Jews of Frankfurt found out how Sarah and Avraham had sought shelter in their city, they welcomed them warmly.

"I want to tell you a secret," she whispered to Avraham. "Not too many years ago... it was a Shabbat afternoon... I was playing at my mother's feet ... she was dozing, or daydreaming ... I don't know which ... but I heard her mumble ... what will the young man who marries my daughter be like? Will he be a scholar or a merchant or both? There was more to her mumbling, but that is not important now. I think that there are so many opportunities for you to be both, if we remain in Frankfurt.

"Why don't we settle here and try to rebuild our lives?"

∽

A SACRED TRUST

— COMMENTARY —

MAJESTY OF THE NUMBER SEVEN

❧

"The Black Death (1347 - 1350) was one of humanity's epochal scourges. For the Jews, it was a tragedy to which, after the fall of *Yerushalayim*, only the horrors of 1096 (The First Crusade) were comparable.

Bewildered by the plague's ravages, people looked for a cause. Before long, the inevitable scapegoat was found—the Jews.

Attempts were made by the authorities and the members of the higher classes to defend the Jews, but they were fruitless. So were those of Pope Clement VI (1342 - 1352) who intervened twice, condemning violence against Jews, forbidding forced baptism, and declaring them innocent of the calumnies against them.

Emperor Charles IV made efforts to protect "his" Jews, but only half heartedly. As often as he offered aid, he granted immunity to the attackers or conceded Jewish property to favorites even before a massacre took place."

Father Edward H. Flannery
The Anguish of the Jews
New York. The Macmillan Company. 1965

❧

Chapter Eighteen

THE MAJESTY OF THE NUMBER SEVEN

Time Line

70 c.e.	600 c.e.	1000 c.e.	1400 c.e.	1600 c.e.	1800 c.e.	2000 c.e.

— Location: Germany —

Two men stood facing each other, unflinching, starring, centuries old animosity etched across the lines of their foreheads and the curves of their chins.

Shlomo Hanagid, the man on the right, stood his ground proudly. He was so respected in his community by both Jew and non-Jew, that people affectionately said of him: "'He epitomizes both Torah and greatness'[1] for he possessed both *halachic* learning, wealth, and the reputation for dealing kindly with his fellow man."

The man on the left was garbed in the black cassock of a parish priest. He stared intently at Shlomo Hanagid, who he planned to beseech for a loan of seven hundred gulden.

"I know why I hate him so much ," thought the priest. "I don't want to be beholden to a despised Jew!" Silently, glumly, he reviewed in his mind the reasons for his blind hatred. "My father was one of them. He married a Christian woman. My playmates always mocked me because the whole town knew of my mixed parentage. I remember how they laughed when they fabricated stories about the Jews. I have been trying to erase the stain of my birth all my life, to prove that I am a true Christian, that I am loyal to my church. The only way that I can prove that I am a 100% true Christian is to show by my actions how much I hate them! This means that I must exhort my parishioners to act violently against them in the same way that I was taught by my teachers, the Dominican and Franciscan monks. I have been doing this for years, and now, woe is me, I have no choice but to beg this Jew for a loan!

[**Ed.** The order of Franciscans Friars was established by Francis of Assisi with the approbation of Pope Innocent III in 1209. The order of Dominican Friars was sanctioned by Pope Honorius III in 1216 with a mandate to preach against Albigenses and Waldenses (sects) heretics. Both religious orders focused their major activity against Jews, especially those who had converted to Christianity and then returned to Judaism. They led the acts of violence perpetrated against the Jews during the middle ages, notably confiscation and burning books of the Talmud, arranging public disputations in which Jews were forced to send representatives to defend the validity of Judaism, compelling Jews to listen to sermons whose purpose was to convert them, staging blood libels and massacres, and persuading dukes to decree expulsions. The wide spread indebtedness of the general population to Jewish moneylenders served as a focus for implementing anti-Jewish legislation which included physical segregation, wearing of badges, and the restriction of financial activities. Their magnetic sermons before enormous crowds, exhorting the people to repentance, encouraged them to increase their acts of violence against those who refused to convert."][2]

Listen to me Jew! I am in desperate straits! I need to borrow seven hundred gulden," he mumbled obsequiously.

Shlomo thought: "If I lend him the money without collecting security, without forcing him to sign a promissory note describing his intentions for repayment, maybe, he will understand that we Jews are not his enemies. Maybe, if I am exceptionally kind to him, he will change his hateful attitude to my people."

[**Ed.** As a result of the development of feudalism, Jews were increasingly cut off from commerce, trade and artisan guilds, civil and military functions, professions, and landownership. In 1179, church fathers decreed Canon Law forbidding Christians to take interest (usury) and threatened excommunication. The Jews, searching for a way to support themselves, became money lenders and pawn brokers, in order to subsist in a hostile environment in which they had no other recourse.][3]

He opened a drawer, removed the requested sum, and smiling, handed it to the priest, without saying a word.

The priest could not contain himself. He taunted: "Jew, aren't you afraid that loaning me money is a tremendous risk, that I won't repay you?"

"I'm not worried," Shlomo spoke softly. "Seven is a significant number for the Jewish people. I'm sure that I will be repaid."

[**Ed.** Seven is a very significant number within Jewish tradition. Among the significant sevens are: the seven days of creation (Shabbat), seven windings of the *tefilin* (phylacteries) around the arm, seven processions with the Torah on Simchat Torah, counting seven weeks after *Pesach* (Passover) in preparation for receiving the Torah on *Shavuot*, seven aliyot to the Torah, seven species of fruit that are special to the Holy Land, seven circles of the bride around the groom, and the seven blessings of marriage.]

The priest took the money and sulked all the way out the door. He walked down the path, lined on both sides with bare bushes, blackened branches in place of verdant foliage, out the wrought iron gate, tightly clutching the seven hundred gulden.

Shlomo's kindness and his sincere, businesslike manner did not allay the animosity of the parish priest. Rather, it aggravated him to the point where, half way back to the cloister, he began flailing his arms wildly, screaming loudly, agitatedly: "I will find a way never to repay that Jew his money." His devious mind constructed a plot.

"He said that seven is an important number to the Jewish people. I happen to know that seven is a number associated with the devil as are the Jews. They are working with the devil to poison our water wells. That's how the plague is spreading so rapidly. If I can annihilate the Jews, I will be able to stop this plague that is ravishing my people. That's why so many of my parishoners are dying and so many Jews are living. The devil must be protecting them. Some people say that this accusation is ridiculous, but I know that it is true. I also know that most people will not stand up to defend the Jews. I will hide some poison among Shlomo's record keeping books. Then, I will let a few people know my plan. They will break into his house, find the poison, and spread the rumor. The populace will be inflamed. A massacre will follow. The Jewish community will be destroyed, along with all their records, and I won't have to repay the loan. And I am going to act quickly. Tonight is a perfect night, for there will be no visible moon."

[**Ed.** The Black Plague (bubonic plague) destroyed half the population of Central Europe. The disease was carried by rats from Oriental ports and brought to Marseille, France, and by Crusaders returning from the Middle East. It spread across Germany, Italy, France, England, Norway, Russia, India, and China. Persecution of the Jews during this period (1348-1351) parallels the ravages of the plague; massacres were horrific, unequalled until the Holocaust in the twentieth century.][4]

To implement his plan, he bought a tiny leather pouch and filled it with red and black powder. He carefully cracked the shell of an egg, emptied it, placed the pouch inside, and matched the halves of the shell together, so that the crack was barely visible. He prepared a pair of soft fabric-like slippers so that his footsteps would be muffled when he tread around Shlomo's house, searching for his record-keeping books. He would hide the poison filled egg next to it. Then he instructed his servant:

"Tonight, I want you to go and watch Shlomo's house. You can sit beside the tall bushes that surround it. Even though the bushes are bare, he will not be able to see you on this moonless night. Make sure that no one else sees you either. Watch carefully. When you are sure that everyone is asleep, I want you to signal me by striking these seven flints against this iron bar. I will see the flickering sparks. You are not to tell anyone what I asked you to do."

"I have nothing to do now but to wait for the signal," he thought gleefully. "By this time tomorrow, there will not be a Jew left in this town!"

Shlomo trudged slowly along the muddy, sleet covered

roads. Heavy snow flurries blurred his vision, so he bent his head to better watch for fallen branches that lay strewn in his path. His beard sparkled from the wet snow. He grasped his arms in a huddle for warmth, as he gradually inched his way homeward. He had stayed in the marketplace very late that evening, finishing a business deal with a man who couldn't stop talking. By the time their business was concluded, there wasn't a carriage for hire in the marketplace. Darkness had descended rapidly; no stars on this dreary night, and no light from the moon.

He was anxious to reach home. He was cold, tired, hungry and wet. He wanted to kindle the Chanukah lights, eat some hot soup, then sit comfortably by the fireplace which provided both warmth and light. As he walked up the path to his house, he was unaware of a pair of eyes that followed his every step. "Tell the children that I am ready to kindle the Chanukah lights," he called to his wife.

His family gathered around the *chanukeya* (Chanukah menorah) which glittered in the shadows from it's honored place on a table next to the window. Reciting the blessings with great fervor, he slowly kindled the *shamash* and the six wicks in the filled oil cups. When he finished, he lifted his youngest child to his shoulders, grabbed the other children, formed a circle, and began dancing to the words of "*Al Hanisim*, For these Miracles..."

The priest waited patiently for the signal. When he saw the seven lights flickering in the darkness, he edged toward Shlomo's house, the poison filled leather pouch concealed in the egg shell held securely in his hand.

[**Ed.** The sixth night of Chanukah always falls the eve of Rosh Chodesh, the new moon which reflects almost no light.]

Slowly, he made his way toward the door, taking care not to trip over a dead branch. The soft fabric of his slippers absorbed the wetness of the ground. He was uncomfortable and cold. He waited silently in front of the door, listening for any sign of human wakefulness, but could not control his unbridled hate: "Do it! Don't wait!" An inner voice urged him forward. "You can implicate the entire Jewish community by placing the poison in his record keeping books and letting a few trustworthy people know. Hurry!"

Heeding his inner voice and disregarding any sensible precautions, the priest turned the door lock, let himself into the house and found himself standing opposite a flushed faced Shlomo, who had been energetically dancing with his children. Shlomo noticed that the priest clutched something in his hand; a warning bell sounded in his head. He quickly set the child down, and with one swoop step, jumped the priest, knocked him down, motioned for his oldest child to bring him a rope, and tied the priest hand and foot. The egg shell cracked in the scuffle, but Shlomo did not have to open the leather pouch to guess what was inside, what the priest had intended to do.

A few weeks later, the priest, his head bowed, his shoulders hunched, his body shuddering, sat in the accused seat in the crowded courthouse. The people shouted: "Expel the Jews! They can not be trusted. They have poisoned our wells. They are not dying from the plague like we are!"

But the judge demanded silence. "I will read this document before I comment on this case: Pope Clement VI has issued a Canon Bull which condemns the massacre or expulsion of Jews from their homes in reprisal for the belief that they are responsible for spreading the plague. Emperor Charles IV and Duke Albert of Austria declared the Jews innocent and pointed out that the death tolls were as high where Jews lived as elsewhere. Count Ruprecht von der Pfalz has taken the Jews who live in his territory under his personal protection. The charges against the Jews are absurd. As for me, I will not be swayed by my so called 'enlightened' contemporaries, Landgrave Frederic of Thuringia who burned Jews 'for the honor of God,' and advised others to follow his example, and the Margrave of Brandenburg who accepted the best three Jewish houses in Nuremberg 'after the next massacre.' I find the accused guilty."[5]

The din in the courtroom heightened. The judge shouted: "Does the accused have anything to say in his behalf?"

"I didn't know that seven was a significant number to those Jews," he muttered. "I only failed because of the number seven. Seven! Seven!! The next time I will succeed!"

The judge looked at him in amazement. He didn't understand why the priest kept muttering seven, seven. The judge thought that the priest had lost his mind.

∾

A SACRED TRUST
— COMMENTARY —
NETILAT YADAYIM

❧

Struggling with Jewish identity and continuity in the last decade of the twentieth century, we wonder which *mitzvah* will have the greatest impact in insuring a Jewish tomorrow.

Pinchas/Paul's mother struggled with the same issue, but she knew that through the power of a *mitzvah*, it was possible for "One to acquire eternity in a single moment."

Talmud Bavli, Avodah Zarah 10b

❧

Cracow, Poland and Rome, Italy shown with modern bountries.

Chapter Nineteen

THE MITZVAH OF NETILAT YADAYIM

Time Line

| 70 c.e. | 600 c.e. | 1000 c.e. | 1400 c.e. | 1600 c.e. | 1800 c.e. | 2000 c.e. |

— **Location: Poland and Rome** —

[**Ed.** Cracow was the 15th and 16th Century capital of the vast Polish Lithuanian empire, and home to a multitude of Jews. Situated on the banks of the Vistula River, Cracow was a center for trade routes between East and West. It also had commercial ties with Breslau, Danzig, Lvov (Lemberg), and Constantinople. It was a haven for a steady stream of Jewish merchants and immigrants who fled persecution from western Europe.

The Jews had already acquired full Polish citizenship by the middle of the fourteenth century; they were permitted to own land, to build a religious community and to engage in unrestricted commercial activities. They managed the flour mills, the salt mines, the liquor distilleries, the lumber mills, and the estates of the wealthy landed aristocrats that dotted Poland's countryside. The Jews were the middle class that helped develop primitive Poland into a modern society.

The Jewish community flourished under the guidance of its revered *talmeday chachamim*, its rabbis and scholars. Because of the emphasis on learning, many families, desirous to provide an intense Jewish education for their children, hired a *melamed* (a tutor), to instruct them.]

∾

Shmuel and Dena lived in Cracow. Their youngest child Pinchas seemed different than his siblings; he was not happy with simple answers. The *melamed* could not satisfy his curiosity. Pinchas wanted to understand the cause and effect of how and why things worked. When the *melamed* let him out of the classroom to play, he would run to the edge of the river, watch the boats dock, eavesdrop on the conversations of the merchants, wonder what kind of world existed beyond Cracow. The merchants excitedly spoke about the great revival of learning in Italy, the patrons who supported artists and musicians, the unprecedented consideration for Jewish men of culture in Padua, Venice, and Rome, the Jewish physician who attended Pope Sixtus IV,[1] his interest in Jewish mystical thought commissioned to Latin translation. He listened as the merchants talked of how the Pope resisted political pressure and extended to Jews the ability to participate in the cultural activities of the Renaissance. Sometimes, he would wander out toward the edge of the city, following the uncharted paths into the virgin forests, to dream about his future plans.

As Pinchas matured, he aspired to leave Cracow, in order to attend the Sapienza, the university in Rome, to study medicine from the noblest physicians of the time. His parents were horrified that their son wanted to leave their close knit Jewish community.

When a fire broke out in Cracow, Pinchas joined the doctors who rushed to help the injured. He was inspired by them because they endangered their lives to help the victims. He was more convinced than ever before that he had to become a doctor.

The next time he spoke to his parents about his dream, he was adamant: "I am leaving Cracow with or without your permission. I have heard from the merchants that Jews are treated kindly in Rome. They are permitted to study in the university. There I will be able to become a physician. Please, give me your blessings so that I may go in peace to fulfill my lifelong dream."

Dena realized that she could no longer force Pinchas to remain in Cracow, in the protective Jewish environment in which he had grown up.

"All right," she conceded. "I've been told that the environment in Rome is not conducive to Jewish observance, which is why we are opposed to your leaving. But I am a practical person. Since you are so determined, we will grant our permission if you swear to us that you will faithfully observe one *mitzvah* (commandment) that I will chose. This *mitzvah* will remind you all the time that you are a Jew. If you swear to do this, then you will have our blessings."

When he agreed, she chose the *mitzvah* of *netilat yadayim*, the ritual washing of the hands, prior to eating bread.

Pinchas smiled gently, then looked lovingly at his mother's face. "I swear to you, no matter where I go, no matter where I happen to be at meal time, I will always observe the *mitzvah* of *netilat yadayim* before I eat bread."

Shmuel and Dena blessed their son and he set out for Rome, following the merchants along their trade routes.

Pinchas settled in Rome among his Jewish brethren who were mostly craftsmen, money lenders and tailors. He enrolled in the university. The years devoted to studying medicine flew. At the university he was introduced to the non-Jewish world; he admired their emphasis on the new learning, on art and literature which marked the beginning of Europe's transition from medieval times to the modern world.

He wrote home often. He wrote of his progress in medicine, of the exciting cultural renaissance which he experienced. He always concluded each letter by reassuring his mother: "Don't worry, no matter where I eat, I have never failed to keep my promise to you. I always wash *netilat yadayim*."

When he graduated with honors from the university, he changed his name from Pinchas to Paul. Because he wanted his parents to know that he had graduated, he wrote a special letter home.

"Dear Mother and Father," he wrote. "I want you to know that I have graduated from medical school with the highest honors. I have been offered the position of personal physician to the noble Pierleoni family. I have changed my legal name from Pinchas to Paul. Somehow, it seems to fit more into the society in which I mingle. But don't worry, no matter where I go, I always remember my oath to you. I always wash *netilat yadayim.*"

"Paul" was a bright, young, eligible bachelor. He was invited to soirees. He was a most desirable dinner guest. The more he became part of the elite Roman nobility, the less he identified himself as a Jew. He even ate non-kosher food, even on Yom Kippur.

Paul's reputation as an extremely able physician spread throughout Rome and its environs.

Years passed. One day, he was called to attend to an old nobleman who was seriously ill. His estate was located in a valley, skirting the Tiber River, deep in the Apennine mountain range. Hastily, Paul prepared to leave the city for the sick man's estate. Knowing that the trip was a distance, he decided to take some provisions for the way. When some friends found out his destination, they warned him: "If you follow the flow of the Tiber River northward, you will be perfectly safe as long as you don't stop. Know that the forests are inhabited by highwaymen. If you keep riding, they will not bother you, but if you dismount, they will surely attack you. You may not survive."

"I understand," Paul repeated their warning quietly. "I am to ride straight through to the nobleman's estate without stopping."

Paul rode along the river's edge, following its trail as it curled northward. The sun sparkled in the verdant trees overhead. The lovely spring day grew warmer. Beads of perspiration slid down his forehead and cheeks. His horse trotted steadily in the direction of the nobleman's estate.

"I cannot stop, I cannot stop," he kept repeating to himself, as he glanced at the refreshing waters flowing alongside the path.

The hours passed. Paul had food and drink in a basket dangling from his saddle bags. He was hungry and thirsty.

Two voices battled within him. "You can not eat, because you cannot stop for *netilat yadayim*," whispered one voice.

"It doesn't matter," hissed the other voice. "You know you will endanger your life if you stop for *netilat yadayim*. Who will know that you missed the *mitzvah* only once? Eat! Don't be a fool. You might be attacked if you dismount from your horse!"

The clear blue waters of the Tiber River looked enticing.

"I cannot disregard my oath. I will stop for just a minute," he thought. "I can dismount from my horse, bathe my forehead and arms, dry them, wash *netilat yadayim*, jump up on my horse and continue my journey."

He peered into the trees and bushes along the path. He could see no one; not even a shadow was visible on the ground. Paul dismounted from his horse, tiptoed to the river's edge, bent to scoop up handfuls of cool water to pour over his perspiring head. Straightening up, he let the cool water trickle down his head, his shoulders. He scooped more water over his head, soaking his shirt. The breezes cooled him. Refreshed, he bent a third time, for *netilat yadayim*.

At that moment, the sound of a speeding arrow rang out from behind the trees, piercing his heart. Paul lay dead on the shore of the Tiber River. His soul ascended to the Heavenly Court for judgment.

"Whose soul dares penetrate Heaven's gates," roared the prosecuting angel?

"It is the soul of Paul, the boy from Cracow who became the famous doctor in Rome, who swore to observe the *mitzvah* of *netilat yadayim*," meekly answered the defending angel.

"That soul has no place here," roared the prosecuting angel. It did not observe the commandments, it knows no Torah, it did not abide by the dietary code or the Shabbat laws, it gave no charity. That soul has no place in Heaven! If it were up to me, I would ban him from Heaven's gates!"

Suddenly, a great commotion was heard from beyond Heaven's gates. "Wait, wait!" a voice called out. "The prosecuting angel cannot substantiate his charges. That soul always observed the *mitzvah* of *netilat yadayim*."

"Who do you think you are," shouted the prosecuting angel?

"I" the voice answered firmly, "am the *mitzvah* of *netilat yadayim*. I want you to know that Paul observed nothing because he remembered nothing of his childhood upbringing. But I know that soul deserves to repose in Heaven because he observed my *mitzvah* meticulously. He died observing my *mitzvah*."

"You have a point," ceded the prosecuting angel. "But what can we do about lowering our standards? Even if he observed one *mitzvah*, he didn't observe the others. How can we permit him his Heavenly reward for only one *mitzvah*?"

"Listen to my suggestion," said the *mitzvah* of *netilat yadayim*. "You can sentence him to remain outside of Heaven's gate until he learns the essence of Jewish life. Give me a year to teach him. After he has learned everything a Jew should know, you will be able to test him. If he passes, then he must be permitted to repose in Heaven."

The prosecuting angel and the defending angel huddled. They shouted and argued heatedly. Finally, they agreed: "We will accept your proposal. Remember, you must teach him everything a Jew should know!"

The *mitzvah* of *netilat yadayim* began teaching the soul of Paul. "Remember," it began, "everything, every *mitzvah* in our Torah is connected and interrelated." The soul of Paul learned Torah as eagerly as he had learned medicine.

"Let me show you how all the the commandments in the Torah are interrelated. Let's begin by reviewing my *mitzvah*, the *mitzvah* that you died to observe.

I am connected to the laws of the sacrifices, for the high priest had to wash his hands and feet in preparation for bringing offerings on the altar in the Holy Temple when it stood in Jerusalem."[2]

The *mitzvah* of *netilat yadayim* proceeded slowly and thoroughly. The soul of Paul was becoming as well versed in Jewish law as it had been in medicine. The *mitzvah* of *netilat yadayim* and the soul of Paul learned constantly. The *mitzvah* of *netilat yadayim*, a superb teacher, connected the laws of prayer to the laws of *tefilin*, to *mezuzah*, to Shabbat, to the dietary code, and to *tzedakah* (charity).

At the end of the year, the *mitzva*h of *netilat yadayim* was satisfied that the soul of Paul had learned the essence of Jewish life.

"Come with me," he urged, "you are on you way to enter the gates of Heaven."

There was no question between the prosecuting and defending angels that the soul of Paul merited repose in Heaven. The prosecuting angel lifted the ban; the Heavenly chorus welcomed the soul of Paul to its final resting place.

৵

The Rabbi of Cracow, being a great Kabbalist, dreamed the entire story of Pinchas' life on the night that Pinchas' soul was welcomed to Heaven. He understood the significance of his dream. When he awoke the next morning, he recorded it for posterity in the Diary of the City of Cracow. At the end of the story, he noted:

"I now understand that there is no such thing as an insignificant *mitzvah*."[3]

৵

A Sacred Trust
— Commentary —
Shimon the Silent

Even the humblest human being is capable of performing great deeds. None was humbler than Shimon and it was he whose heroism saved a community.

Shimon's greatness was revealed not only in his act of great valor but in the quality of his life; in his refusal to be dragged down to the level of his fellow citizens by engaging in gossip and idle talk.

He had the courage to act and to live by the dictates of his conscience and by his fidelity to Jewish ethical behavior.

> —*Rabbi Sidney Greenberg*
> *Temple Sinai*
> *Dresher, PA*

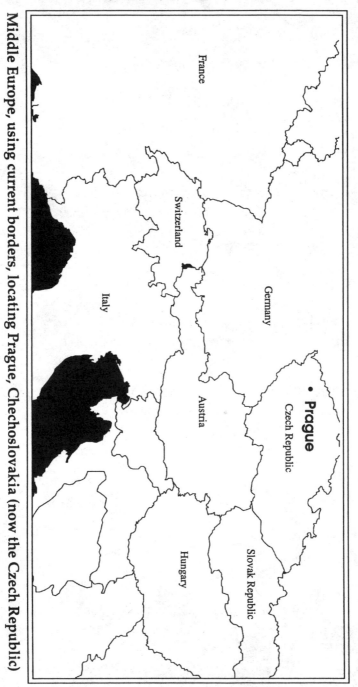

Middle Europe, using current borders, locating Prague, Chechoslovakia (now the Czech Republic)

Chapter Twenty
SHIMON THE SILENT

Time Line

70 c.e.	600 c.e.	1000 c.e.	1400 c.e.	1600 c.e.	1800 c.e.	2000 c.e.

— Location: Prague, Czechoslovakia —

[**Ed.** Prague, Czechoslovakia, on the banks of the Moldau/Ultava River was the location of one of the largest Jewish communities during the Middle Ages. Although they were confined to the ghetto area and restricted in their relationships with the non-Jewish world, the Jews still created a strong, cohesive, independent community. Near the cemetery, they built a synagogue which came to be known as the Alt-neu Shul (old-new, German\Yiddish) after it was refurbished through the generosity of Shmuel Mizrachi between the years 1142 and 1171. Another reason for the name Alt-neu is a play on the Hebrew words *al t'nai* (on the condition), meaning that we will pray here on the condition that when the Messiah comes, we will return to *Yerushalayim* to pray. The people believed that the Alt-neu Shul was so holy that it literally bridged heaven and earth in Prague much as the ancient Holy Temple bridged heaven and earth in *Yerushalayim*.]

Shimon, the tailor in the Prague ghetto was a man of very few words. The people called him Shimon the Silent. Because he refused to take part in the everyday prattle and gossip of the marketplace, they mocked and scorned him. Shimon paid no attention to them. He sewed for his customers and provided a decent livelihood for his family. He started and ended each day by praying with the *minyon* in the Alt-neu Shul.

Shimon's mother, the caretaker of the women's section in the Alt-neu Shul, paid no attention either to the people making fun of her son. Rather, she spoke up for him. The worst offenders were the women who sat there on Shabbat morning disdainfully sneering at him, rather than praying or following the reading of the Torah.

Only Shimon's wife cringed when she overheard people attacking her husband; she avoided most of the people in the ghetto.

Just before the holiday of Shavuot, the communal leaders received a message that the king wanted to inspect the ghetto. Because the Jews knew that security depended upon a peaceful relationship with the king, the *parnas* (the president of the community) asked everyone to do his share to clean the ghetto streets, to decorate the windows with flowers, to adorn the marketplace with colorful fabric streamers to honor the king.

The king was very pleased as he toured the ghetto a few days later. He walked around inspecting the market stalls, chatting with the people who lined the streets to greet him, to bid him peace. Suddenly, the calm was broken! From a nearby rooftop, a sharp stone was thrown, clearly aimed at the king's head, but missing him by one centimeter. People scattered, scurrying for cover, shocked at the horrible incident, not knowing if more stones would be thrown, not knowing the reaction of the king.

"If the culprit is not found in eight days," the king growled furiously, "I will open the gates to the mob and permit them to do whatever they want to the entire Jewish community!" The king stormed out of the ghetto.

The *parnas* pleaded with every person in the ghetto to become a detective, to search for any clue that might lead to the discovery of the would be murderer. But on the eighth day, the people were no closer than on the first day in discovering who had plotted to kill the king, thereby jeopardizing the entire Jewish community.

The mob, waiting for the king's signal outside the ghetto walls, grew more and more impatient. Every Jew, watching the hours pass helplessly, gathered the morning of the eighth day in the Alt-neu Shul to pray for deliverance.

The only person who was missing from the Alt-neu Shul was Shimon. Early that morning, he bid his wife goodbye as he did every morning before going off to his stall in the marketplace to sew garments. This day, however, he went directly to the police constable.

"I want you to know," he said, "that I am confessing to the crime perpetrated against the king last week. I was the one who threw the stone."

The constable immediately took Shimon into custody. He asked no questions. He had his confession. He sent word to the king that he had the confessed murderer in custody.

The king immediately issued two decrees: "I hereby absolve the entire Jewish community from complicity in the crime perpetrated against me. I order the mob to retreat from the area surrounding the ghetto. I further decree that the confessed criminal be thrown off the same roof from where he had thrown the stone the week before; soldiers will be stationed on the street below holding outstretched bayonets to cut the murderer's body to shreds when he falls. The inhabitants of the ghetto must watch the execution as a lesson to anyone who dares threaten the life of the king. The execution will take place immediately."

They trembled in their anger at the discovery that it was Shimon who had endangered all their lives. The Jews now felt justified for the way they had treated him. Scowls crossed their faces as Shimon the Silent was pushed from the edge of the roof.

Only Shimon's mother understood the truth; that her son was innocent. Realizing that he had given his life to save the entire Jewish community, she staggered into the Alt-neu Shul, crawled up to the Holy Ark, and opened the curtain. Tears streaming down her cheeks, her shoulders heaving in uncontrolled anguish, she prayed: "Thank you, my God, for including me among the righteous mothers of the Jewish people. As Sarah's son Isaac was willing to sacrifice himself, so my Shimon sacrificed himself. As mother Sarah died when she heard the news of the binding of her son, so let my soul depart."[1] She fell lifeless on the *bemah*.

A few months later, the Mayor of Prague, Vladislov von Rosenberg lay on his deathbed. His conscience gnawed at him; he had something to confess before he died. "Call the Rabbi of the Jews," he demanded of his servant. "I must speak to him."

By the time the Rabbi stood before the dying mayor in his luxuriously furnished bedroom, his strength had ebbed considerably. He whispered: "I want you to know that it was I who hired the person who threw the stone at the king. I wanted to cause trouble for the Jews. I want you to forgive me, so that I may die in peace."

"Our religion is different than yours," said the Rabbi harshly. "It is not in my power to grant forgiveness. However, I suggest, in order to ease your conscience, that you show how sorry you are by leaving instructions in your will that your fortune be inherited by the family of Shimon the Silent. Without their husband and father, they have little means of support, except for the charity of the Jewish community. If you leave them your fortune, you will ease their suffering in this world, and hopefully, your act of decency will help atone for what you did."

Just moments before he died, Mayor Vladislov von Rosenberg signed over his fortune to the family of Shimon the Silent in the presence of the Rabbi. When the Rabbi returned to the ghetto, he called all the Jews to the Alt-neu Shul. He told them what the mayor had revealed to him.

"Forgive us, forgive us," they pleaded, for they were ashamed of the way they had treated Shimon the Silent, the man who had sacrificed his own life in order to save their's.

∽

A Sacred Trust

— Commentary —

Joselman, Luther and the Emperor

The early 16th century was a period of continuing challenges for the Jewish community of western Germany. Two major factors influenced Jewish life: the emergence of an economic middle class and the rise of Protestantism.

The age of exploration, which occurred during this period resulted in new economic arrangements throughout Europe. The development of new transportation routes increased world trade, creating new wealth and expanding the demand for goods. This gave rise to a petty merchant class, consisting both of artisans who produced finished goods and traders who carried these goods from town to town. While the Jews flourished in this economy, competition among artisans, peddlers and merchants was intense and the Jews were often seen as a threat to Christian business people. Some of the accusations against Jews were motivated by local economic competition and required the intervention of a central authority, the Emperor, to settle disputes.

The burgeoning economic system also facilitated the growth of Protestantism, which challenged the Jews on two fronts. The existing Catholic church, in defending itself against Protestantism, increased pressure on the Jews in its fight against heresies. The central authority, the Emperor, in seeking to strengthen its position, often relied upon the Jews as a source of support and stability as both Catholics and Protestants sought the support of monarchs in their struggle with each other. Thus, the leaders of the Jewish community often found themselves defending Jews and Judaism against both economic and religious forces which viewed the Jews as either potential allies or adversaries in the competition for control and supremacy. In this period, Rabbi Joselman emerged as the Jewish leader with responsibility for maintaining the position of the Jewish community in the western Germanic lands.

—Rabbi Art Vernon,
Director of Educational Development.
Jewish Educational Services of North America, (JESNA)

The Rhine River Valley, using today's boundries, listing general
locations of many cities and towns mentioned in the
Medieval and Renaissance stories.

JOSELMAN, LUTHER AND THE EMPEROR

Time Line

| 70 c.e. | 600 c.e. | 1000 c.e. | 1400 c.e. | 1600 c.e. | 1800 c.e. | 2000 c.e. |

— Location: Germany —

[Ed. Rabbi Yoseph Joselman ben Gershom, (1478-1554), a descendant of Rashi, was born in Rosheim, Alsace, during a time when life for the majority of the population was characterized by wars fought between dukes, lords, princes, and nobles with the aid of mercenaries. Temporary peace settlements unleashed the vengeance of the unemployed mercenaries and they rampaged and plundered mercilessly, choosing Jews as their prime victims. The Jews fled from towns all over the Germanic lands in search of respite from their wanderings. Often, they resettled for a short while, and were banished at the whim of the leaders of town councils. Repeated threats fulfilled the prophecy of the "wandering Jew," and they turned to Rabbi Joselman time and time again to use his "letters of protection," issued to him by the emperor, to plead for the nullification of the decrees.[1]]

"I am giving Rabbi Joselman of Rosheim 'letters of protection' in his role as governor and chief of all Jewry in the Germanic lands. He is so unselfish, so concerned for the welfare of his brethren, so clever in dealing with people. I guaranteed him that as long as I ruled, his pleas on behalf of his people to my imperial throne would never go unanswered. Why, if Rabbi Joselman had been born a Christian, I would have appointed him my chancellor," mused Emperor Maximilian.

"He exemplifies what a learned and caring human being can achieve toward bringing universal peace. I remember how he trapped Johann Pfefferkorn, by refuting his argument that the writings of the Talmud constituted blasphemy against the church.[2] At first, I was impressed by Pfefferkorn's writings.[3] But I was no longer impressed when Rabbi Joselman showed me that his allegations proved ignorant of rabbinic literature. He patiently taught me a page of the Talmud. When I questioned Pfefferkorn about it, he could not answer the simplest questions, even though he boasted that he was a Talmudic scholar. He is such a sad case; an apostate, once born a Jew, and now functions with the sole objective of harming his people of origin. He wants me to confiscate all copies of the Talmud and other Jewish books and burn them. I have ordered that the books be kept in safekeeping until I decide what to do about his demands."

Rabbi Joselman knew that Pfefferkorn would continue to search for ways to burn books. "Besides the Emperor, I must seek additional help from other sources to prepare for the time when the fiend strikes again," he thought. "I will try to enlist the aid of Johann Reuchlin, the leader of the cultural renaissance in Germany.[4] He is a respected judge and an intellect, fluent in German, Latin, and Hebrew. I have even heard that he studied in Rome with Rabbi Ovadiah Sforno, the famous commentator and *halachist*, because he wanted to become familiar with the Torah.[5] After all, if Pfefferkorn succeeds, the loss to the Jewish people will be inestimable, since printing is such a new invention, and many of our Holy Books are still in manuscript form. Moreover, I must find a way to stop him from burning the Word of God."

He set out for Tubingen, to beseech Reuchlin personally. He received him warmly. "How can I help you?" he inquired.

"Pfefferkorn, the apostate, has convinced the Emperor to confiscate Jewish books on the grounds that they are hostile to Christianity. The Emperor has ordered that the books be stored temporarily until he decides what to do with Pfefferkorn's demands. If the emperor should decide in favor of Pfefferkorn and the Dominican monks, then our books will be desecrated. And I know that Pfefferkorn's threat is merely a means of extorting money. He has already made it known that when the Emperor releases the books, he wants 100,000 gold gulden, an amount that is more than the total wealth of all the Jews of Frankfurt, not to burn them. I came here to appeal to you, as the only non-Jew in all of Germany who is conversant with the Hebrew language, to disprove his accusation by your personal examination of our sacred books."

Reuchlin replied: "I hear the urgency in your voice, and I want to assure you that I will do everything in my power to help save your precious books from the flames. From my studies with Rabbi Ovadiah Sforno, I know that there is great wisdom in your Torah and your sacred books. I refuse to condemn the Talmud and, unlike most of my contemporaries, I will not agree to damn what I myself do not thoroughly know and understand. The Talmud was not composed for every blackguard to trample with unwashed feet and then to say that he knew all of it. Furthermore, I will demand that the Jews be accorded proper treatment as members of the empire and their leaders be respected as imperial burghers."

Rabbi Joselman dedicated so much of his time traveling from one German town to another freeing Jews from torture and burning, pleading with burgomasters to rescind decrees of expulsion, righting slanderous accusations, that he had very little family life. But he accepted this sacrifice because he was the *Shtadlan*, governor and chief of all German Jewry, and there was no one to speak on their behalf or defend them beside him.

[Ed. *Shtadlan* was an honorary title bestowed upon the leaders of the Jewish community living in the Germanic lands. It referred to their role as pleaders for the cause of the Jewish people in the court of the Emperor.]

In January, 1516, delegates representing the Mainz Elector voted to banish the Jews from their territories.

[Ed. The Mainz Elector controlled the territories of Frankfort, Hesse-Darmstadt, Babenhousen, Wiesbaden, Solms, Amtheyem, Gelnehausen and Virymze.]

Rabbi Joselman always tried to use the authority granted to him by the Emperor to help his people, without seeking a personal audience with him. But this time, he clearly realized that the situation was too serious; he feared the outcome if the delegates refused to heed his plea. He therefore decided to seek a personal audience with the Emperor who was holding court in the imperial city of Kaufbeuren.

Rabbi Joselman stopped in Mainz to pray in the Jewish cemetery at the graves of the righteous and holy people who had lived in the Germanic lands centuries before him prior to appealing to the Emperor. Walking through the burial ground, he was dismayed at the desecrated graves that had no tombstones because they had been stolen, and the few remaining tombstones that had been broken. He knew that Rabaynu Gershom, Rabbi Meshullam ben Kalonyumos, Rabbi Shimon Hagadol had been buried there, but he could not find their graves.[6] "Master of the World, " he prayed, "please put words in my mouth that will find favor with the emperor. "

Rabbi Joselman's audience with Emperor Maximilian resulted in an imperial decree addressed to the Elector of Mainz forbidding him to banish the Jews in his territories.

∽

Unexpectedly, a new threat to the security of the Jews was brewing from a totally different source. On October 31, 1517, Martin Luther, famous as a scholar and an orator, a professor of theology and a biblical commentator at the University of Wittenberg nailed his *Disputation on the Power and Efficacy of Indulgences,* a ninety-five point thesis, to the door of the castle church in Wittenberg. Among his grievances, he demanded to know why the Pope would not build St. Peter's Bascillica in Rome with his own money rather than with the money of poor believers.

"The real treasure of the Church," he declared, "is not the institution with its wealth and power but the most Holy Gospel and the glory and grace of God ... and they were not for sale; but a free gift."

He had criticized the Papacy but praised the Hebrew Bible and the Jewish people. He believed that they were the Chosen People of God, the real aristocracy of the ancient world, superior to pagan Greeks and Romans.

"Luther is proposing very radical ideas, very different than official Church theology," thought Rabbi Joselman. "I think I should seek him out to determine what his real position is concerning my people. Maybe, if he has the opportunity to speak to the Emperor, and he convinces him that we are not guilty of all the crimes of which we have been accused, that we are all really the children of Abraham ... maybe, then there will be some respite from the hundreds of years of persecution."

They met in Rabbi Josleman's house in Frankfurt.

"I am grateful to you for what you have written opposing the persecution of my people," began Rabbi Joselman.

"You are a wise man, " interrupted Luther. "I recognize Jewish contribution to Christianity, but times are changing, and you and your people persist in clinging to your old fashioned ways, your outmoded rituals and observances. Why don't you convert as an example to all your people?"

Rabbi Joselman was taken aback by Luther's audacious request, however, he was not at a loss for words. "We believe in One God. He has exhorted us to choose life by living according to His commandments. Our religion is one of *mitzvot*, of actions. It is totally contradictory to your doctrine of living by faith alone."

"I hope that all your people are not as a stubborn as you. I will still try to convert them. I will continue to seek out your leaders, and try to convince them to convert. But if they don't follow me, let them beware!"

Luther did not give up. He continued trying to attract Jews to his cause with a treatise, *That Jesus Christ Was Born a Jew*.[7] In it, he reminded his contemporaries that the "historical setting for the redemption of the world was Judaism."

"Why should Jews chose to convert to Christianity, after the way they have been mistreated for all these centuries," he demanded. "If we change our treatment of them, and show them true Christian love, we will be successful."

But when his meetings with Rabbis and Jewish communal leaders proved fruitless on one hand, and attacks against him by Catholic churchmen labeling him a "Jew father, and a Judaizer," gained popularity on the other hand, he succumbed to the old established anti-Jewish ideology and concluded that "fifteen hundred years of exile did not humble the Jewish people ... it will be impossible to convert them."

Rabbi Joselman watched the controversy grow between the leaders of the Catholic Church and Martin Luther, its critic.

[**Ed.** The Church leaders denounced Luther as a heretic, and sought to deny him the 'protection of civil law in this life and the solace of the sacraments for the life to come.' The Imperial Diet summoned him to Virmyze and demanded that he retract his errors. He refused and declared instead: "It is neither safe nor honest to act against conscience. Here I stand. I cannot do otherwise. God help me. Amen."]

"If only Luther remains absorbed in his controversy with the Church," reasoned Rabbi Joselman, "he will give up trying to convert my people to his cause." But it was not to be. Rabbi Joselman watched as Luther became more and more critical of the Jews, for he was steeped in medieval hatred of the Jewish people. He vented his anger and frustration against them, and toward the end of his life, he wrote, *On the Jews and Their Lies.*[8]

[**Ed.** In this treatise, he recommended the total segregation of Jews from Christians by burning their synagogues, schools, houses, prayer books and Talmudic writings, forbidding Rabbis to teach, abolishing their safe conduct on the highways, confiscating all cash, silver and gold and using it to support converts, and forcing their young to work at manual labor.]

Rabbi Joselman sat at his study table in his home in Frankfurt, sighing as he read Luther's newest treatise. Then he closed his eyes and reflected. "We chant at every *Pesach Seder: And it is this that has stood by our fathers and us; for not only one has risen up against us to destroy us, but in all ages they rise up against us to destroy us; and the Holy One, blessed be He, rescues us from their hands.*"

"I see this prophecy being played out continuously: the slavery in Egypt, Haman's attempted physical annihilation (the miracle of Purim) and Antiochus' attempted spiritual annihilation (the miracle of Chanukah), the destruction of both of our Holy Temples, our exile from our ancestral homeland and dispersion among the nations of the world, the Crusades, the blood libels, the disputations, and the banishments. Will it never end? Yet, I must believe that somehow, we will survive. Somehow we will live!"

꙾

A Sacred Trust
— Commentary —
The Golem

Once the Christian world believed that Jesus was God and that the Jews had killed him, no crime seemed too bizarre or horrific to attribute to them. The blood libel—the accusation that Jews murder non-Jews in a religious ritual and then drink their blood, originated in twelfth-century England. Over the next seven hundred years, it led to the murder of tens of thousands of Jews.

The particular irony of the blood libel is that it was directed against the first nation in history to outlaw human sacrifice (see Genesis 22 and Deuteronomy 18:10), and the only people in the ancient Near East to prohibit the consumption of *any* blood (Leviticus 3:17; 7:26; 17:10-14; Deuteronomy 12:16; 12:23-25).

The fact that so many Christians believed and spread this lie for hundreds of years led the early Zionist thinker Ahad Ha-am to note one "consolation" in the blood libel: It enabled Jews to resist internalizing the world's negative portrayal of them. "Every Jew who has been brought up among Jews, knows as an indisputable fact that throughout the length and breadth of Jewry there is not a single individual who drinks human blood for religious purposes. 'But,' you ask, 'is it possible that everybody can be wrong, and the Jews right?' 'Yes, it is possible: the blood accusation proves it possible."

Rabbi Joseph Telushkin
Author of "Jewish Literacy,"
"Jewish Humor" and "Jewish Wisdom"
Taken from *Jewish Literacy*, with permission of the author

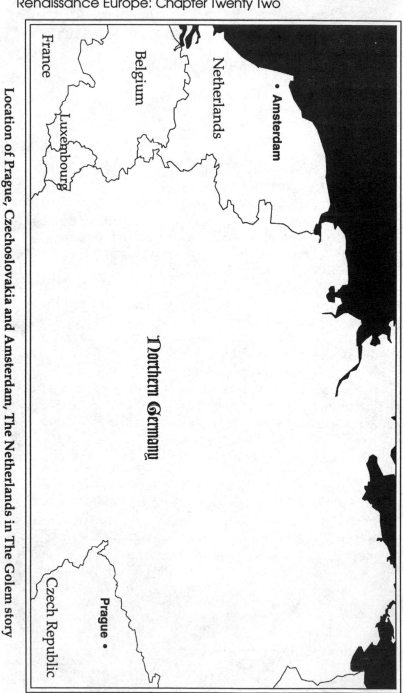

Location of Prague, Czechoslovakia and Amsterdam, The Netherlands in The Golem story

THE GOLEM COMES TO PRAGUE

Time Line

| 70 c.e. | 600 c.e. | 1000 c.e. | 1400 c.e. | 1600 c.e. | 1800 c.e. | 2000 c.e. |

— Location: Czechoslovakia and The Netherlands —

[Ed. Rabbi Yehuda Loew ben Bezalel was known by the acronym of his name, *Maharal*, [1512-1609]. Besides being an outstanding Talmudist, he was also a mathematician, a prolific writer, a profound philosopher and a Kabbalist. The *Maharal* is credited with having created the Golem, whom he infused with life by applying secrets of the Kabbalah (mysticism), in order to rescue the Jewish people from the infamous blood libels.[1]

"*Mameh*, I see *Tateh* (Rabbi Yehuda Loew ben Bezalel), my husband Yitzchak and Yaakov (Rabbi Yaakov HaLayve) trudging along the crooked cobblestoned streets that wind their way up from the river's edge into the ghetto," Faygel whispered as she peered out the dormer window at the moonlit shadowed shapes drawing closer and closer. "The three of them went down to the river bank many hours ago, and now I see four. Who is the other person that accompanies them?"

Perele shrugged her shoulders: "I really don't know. Maybe *Tateh* has been involved in some mysterious activity. I'm sure he will introduce us to him when they come in. Meantime, they must be very hungry, since they've been away for such a long time. Let's put some food on the table, so that they can refresh themselves as soon as they reach the house."

Three men entered the house, followed by the stranger. He was exceedingly tall and thin, wide shouldered, but very bony. His eyes were deep set in their sockets, and he stared straight ahead with a waxy glare. He was dressed in the garb of the caretaker of the synagogue, except that a brimmed cap sat perched askew on his head, long curly hair protruded from it and intertwined between his head and his beard. His arms hung motionless at his side.

The *Maharal* beckoned him to sit at the table. He sat down, bent his elbows on the table, immediately cradling his head between them and waited. He did not utter a word.

"You have nothing to fear from our guest," the *Maharal* said to his family. "Even though he cannot speak, he understands. I will show him how to assist Chayim, the caretaker of the shul. His name is Yossele Golem."

[**Ed.** The root of the Hebrew word 'golem' means shapeless matter, awkward person, robot, boor.[2]]

Then he turned to Yossele Golem. "I want you to know that I have formed you from the clay of the Ultava/Moldau riverbank, with my knowledge of *Kabbalah* (Jewish mysticism) and with the help of God, for the express purpose of saving the Jewish people from any harm. I have endowed you with supernatural strength, so you will always be able to execute the most difficult of my commands. You will always do my bidding, even if you have to jump from roofs, crawl through tunnels, or ride by yourself to distant cities. You will live in my house.

"Let me explain why I formed this Golem," he continued, turning to his wife and daughter. "Relationships between the Jewish people and their non-Jewish neighbors had been relatively peaceful in the years before I was born on the first Seder night, in Virmyze. My mother told me how things changed on that night. She remembered the details distinctly, for as the Seder proceeded, her labor contractions increased. Trying to distract herself, she glanced out of the window and saw the shadow of a man reflected by the moonlight. He was hovering near the hedge. Suddenly she screamed from a very sharp contraction. My father motioned to two men to run to call the midwife. In the confusion that followed, the "shadow" that had been hiding near the hedge, not knowing what happened, thought it was the opportune moment to throw into the house his sack in which was the body of a dead child. He was caught in the act, and dragged to the constable who incarcerated him on the pretext of perpetrating a blood libel.

As my father heard my first cries, he said:"This child will save the Jewish people from many more blood libels."

Until recently, I did not feel that we were in any particular danger. Now, however, the priest Thaddeus has settled in Prague. He is an avowed hater of the Jewish people. He has instigated blood libels in other cities before. There is no doubt in my mind that he will do the same here, since it is close to *Pesach* (Passover)."

[**Ed.** Blood libels usually coincided with *Pesach*. The perpetrator alleged that the Jews killed a Christian child and used its blood to bake *matzot*.]

"I decided that I have to be prepared to deal with any hateful act that he may perpetrate against us. I hope that Yossele Golem will help us thwart any of Thaddeus' plots."

Father Thaddeus settled in the cloister not far from the ghetto and immediately busied himself with discreet inquiries among the nobles: "Who owes any money to Jewish money lenders?"

He found out that Count Batislav von Lehn had borrowed a great deal of money to finance a risky business venture which had failed. He was searching for a way out of repaying the loan.

"On the Jewish Sabbath, before their spring holiday, you and I will stand in the doorway of the Alt-neu Shul, and demand that they return your daughter unharmed!" he plotted with the count.

[**Ed.** See beginning of Chapter Twenty regarding the Alt-neu Shul.]

"We will already have slaughtered a pig, poured its blood into bottles, and placed it in their Holy Ark, behind the Torah scrolls as evidence. We will have hidden your daughter in the dungeon of your mansion where she will be safe. No one will know that we planted the evidence. We will incite the mob by telling them the the Jews killed your daughter. They will follow us, and disrupt their prayers with their frenzied demands. Signalling them to break into the merchant's house to whom you are in debt, they will destroy his records and then you will not have to repay the loan."

Father Thaddeus did not know that Yossele Golem, upon the command of the *Maharal*, would be able to find the Count's daughter, dirty, frightened, but unharmed and exonerate the Jews of Prague. He acted so quickly, that the mob never reached the merchant's house.

Father Thaddeus gritted his teeth and wrung his hands in despair. "An unexpected interference," he muttered." But someday, somehow, somewhere, I will remove the Golem from the scene. This is only a temporary setback. And if I can not arrange a successful blood libel, then I will continue to kidnap Jewish girls for conversion purposes."

∽

THE SHIDDUCH (THE MATCH)

"Johann, bring me a bottle of wine from the cellar," shouted Father Thaddeus at his valet. After pouring a glassful, Johann respectfully departed. Father Thaddues stared at the label on the bottle: Berger Winery! An idea gradually shaped itself in his mind. "I don't go to the winery very often," he mused, "because I send Johann to buy what I need. But, on the few occasions that I have been there, I noticed that it is managed by the Berger's daughter. I think her name is Malka. She is their only child. Wouldn't it be a coup if I could kidnap her and convert her to my religion? How shall I do it?"

He played with a few different schemes.

"It will not be easy for me to persuade her if I go to the winery. I have to think of a plan to get her to come here.... I know how to do it. I will find fault with the bill. She has charged me for ten bottles that I did not buy. If that fails, I can argue that the wine she sold me tastes like vinegar, and that I should not be required to pay for an inferior product. I will send Johann to the winery to invite her to come here to settle my account."

Malka refuted Johann's inquiry about the amount due on the bill. "I have never erred in my calculations," she said adamantly.

"My master will be very happy if you will come to the cloister to discuss it personally with him, " he responded.

Angrily, Malka picked up the notebook listing the money owed her, locked the door, and followed Johann.

Thaddeus was overjoyed when he saw Malka walking up the path. He tried to stay calm. "Once I finish the episode of the charges on my bill, then I can talk to her. I will praise her a lot. I will have her in my clutches, soon."

"Thank you so much for coming," sang Thaddeus sweetly. "I'm really sorry that I had to put you through so much trouble, but I can't be expected to pay for something that I did not buy."

Malka responded adamantly: "It is written in my notebook, black and white, that you owe the winery for ten bottles. Does the Father think that I would add to his debt?"

"No, I don't know too many intelligent and honest girls like you." he flattered. "Wait, I might have an explanation for the overcharge. I remember now, the wine in those bottles tasted like vinegar. I put them aside to return them. Johann, bring those bottles. They are in the southwest corner of the cellar."

"Here, why don't you taste the wine?"

She poured a little into a glass, sipped it, and said, "Why, this wine is delicious. There is nothing wrong with it."

He suggested they try two other bottles. By the time Malka had tasted wine from all the bottles, her reserve had been penetrated. Instead of returning to the winery immediately,

Thaddeus convinced her to stay and talk.

When she rose to leave, he said softly: "I hope to see you again soon. Maybe, you can write me a letter and send it with Johann when he comes to buy wine."

As soon as she was out the door, he chuckled gleefully: "by the look in her eyes it won't take too long for me to hear from her. It won't take long for me to spring my trap."

Malka did not see anything wrong with talking to the priest. He seemed so intelligent; he acted like such a gentleman; he always made her feel so good about herself. So when business slowed down in the afternoon, she developed the habit of closing the winery, walking over to the cloister, and spending an hour or two with Father Thaddeus. At first she went to the cloister once a week, then more often. She reopened the winery later and later in the evening hours. People began whispering that Malka was visiting Father Thaddeus; they reasoned that her frequent visits were not on business. Her parents noticed a gradual change in her attitude toward them, but they felt helpless to act.

Then, one evening, she did not reopen the winery; by ten that night, she had still not returned home. Michal, her father, paced back and forth across the dining room floor, worry written all across his face. Leah, her mother sat at the table, hunched over, tears streaming down her blurry eyes: "I fear something terrible has happened to our only daughter," she sobbed uncontrollably. "She has changed so much in the past few months. She acts as if some terrible outside force is controlling her, as if she has no will of her own! That Thaddeus! I have heard that he has a way with Jewish girls. What if our Malka is under his influence?"

"If all the rumors I've heard are true," choked Michal, "then we must not sit here by ourselves and cry. We must try to seek the help of the *Maharal*. But, first, let's go to the cloister to find out if Thaddeus has hidden her. We will demand her release."

They ran as fast as they could. Breathlessly, they pounded on the door, demanding to see Thaddeus.

"What is the meaning of this disturbance in the middle of the night?" sputtered Johann, as he opened the door.

"We have every reason to believe that our daughter is here. We want to see Thaddeus," they shouted.

Finally, the priest appeared. His face scowled with satisfaction at the cruel evil he had perpetrated. "How dare you Jews disturb me in the middle of the night," he sneered. "Your daughter is not here. You are utterly mistaken. Now, be off, immediately, and don't come back!" He slammed the door in their faces.

Hysterical, sure that he was lying, they staggered back down the path that they had run up a few minutes before. They hurried toward the *Maharal's* house. He listened compassionately to their plea for help.

"Your must understand," he began, "that in whatever way I am able to help your daughter, it must be done with utmost secrecy. Thaddeus has convinced Jewish girls to convert before. His defense has always been that they convert by their own free will. I know this is not true, and tragically, you know this is not true also. But I don't want to provide him with any reason to believe that I am interfering in his affairs. Do you have any relatives that live far from here?"

"Yes," Michal replied, "I have a brother who lives in Amsterdam."

"Good," continued the *Maharal*. "There are three things that you must do: first, you must fast for the next three days. You may only eat a little after dark to sustain yourselves Second, each day of these three days, recite all 150 chapters of *Tehillim* (Psalms). Pray to God, with all your heart and with all your strength to help you. Third, prepare a carriage with food and water for a long trip. Hire two trusted people who can leave Prague on a moment's notice, who will accompany Malka to Amsterdam. Then wait."

Thaddeus realized that the only way he would win Malka over to Christianity was if he could persuade her to leave her Jewish environment. That night was the first that Malka spent in the guest quarters of the cloister. Thaddeus provided for her every comfort in the large room on the top floor; beautiful linens and wonderful books to keep her occupied when he wasn't talking to her.

The next morning he said to her: "I hope you are happy here. Since you must be lonely while I go about my clerical duties, I want you to know that I have planned a party for tomorrow night. I have invited the nobility to meet you. I want to introduce you to all the people with whom you will mingle after your conversion. By the way, you must begin studying soon. Why don't we begin the first lesson this afternoon?"

Malka listened fitfully while Thaddeus droned on and on. He talked about vague, obscure ideas. She couldn't concentrate. Finally, she turned her mind off completely. The second lesson was a repetition of the first.

When he saw that he was not making too much progress, he coaxed: "Come, put on your prettiest dress. Our guests will arrive soon. I want you to pay particular attention to Hans, the young son of Baron Ramches."

The young people were officially introduced and then they sauntered off to talk. Malka became more animated as the evening wore on. Hans could not take his eyes off her.

Thaddeus realized how successful his efforts were at matchmaking. He withdrew the Baron to a corner and whispered: "After she converts next week, I think they should be married."

Before Hans and his father left the party, he had placed a ring on her finger. "This ring was my mother's," he said. "I am giving it to you as a symbol of the bond that we will soon share our lives together." The gold ring was set with precious stones that surrounded the engraved insignia of the Baron's family "coat-of-arms."

The next day, Father Thaddeus received a message from the Bishop in which he wrote that an emergency had arisen. "I am urging all the priests in the diocese to join me at Karlsbad (Karlovy Vary, a small city west of Prague) to discuss the issues in order to decide a course of action."

Thaddeus was so flattered that the Bishop considered his opinion important, that he ignored his inner conflict between leaving Malka alone in the cloister and his need to participate in the conference.

"I know I exerted much time and effort to convince her to convert," he reasoned. "She is looking forward to marrying Hans, and I'm sure she will be well taken care of by Johann during my absence. After all, I'll only be away from Prague for a few days. What can possibly happen in a short time?"

He called Johann: "I expect you to guard Malka with your life. Prepare the best food for her, talk to her, grant her every wish. Do not let her leave the cloister."

Johann promised to watch her closely, and Thaddeus left for the conference singing wedding songs.

As soon as Thaddeus was away from the cloister, Malka felt a gnawing anxiety within. "He always made time to talk to me, to discuss my doubts. It is as if he has some uncanny power of persuasion. Now he is not here." Her head ached, and her heart palpitated. She lay down on her bed to think.

"What am I doing here in the cloister?" she whispered weakly. "What will my parents say when they find out what I am about to do? I don't even have to answer that question. They will be devastated. If only I could find a way out of here!"

She looked at the ring on her finger, pictured Hans'

handsome face, but she couldn't answer her own question. When Johann knocked at her door with her dinner tray, she refused the food. She paced the floor, sat on the edge of the bed, lit a lantern, picked up a book hoping reading might distract her. But nothing made sense. Finally, she lay down, fell into a deeply troubled sleep, and dreamed one horror after another.

She awoke, terrified, to find a tall, bony looking, wide shouldered man in her room. He carried a sack in his left hand and a piece of paper in his right. He beckoned her not to scream, to follow him to the window. Extending the paper through the window bars so that the light of the moon shone on it, she read the big letters: "I have come to save you. Do not hesitate. Crawl into the sack, and I will carry you back to your parents house. They are waiting anxiously for you."

Malka crawled into the sack. She felt herself being lifted, jolted, and carried—she did not know where. Then it seemed that the man was running. At last the sack was laid gently on the ground, and Malka was pulled out. Then the man disappeared. She looked around, and found that she was standing on the path leading up to her parent's house. She ran inside.

Her parents had been unable to sleep.

"Can you forgive me for all the anguish I have caused you," she pleaded.

"We forgive you, we forgive you. But Malka, there isn't much time. Change your clothes and dress warmly. Your life will be in danger when the priest finds out that you escaped from the cloister. Hurry! You realize that you can't stay here. Every minute counts. These two family friends will take you to Amsterdam. Give this letter to my brother Chaim. He will be happy to have you live with him and his family. You will be safe there."

The next morning there was no response to Johann's knock. He held the breakfast tray in one hand, and shook the door knob desperately. When there was still no response, he opened the door, placed the tray on a table, walked over to the bed and reacted hysterically when he found that it was empty.

"Thaddeus will blame me for her disappearance. I promised to guard her at all costs. He will fire me from this job that I have held for years. He might kill me and leave my wife without a husband and my children without a father. What shall do? Only the devil could have helped her escape. After all, there are bars on the windows. I have to remove the suspicion of negligence from myself. I must try to calm myself. I can't think in this condition."

He imagined how he would execute the plan that developed in his mind. He waited until nightfall, went to the graveyard behind the cloister, dug up a full skeleton of bones, carried them to Malka's room, laid them on the bed, poured oil around the room and set it ablaze. The entire guest quarter of the cloister burned before the fire was contained.

The constable investigated the fire and concluded that it was accidental.

Thaddeus returned a few days later. He blamed himself for leaving the cloister, but refused to accept Johann's plea that the fire was accidental.

"When those Jews found out that I left the city they must have used the opportunity to gather a great deal of money to bribe you to release the girl," he growled. "I wager that you planted those bones to make the constable believe that she was killed in the fire. I will not rest until I convert one of their's. Better yet, I will await the opportunity for another blood libel."

Days later, the three travellers arrived at Chaim's house in Amsterdam. He finished reading his brother Michal's letter, looked at Malka and said: "Your father has written that he has been unable to find an appropriate husband for you in Prague. He knows that I am very involved in the Jewish community here in Amsterdam, that I have many contacts with people from other countries because of my business. He asked me to do my best to introduce you to appropriate young men. Of course, I will. In the meantime, you will live in my house, and I will treat you as one of my own children."

Malka quickly became accustomed to living in Amsterdam. As part of her uncle's family, it was expected that she help those who were less fortunate, and she lovingly attended to the needs of widows, cared for their children, taught them to read and write, visited the sick, always bringing them hot food. People talked about Chaim's niece, not only praising her beautiful appearance but commending her for her kindness. It didn't take long for fathers with eligible sons to make proposals to Chaim; but Malka found fault with each one of the young men. In quiet moments, she relived the terror of her escape from the cloister, the horrible thought of what she had almost done, the anguish she must have caused her parents. She tried to push these things out of her mind, but she could not erase the image of handsome Hans, whose ring she still wore.

Three years passed, and Malka had rejected the best young men. Her Uncle began to worry about her future prospects for marriage.

One day, the *shadchan* (match-maker) came to Chaim and said: "A young man has arrived in our city to study at the *yeshiva*. His name is Avraham, and he comes from Friedburg. His letters of recommendation extol his brilliant mind and his wonderful qualities. I would like him to meet Malka this evening."

Malka was weary of meeting prospective bridegrooms: "It must be another one of those that I will find fault with. I'm really getting tired of meeting 'proper' young men."

But when she entered the room where Avraham stood, she noticed something familiar about him. She tried to imagine what he would look like without the beard. They began talking; the conversation became animated.

The *shadchan* pulled Chaim aside and boasted: "This time I've been successful. It seems to me that those two young people like each other. I think you can make plans for their wedding!"

The good news spread quickly through the Jewish community of Amsterdam: the beautiful Malka was engaged to Avraham from Friedburg!

Two days later, Avraham arrived at Chaim's house carrying many gifts for his bride to be. Among the gifts was a ring. Malka started to remove Han's ring, in order to place Avraham's on her finger. He was watching her closely, but a second later, he lay faint on the floor.

She screamed for help. Two servants carried him to a couch, called for cold towels and spirits in an effort to revive him.

Slowly, he opened his eyes and struggled to sit up. "That ring, where did you get that ring?" he murmured.

"Why do you want to know?"

"Its insignia is engraved with the "coat of arms" of the family name I used many years ago."

"Hans? Hans?" she whispered. "But your name is Avraham."

"I am a convert. Let me tell you how it happened:

"When your bones were found after the fire in the cloister, I was beside myself with grief. I could not forget the look in your eyes, your soft smile, the excitement in your words when we spoke. I knew that there was something special about you. I had to find out what this special quality was. As I searched, I found that within Judaism there existed guidelines for man's relationship to man and man's relationship to God. The more I searched, the more I wanted to become a part of a people that I perceived to be holy in their way of life. I started to study Torah secretly, but I realized that I wanted to learn more than I could master on my own.

Then I had to face two problems: first, I could not progress further without the help of Jews who really knew Torah and who could answer my questions, and second, I knew my father would disown me if I converted. So, I told him that I wanted to establish a branch of our family business in Vienna. With his blessings, I went there to live, and started writing letters to him from my new address.

I found that I would be able to study with Rabbi Yaakov Ginzburg in Friedburg, a distance from Vienna, so I arranged with my landlady to hold my mail and forward it to me. I always kept in contact with my father; my letters told him about the expansion of our business. Sometimes I mentioned how much I liked living in Vienna because I was meeting interesting people who were helping me forget my anguish over your horrible death.

When Rabbi Ginzburg determined I was ready, he circumcised me, took me to the *mikveh* (ritual bath), and named me Avraham Yeshurun. He spent a lot of time studying with me, for I had come to realize that a Jew never stops studying. Shortly after I became a Jew, I received word that my father had passed away and I was named his sole heir. I had to make arrangements to maintain his estate and holdings. I realized I would have to return to Prague at some future point.

Rabbi Ginzburg suggested that it was time that I married. He told me that Amsterdam had a big *yeshiva*, and a fine Jewish community. He blessed me that I might find my soul mate here. How wonderous are the ways of God Who guides the footsteps of man!

Avraham looked lovingly at Malka. Tears streamed down her face. A joyous smile played around the edges of her lips.

Avraham and Malka were married and returned to Prague where Michal and Leah witnessed the fulfillment of the blessing: *"And you shall see the children of your children. Peace upon Israel."*[3]

A Sacred Trust

— Commentary —

Diary of a Lady

Through history we learn about events which shape people's lives and future generations, but through autobiography we see how individuals, because of their unique personalities and values, shape and interpret the events about them. Gluckel of Hameln, a pre-modern woman who set down her memoirs for her children and grandchildren, provides us a window on how traditional Jewish women viewed their lives as well as on "the struggles and aspirations of the Jewish people to survive in an unfriendly world." Through Gluckel's diaries we see the *Sabbatean* movement as a rift which divided families; the Plague as a threat to Jews' lives, even when they were not infected by it; business ventures as a means to be able to achieve the highest levels of *tzedakah* as well as to dower one's own children properly.

Gluckel's memoirs illuminate how the traditional Jewish values of family, *tzedakah* and learning were played out in lives fully lived. Gluckel's relationship with her husband invites admiration and emulation. He was her "dearest friend" and she his business confidante and partner. The worldly success he achieved brought with it responsibility to help others, he practiced the highest form of *tzedakah* by assisting others to start their own businesses.

Love of Torah learning was a value he carried with him everywhere. On his business journeys he would frequently visit rabbinical courts to hear how disputes were adjudicated. Both his business and his love of rabbinic argumentation he shared with his wife, his partner in worldly as well as domestic affairs.

Together they were parents of twelve children—by today's standards an overwhelming burden, but not to Gluckel, who wrote "I feel blessed like a fruitful olive plant when they sit around my table." As she set down her memoirs in later life, she was truly *"s'meicha bechelka,"* happy with her lot in life, seeing her children well-married, her husband's business affairs successfully managed in her own hands, and her values articulated to her offspring through the writing of her memoirs.

—*Roselyn Bell Baskin,*
Managing Editor, Jewish Education News
(CAJE), Coalition for the Advancement of Jewish Education

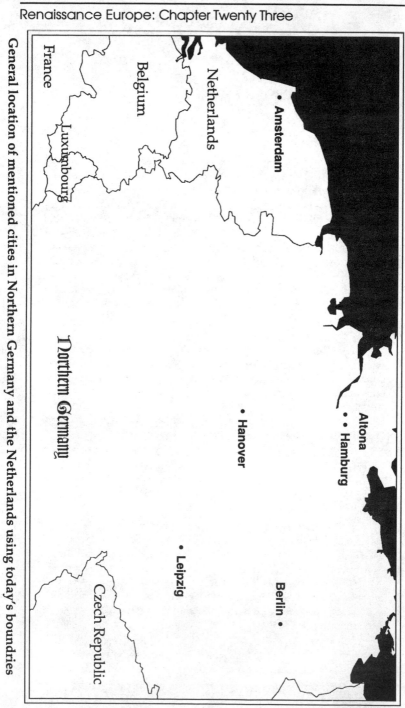

General location of mentioned cities in Northern Germany and the Netherlands using today's boundries

DIARY OF A LADY:
OUT OF THE GHETTOS

Time Line

| 70 c.e. | 600 c.e. | 1000 c.e. | 1400 c.e. | 1600 c.e. | 1800 c.e. | 2000 c.e. |

— Location: Germany —

[**Ed.** Through the diary of Gluckel of Hameln (1645-1724) we can understand how the Jews of western Europe lived as the ghetto walls crumbled and gradually permitted them to take their place in society.]

Did you ever wonder what is was like to be a Jewish woman in seventeenth century Germany? I actually did not set out to write my memoirs for posterity, but maybe historians will use them to describe the rich panorama of Jewish life in such major communities as Hamburg, Altona, Hanover, Metz, Berlin, and Amsterdam. My original intention in writing these memoirs was to acquaint my children and grandchildren with their family background. I was also searching for something to do to lift my spirits from the dark veil of depression that descended upon me after the death of my husband. The nights were long, lonely, and sleepless, so I wrote to pass the time.

To begin, I want you to know that I was only three years old when the Thirty Years' War ended.[1] It was a devastating war, fought between Catholics and Protestants for territorial gain and political power. The usual effect of war on the Jews that were living near the battlefields was reminiscent of the persecution of the middle ages; acts of violence, banishment, blood libels, kidnappings, restricted neighborhoods, mandatory residence permits, near ruinous taxes. Yet, my story is the story of the struggles and aspirations of the Jewish people to survive in an unfriendly world, a world whose values are very different from ours.

I remember so many things from my father's house. His insistence that both his sons and daughters receive the best in religious as well as secular education stands out most in my mind. He was totally devoted to the acts of kindness, which our tradition teaches, has no limits: feeding the hungry, dowering the bride, providing for the sick, comforting the bereaved.[2]

He was the *parnas* (elected head) of the Hamburg Jewish community, and it prospered so much under his leadership that the community was not in debt.

[**Ed.** Records of Jewish settlement in the cities of Hamburg, Altona, and Wandsbeck (Northwestern Germany, Schleswig-Holstein) date to the sixteenth century, when Conversos, fleeing from the Spanish Inquisition settled in the area. The city councils welcomed them on the basis of perceived economic benefits; the Jews did not disappoint them. They were financiers, shipbuilders, importers, weavers, and goldsmiths. From the early 1600s, Germanic Jews migrated northward, swelling the Jewish population. The Jews of Hamburg were subject to medieval decrees of banishment, and were expelled in 1649, not being permitted to return until 1656. Because Wandsbeck and Altona were ruled by the Danish kings until 1864, it was easier to build three synagogues there and maintain the jointly owned cemetery, located in Altona.]

Many more Jews lived in neighboring Altona, a quarter hour ride by carriage. They carried on their business in Hamburg and traveled back and forth, since they needed special permits to engage in business there. The permits were purchased from the burgomaster for one ducat, and had to be renewed monthly. This system complicated their lives, for they left their homes very early each morning for the synagogue, traveled to Hamburg immediately after the services, engaged in business only until early evening, and were forced to leave Hamburg before the gates closed. Danger always lurked on the roadways, for mercenaries who had been hired by various dukes or monarchs for temporary battle and then found themselves unemployed, overran the land and attacked travelers in an effort to earn a livelihood.

My father betrothed me when I was twelve, and I was married at fourteen. My husband Chaim and I went to live with his parents, in Hameln, a back country town with only two other Jewish families. The three families lived close together A brick wall surrounded the outside of the houses which faced into a common courtyard.

[**Ed.** Throughout Medieval Europe, Jews lived in close quarters for security and sense of community.]

In my new, strange environment, I found the most comforting moments when, from behind my bedroom door, I listened to the melodious notes of my pious father-in-law Yoseph chanting the Shabbat morning service at the break of dawn. His voice was angelic, and his song echoed as a heavenly choir. I was very surprised, when a few years later, he joined the Shabbatean movement.

[**Ed.** The followers of the Shabbatean movement believed that Shabbetai Tzvi was the Messiah. The movement divided Jewry into two camps; those that believed in him and those who believed that he was a fraud. Only when he converted to Islam to save his life from the Sultan's (of Constantinople, Turkey) death threat, did some people admit that they had been deceived.]

Letters had arrived from Smyrna, Turkey, announcing the arrival of the Messiah, and both young and old ran to the synagogue, dressed in their Shabbat finery to listen to their public reading. As a result, my father-in-law, and many of his contemporaries, sold their homes and lands, packed their belongings, and waited for the day that the Jewish people would be redeemed. My father-in-law expected to set sail to the Holy Land from the port of Hamburg, but asked us to hold two casks with provisions of peas, beans, dried meats, and household linens while he made arrangements to emigrate. He waited in vain for three years, finally settled in Hildesheim, twenty five miles from Hameln, and died at a ripe old age without having seen the Holy Land.

෴

During the first year of our marriage, Chaim tried to establish himself in business, but there was no trade center in Hameln, and he didn't want to spend his life as a money lender. My father offered to support us if we returned to Hamburg for the next two years on the condition that Chaim spend half of each day studying Torah, and the other half trying to build a business. In those days, gold chains were very fashionable, so my husband invested in raw gold metal, turned it over to a goldsmith for design, and sold the finished product profitably. It did not take long for us to be able to move into our own home.

When we had accumulated enough to invest, we ventured into trading precious stones. Chaim had to travel to the fairs in Amsterdam, Berlin, Frankfurt and Leipzig. Because we both feared his becoming ill, encountering with an accident, or dying in a strange city, he shared every phase of his business with me. He wanted me to be protected from the government confiscating our property if something happened to him. As time went on, I was as comfortable in the business world as I was in my kitchen or in my children's nursery. Thirty years later, when Chaim lay dying, friends asked him if he had any last wishes as to my care. "None," he answered. "My wife knows everything about our business. Her decisions were always equal to mine. She will be able to carry on without me much as she has been my right hand until now."

Indeed, we were very good friends, companions, not only man and wife. In business matters, Chaim sought advice from me always, never making a decision without consulting me. He referred to me as the apple of his eye. He loved to share all his experiences from the fairs with me, particularly descriptions of the civil cases that were presented to the rabbinical courts, adjudicated by leading scholars. The Jewish community considered it shameful to settle their private civil cases a in secular courts. The courts usually sat in session at the same time as the fairs, and when he had time, he would attend. The details he shared fascinated me.

Are you wondering how I could be a wife, a companion, a business partner, and the mother of twelve children? To confess my true feelings, I want you to know that it was not an easy task. Often, especially when the children were very young, and most of them were two years apart in age, I thought I was more burdened than anyone else I knew. Yet, now, that they are grown, I feel blessed like a fruitful olive plant when they sit around my table.[3]

Often, during a pregnancy, I yearned for certain foods. Well, when I was in my ninth month with my son Yoseph, my mother and I passed a fruit stand that sold medlars.[4] I made a mental note to stop at the stand before returning home. By the time we finished our business, it was very late, and I forgot about purchasing the fruit. Returning home, I was pre-occupied with a yearning for this fruit. Soon afterward, I gave birth, but the midwife whispered that the baby was covered from head to foot with strange brown spots. He refused to nurse, and grew weaker and weaker day by day. Finally, I sent my maid to the market to purchase the medlars. When she brought me the fruit, I mashed it into pulp, and touched it to the baby's lips. Amazingly, he opened his mouth, and began to suckle. He suckled the fruit of an entire medlar, than I placed him near my side to nurse. He suckled heartily, gradually regained his strength, and all the brown spots disappeared by the day of his circumcision. I am recording this in my memoirs so that you will know that not all whims are folly, not all yearning of women are nonsense.

∾

Alsatian Jews had a very special custom, that, as far as I know, was unheard of in other communities. Mothers of newborn sons preserved the diapers which their babies wore to their *brit mila*, (the circumcision ceremony). It was called a *mappa*, and it was cut into long strips, embroidered with the child's name and birth date. It was stored in the synagogue after the child reached the age of three, and used as the binder for the Torah on the day of his Bar Mitzvah. When a census was taken, all the *mappot* (plural of *mappa*) were counted to determine the number of males in the community.[5]

❧

I musn't forget to tell about our encounter with the plague. We were naturally frightened about rumors of illness, especially of the spread of the bubonic plague. We had no cures, and didn't understand how it spread from one community to another. Anyway, we found that there were some afflicted families among us. One morning, as I was dressing my daughter Zipporah, I noticed large sores near her armpits. My husband had similar sores. The barber had covered them with a plaster and some ointment. So I instructed my maid to take her to the barber, never thinking the worst. On the way they met a woman who claimed to be a healer. When the healer saw the sores, she started screaming, "plague! plague!" and fled.

My maid returned to me, baffled. I had to think of a plan to hide them, lest the authorities be notified and blame the Jews. I arranged for them to stay with a peasant family in an outlying village. They agreed to shelter Zipporah and my maid in their cottage for a very high fee, explaining that they were exposing themselves to tremendous risk. Within a week, Zipporah was cured of the sore, and they returned to our home.

❧

Although I did not intend my memoirs to be lessons in morality or proper behavior, I can not help but share with you a small part of my ethical will. This ethical will was intended to guide my children when they reached adulthood; I instructed them to read it often. The kernel of the Torah is *'you shall love your neighbor as yourself.'*[6] But in our days, we seldom

find it so, and few are they who love their fellowman with all
their heart. On the contrary, if a man can contrive to ruin his
neighbor, nothing pleases him more.

The best thing for you, my children, is to serve God from
the heart, without falsehood or sham, not pretending that
you are one thing while, God forbid, in your heart you are
another. Say your prayers with awe and devotion. During the
time for prayers, do not stand about and talk of other things.
While prayers are being offered to the Creator of the world,
hold it a great sin to engage another man in talk about an
entirely different matter — shall God be kept waiting until
you have finished your business? Moreover, put aside a fixed
time for the study of the Torah as best you know how.[7] Then
diligently go about your business, for providing your wife
and children a decent livelihood is likewise a *mitzvah*—the
command of God and the duty of man."

I really never understood why things happen in this
world; why some business partnerships ended with hard
feelings, why many of our losses were replaced by better
opportunities, why one of my children died so young, why
I was able to find such wonderful matches for the other
children. I only know that I taught my children to accept the
joys as well as the burdens, to live according to God's commandments, and yield to His Will.

I think it is because Chaim and I were leaders of our
community, that we were able to marry our children to 'good
and just people.' Many of them were pious scholars and
children of *parnassim* of their respective communities. We
were able to provide each child with an appropriate dowry,
in the thousands of reichthalers. We have particular satisfaction from our daughter Esther. She invites a Rabbi and a
Talmud student to dine at her table every day, and she metes
out honor to rich and poor alike.

∽

We became prosperous. Since helping a poor person establish his own business is considered to be the highest form of charity, we decided to set aside the money we had designated for *tzedakah* (charity), for this purpose.

It is interesting that most of the people we helped start their own businesses became very wealthy. These people never befriended us. It seems to be the way of the world not to recognize the good that people do. I can recall the names of those people who Chaim invited into partnership. Often, when they had his letters of credit, they turned their back on him and became his competitors. There was the incident with the seed pearls that had no buyers, the precious stones that were stolen, and the promised equal sum of money to match his investment that never arrived at the bank. Truly, Chaim had such a pulse for the market; he had innate intuition when to buy and when to sell.

∽

I was married to Chaim for thirty years, always thinking that our life would go on forever, or at least that my own death would precede his. I could not imagine caring for the unmarried children without him. But it was not to be. On Tuesday, the 19th of Tevet, 5449,[8] he went to a business meeting. As he neared the other merchant's house, he tripped over a sharp stone. The best doctors could not stitch the gash in his abdomen. By Shabbat, we all knew that his wound was fatal. He called in the members of our family, one by one, and asked them for forgiveness. He bade them to comfort me after his death. He insisted that I would know how to carry on by myself . Then, he asked everyone to leave the room, with the exception of Rabbi Feibisch Layve who told me later that his strength ebbed slowly and he died with the words *Sh'ma Yisrael* on his lips. I truly believed that I would never cease to mourn for my dearest friend.

The entire community attended his burial rites on Sunday. It was the 24th day of Tevet, 5449. I observed the seven days of mourning, sitting on the ground, surrounded by our twelve fatherless children. A *minyon* prayed daily in our house during that week, so that our children could recite *kaddish*. After two or three weeks, visits of consolation stopped, and I, a widow, had the responsibility of providing for them.

After thirty days of mourning, I sat down to take an accounting of my affairs. Since I knew about every entry in the ledger, there were no surprises. I balanced my accounts, called an auction, sold some merchandise for a profit, and loaned the extra money out at interest. During the next few years, I continued our business and arranged matches for our unmarried children.

My memoirs describe what it was like to be a Jewish female in northern Germany during the seventeenth century. I wonder if there will be much diffrence in future generations between the way I lived my life and the way women will live theirs?

Part Three

THE SEPHARDIC EXPERIENCE

Time Line

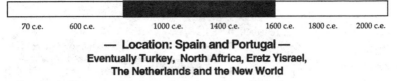

| 70 c.e. | 600 c.e. | 1000 c.e. | 1400 c.e. | 1600 c.e. | 1800 c.e. | 2000 c.e. |

— Location: Spain and Portugal —
Eventually Turkey, North Africa, Eretz Yisrael,
The Netherlands and the New World

Evidence of Jewish settlement in the Iberian Peninsula dates from the time of King Solomon.

"For the king had a Tarshish fleet on the sea along with Hiram's fleet. Once every three years, the Tarshish fleet came in, bearing gold, silver, ivory, apes and peacocks."[1]

The prophet *Yonah* (Jonah) attempted to flee to Tarshish when God commanded him to go to Nineveh to instruct the people to repent.

"But Yonah rose up to flee to Tarshish from the presence of the Lord."[2]

According to many archaeologists, Tarshish was an island off the coast of Spain. The few Jews who lived in Spain in early times were mostly merchants, and they were ruled by the Visigoths, representatives of the Catholic Church.

Kings ruled by Divine Right, and their attitude to the Jews was expressed in anti-Jewish discriminatory legislation. Jews were prohibited from owning Christian slaves, from celebrating *Pesach* (Passover) before Easter, from reading their Bible in Hebrew, from studying *Mishna*. Torturous deaths were meted out to Jews for not believing in Jesus and the Resurrection. Forced baptism was a common practice.

It is no wonder than, that the Jews joined forces with the Moorish (Islam) conquerors to oust the Visigothic rulers in 711, hoping that a change of rulers would change their lot.

Almost five centuries of mutual coexistence, fostering the Golden Age in Spain, ensued. Art, science, literature, law, medicine, philosophy, grammar, flourished. Jews lived side by side with their Moslem neighbors. They became advisors and prime ministers to caliphs, as well as developers of a middle class merchant economy. (*Medieval Connections,* Chapter Twenty Four; *Reminiscence,* Chapter Twenty Five.)

Except for sporadic instances of persecution by fanatic Moslem tribes, the Jews were safe and comfortable until the Christian reconquest of the Iberian peninsula began in the thirteenth century. At first, the new conquerors, needing the administrative and economic services of the Jews, followed precedent and permitted them to continue living in freedom. However, gradually, replacing the Jewish middle class with Christians, they imported the racially discriminatory laws from medieval Europe. (*The Disputation at Barcelona,* Chapter Twenty Six.) Persecution followed. Many Jews sought refuge in other lands, but many remained, hoping that the persecution was temporary. (*Women Show the Way*, Chapter Twenty Seven.)

To cope with the oppression, some converted superficially, becoming Conversos. On the surface, they lived according to Catholicism; in private they observed Judaism. (*Kol Nidrei,* Chapter Twenty Eight.)

Others converted outright, in order to continue the lifestyle they had lived for generations. The Church set up the Inquisition to ferret out heretics, as the new Christians were called. Instituting *auto-da-fe's* and other forms of torture, the Inquisition tried to make Spain *limpieza de sangria,* free of people with Jewish blood. (*Tales of Conversos,* Chapter Twenty Nine.).

The Expulsion Order, (The Alhambra Decre) issued on March 31, 1492, decreed that all Jews must leave Spain by August 1, 1492. Sephardic (Spanish) Jews scattered all over the Mediterranean basin. Some fled to countries in the Ottoman Turkish Empire and farther East; some returned home to Eretz Yisrael (Israel), where Lurianic *Kabballah* developed. (*Why?* Chapter Thirty One.)

Some searched for religious freedom in the New World. (*Sailing with Columbus,* Chapter Thirty.)

These are the stories of our medieval Sephardic ancestors.

A Sacred Trust
— Commentary —
Medieval Connections

In order to understand the eternity of the Jewish people, one must appreciate the promises which G-d made to our forefathers. We were told that the Almighty will scatter us among the nations of the world, but, instead of weakening our spirit as a result of this dispersion, we would become a beacon of light for the rest of civilization.

Miraculously, this prediction, although it has caused jealousy and anti-Semitism, has come true over and over again. We have continuously networked with Jews throughout the world, as well as influenced others to our ways

As you read about the Kingdom of Khazaria, consider the impact of the Jews on other people throughout the ages.

—*Rabbi Eugene I. Kwalwasser*
Principal
Yavneh Academy
Paramus, NJ

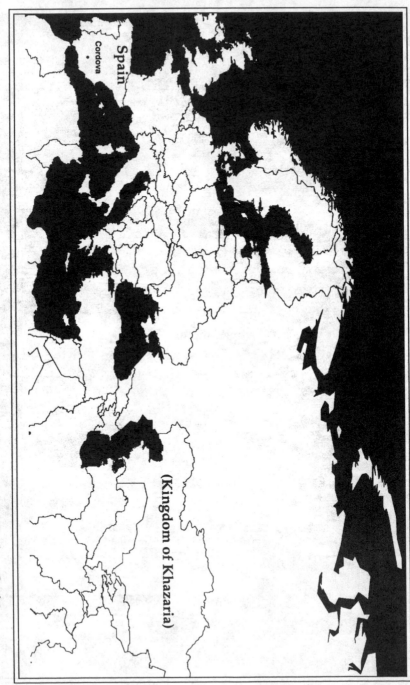

Kingdom of Khazaria, between the Caspian Sea and the Caucasus Mountains, and Cordova, Spain.

MEDIEVAL CONNECTIONS

Time Line

70 c.e.	600 c.e.	1000 c.e.	1400 c.e.	1600 c.e.	1800 c.e.	2000 c.e.

— Location: Cordova, Spain and the Kingdom of Khazaria —

It was siesta time on a very warm summer afternoon. The servants were lazily lounging around. His secretary was sleeping. Chasdai ibn Shaprut stretched out on his large, comfortable couch in the study of his magnificent villa in Cordova. He placed his hands under his head, closed his eyes and daydreamed.

"In neighboring Christian Germany and France my brothers face daily discrimination and increasing outbursts of violent persecution for no other reason than they were born Jews. Here in Spain, we have achieved a welcome respite from our wanderings. We mutually co-exist with our Moslem neighbors; only religion differentiates us. With all my political connections, with my favored status as part of Caliph Abd al-Rahman III's royal inner circle, I have the ability to find out if the rumors I've been hearing about an independent Jewish kingdom in far off Khazaria are true. I must find out how it is possible for Jews to live independently outside of the Holy Land. I will have to draw up a few plans for my emissary to follow, in order to determine the truth of these rumors."

~

"Isaac (bar Nathan), you are one of my most trusted courtiers. You know that I have been intrigued by the rumors that an independent Jewish kingdom exists in Khazaria. In the past, these rumors were carried by merchants. Yesterday, an envoy from the Byzantine court appeared here, in Cordova.

When I questioned him, he admitted that his country had commercial ties with the Khazar kingdom. I have consulted with geographers to determine the exact location of this alleged kingdom of the Jews. I want you to undertake a serious mission; the journey will be long and difficult. I want you to authenticate the reports that I have been hearing.

I will furnish you with letters of introduction, gifts to the King of the Khazars, and sufficient money for the trip. The preferred way to travel is to sail eastward across the Mediterranean toward Constantinople, secure permission from the Byzantine ruler to cross his country, and continue your voyage northeast across the Black Sea, to Khazaria, which is located in southern Asiatic Russia, just west of the Caspian Sea. The trip across the Medeterranean and Black Seas will take you nine days, and land travel will take you 28 days.

If the Byzantine ruler will not give you permission to cross his land, then proceed eastward to the Holy Land. You know that I have been in constant touch with Jews residing there. When you reach Yaffo, hire a wagon driver to take you to Tiberias. A large Jewish community lives there and thrives on creating beautiful tapestries and textiles. Since they communicate regularly with the *yeshivot* (Jewish academies) in Babylonia/Persia, they will probably ask you to wait until their next mission there. This way someone will accompany you part of the way; then you can travel north by yourself toward Armenia until you reach the land of the Khazars."

After what seemed a lifetime of waiting, Chasdai welcomed Isaac back to Cordova. He carried with him a letter from the king of the Khazars. The king had written:

To Hasdai ibn Shaprut, honored nasi (prince) and adviser to the Andulusian Caliph of the Umayyad Dynasty Abd al-Rahman al-Nasir:

In answer to the questions of your ambassador Isaac bar Nathan: Originally we were Turkish nomads, and we settled between the Caspian Sea and the Caucasus Mountains at the end of the sixth century. At first, we tried to live harmoniously with the surrounding rulers, but they refused to accept our sovereignty. Increasingly, passing merchants sought us out as customers; and Jews, fleeing from persecution in Byzantine lands emigrated here. The ritual of these Jews intrigued King Sabriel and Queen Serah, for they were monotheistic, although their religious ritual was not clearly defined.

Tradition has it in our country, that an angel appeared to a God fearing man named Bulan in a dream and instructed him to convert all the people. He informed the King and Queen of his dream. Since they knew Greek clerics professing Christianity and Moslem theologians, they, with the guidance of Bulan, invited them to debate upon the scriptures to decipher the most desirable and true faith. When each of them agreed that Judaism was the mother religion, they understood the meaning of the dream. The King and Queen converted and urged their subjects to convert to Judaism, also. All the males in the kingdom were circumcised, but few kept Shabbat.

King Sabriel then invited Jews from Babylonia/Persia to Khazaria, in order to further teach his people the tenets of Judaism. They became acquainted with Torah, Mishna, Talmud, and liturgy. One of the Rabbis was appointed as the judge. Bulan's grandson, Obadiah, a man noted for his generosity and piety, built synagogues and schools.

King Sabriel and Queen Serah had a son. I, Joseph am that son. I invite you to come to Khazaria to visit.[1]

A Sacred Trust
— Commentary —
Reminiscence

Many dazzling innovations have been made in our fast-moving technological age. The means of communication now include the computer, the fax machine, the cellular phone, etc. But the caution we need to exercise in the use of our speech, whether written or oral, is just as compelling as ever, if not more so.

Words are still the bearers of good or evil, hurt or healing, conflict or compassion. What we say to each other is as important as to how we express our thoughts and feelings.

These days we have tended to become a bit more callous. We forget that in the list of 44 sins (*Al Chet*) that we declare on Yom Kippur, more than a third are sins of speech. Words can be wonderful or dangerous tools and we must be careful how we use them.

Rabbi Harry Essrig

Publisher of "The American Rabbi"

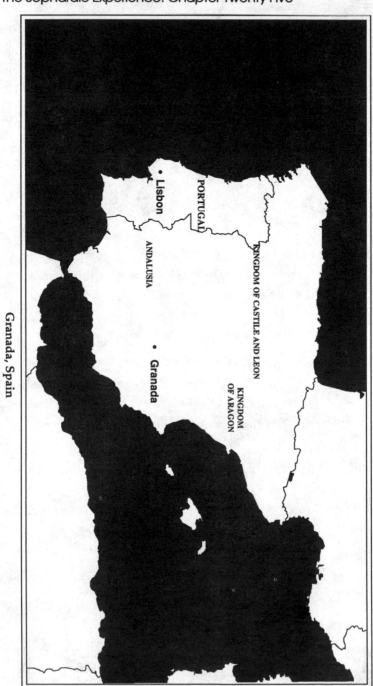

Granada, Spain

REMINISCENCE

Time Line

| 70 c.e. | 600 c.e. | 1000 c.e. | 1400 c.e. | 1600 c.e. | 1800 c.e. | 2000 c.e. |

— Location: Granada, Spain —

[**Ed.** Rabbaynu Chananel (965-1057) was one of the most celebrated medieval Jewish scholars, known for his commentary on the entire Talmud Bavli (the Babylonian Talmud). The portions of the commentary that have survived through the ages can be found on the outside columns of each page of the Talmud. He was the teacher of Rabbaynu Gershom (960 - 1028).]¹

"I, Rabbi Shmuel Ibn Naghrela, HaNagid, remember the letter of consolation that I wrote from my home in Granada to Rabbaynu Chananel. I had just found out that his father Rabbi Chushiel had passed away. Rabbi Chushiel was one of the four Rabbis captured by the pirates, the one that was redeemed in Kairoun, Tunisia."²

This is what I wrote: "To him who is surrounded by a halo of rays like *Moshe Rabbaynu* (Moses), for whose sake his people is distinguished, to our friend, Rabbaynu Chananel, the humblest of all sages, peace and consolation!

It is known to my master that, although his fortune is in ruins, and his sorrow as great as the sea because his father was called to the assembly of the Heavenly Hosts, it is not for him alone that the light has been taken away. The torch has been extinguished, the table shattered and pulled down for all inhabitants of the earth under the Heaven. We are all aware that a misfortune has befallen the whole world, for all men become kin when a sage has passed away, particularly from among us, the teachers of the Torah. From us the garment of honor has been stolen, the pearl hidden away, the crown has fallen from our head, and beauty has banished from our midst. We have lost a man. O, that I were able to ransom my master with my life! I would offer scores of precious stones in order to acquire a merit for many."

You might ask where I learned to write with such expressive metaphors. Actually, writing is a craft that can be developed with a lot of practice. You see, I used to own a spice shop. It was located next to the courtyard of Ibn al-Arif, who was the scribe to Caliph Habbus ibn Maksan, the Berber king who ruled Granada. The scribe had a maidservant, and she always asked me to write letters for her, since she did not know how to read or write. He always complimented her on the beauty of her writing style and her choice of metaphors. It happened that Ibn al-Arif wanted to take temporary leave from his duties in the royal court, but he needed to find a person who would be able to replace him. He asked his maid servant who wrote the letters for her.

She replied, "You are perhaps acquainted with the Jewish man who owns the spice shop next to your courtyard? He writes those letters for me."

The scribe, very happy that he found a perfect replacement, invited me to become the scribe for Caliph Habbus while he was on leave. Caliph Habbus was so impressed with my ability, that, even after his scribe returned to the court, he insisted that I remain as the advisor to the scribe of the king. When the scribe passed away, Caliph Habbus appointed me as his permanent official scribe. He not only appreciated the way I wrote; he valued my advice and counsel. Eventually, he appointed me to the position of Vizier (Prime Minister).

Life in the court of the Caliph was exciting, to say the least. There existed much jealousy between the Caliph's two sons, Badis, the elder, and Buluggin, the younger. Every person in Granada, had his own reason for supporting one or the other as the future heir to the throne. It seems that I inadvertently became involved in the dispute. I found out how much trouble this would cause one day during a royal procession.

I was riding with Caliph Habbus at the head of the procession. His sons followed in the second carriage. The nobility followed behind them. Barriers had been erected on the streets to protect the royal procession. Suddenly, a prominent merchant, pushed his way through the barrier, jumped over the ropes, and began cursing me. The Caliph was incensed at the man's audacity.

"That man has no reason to use his tongue for such evil purposes. He cannot insult my esteemed minister without paying for his indiscretion. Have it cut it out!" he commanded me.

We returned to the palace, and I tried to find a way to follow the king's order without physically harming the merchant who had cursed me. I ordered him to the palace. He arrived, fearful, agitated, expecting the worse. Gently, I assured him that I would not harm him physically; he only had to regret his wrongdoing and swear that he would not curse anybody, ever again.

The following year, the Caliph and I led his royal court once again in procession. The merchant waited as the Caliph's coach neared where he stood. He stepped forward, bowed deeply, and shouted: "Allah be blessed! May the God of Vizier Shmuel be blessed!" Then he retreated behind the barricade.

The Caliph turned to me: "I thought I ordered you to cut out that man's tongue."

"Your majesty! I certainly obeyed your order. I did cut out his angry tongue. And I replaced it with a peaceful one!"

A SACRED TRUST

— COMMENTARY —

DISPUTATION AT BARCELONA

❧

Jewish Self-Esteem: Judaism as a minority religion periodically has been portrayed in denigrating terms. The behavior of Rabbi Moses ben Nachman (the Ramban) models for contemporary Jews the necessity of maintaining a positive Jewish identity and self-esteem regardless of the might of external anti-Judaism. Like the Ramban, we must be prepared to publicly affirm THE CASE IN FAVOR OF JUDAISM!

Aliyah: This episode provides the context in which a prominent rabbi of the Middle Ages decided to leave the Diaspora and to settle permanently in the land of Israel. Ramban indeed became one of the great exponents of the *Mitzvah* of *Yishuv Eretz Yisrael* and of the praiseworthy act of choosing *Aliyah* to our Sacred Land—*Eretz Yisrael*— as a religious obligation.

Kiddush HaShem: In our era, during which Jews living in freedom so often opt out of Torah study, it is compelling to be reminded of pious Jews throughout the ages who were willing to die in defense of the Talmud. The concept of martyrdom in order to preserve God's legacy to us— *Kiddush HaShem*—is a reminder to maintain Judaism as a life-and-death priority for our spiritual survival. God's Torah is most certainly *Etz Chaim;* it is our Tree of Life.

Rabbi Alan Silverstein,
Congregation Agudath Israel, Caldwell, NJ,
President, International Rabbinical Assembly

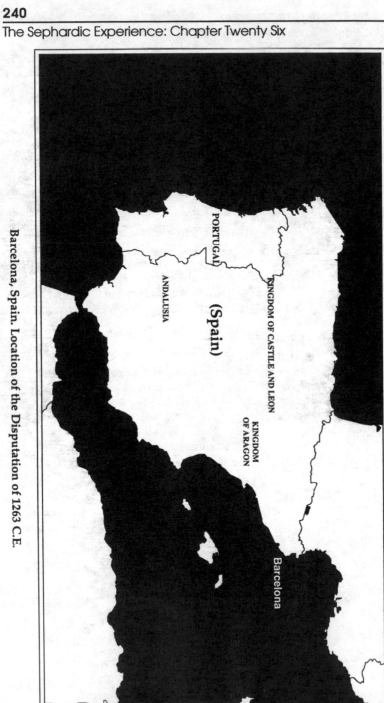

Barcelona, Spain. Location of the Disputation of 1263 C.E.

THE DISPUTATION AT BARCELONA

Time Line

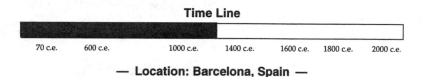

| 70 c.e. | 600 c.e. | 1000 c.e. | 1400 c.e. | 1600 c.e. | 1800 c.e. | 2000 c.e. |

— **Location: Barcelona, Spain** —

Outside, the sun sparkled on the plaza, as its broad boulevards pressed downward toward the Mediterranean Sea. Mountains surrounded the busy port city located in the corner of northeast Spain.

Fray Ramon de Penyafort, head of the Dominican Order, sat with his disciple, the apostate (one who has rejested his Judaism) Monk Pablo Christiani, in the chapel of the monastery in Barcelona, on a fateful day, in July, 1263.

Garbled whispers. Pablo hesitated: "Do you really want to know why I converted to Christianity? Let me tell you. In my studies of Bible and Talmud, I came to realize that the Jews are a rejected people. Now, I want to promulgate the Christian faith among my former brothers. I am convinced it will be for their own good. But wherever I travel, they refuse to listen to my reasoning."

"Would you be interested in arranging a Disputation? prodded Fray Ramon. "Jews will be forced to listen and through persuasive arguments we can lead them to conversion. They will thank us, for then they will receive salvation. We will save their souls."

"You are always well received by King James," suggested Pablo. "Go to him and discuss our plan. If he approves, we should act quickly to make the arrangements. He will ask you who to appoint to dispute for the Jews. Suggest their revered leader, Rabbi Moses ben Nachman. I was schooled in the faith of the Jews before my conversion, and I will be a formidable opponent. When their Rabbi can no longer prove the validity of Judaism, he will lose the Dispuation and then he will have no choice but to convert. And when he converts, they will all follow his example and abandon their faith."

Fray Ramon arranged an immediate audience with King James. "Your Majesty, we have a tremendous opportunity to bring the Jews of your kingdom around to our way of thinking. Why, in Disputation after Disputation, we gain many converts to our faith. It has come to my attention that young Pablo Christiani, a new convert to our faith, well schooled in Jewish texts from his youth, is willing to debate with their revered leader Rabbi Moses ben Nachman."

"I am a fair man, Fray Ramon," thundered King James. "I am not interested in disturbing the harmonious relationship between the people who live in my kingdom the way King Louis of France does."

"But, Your Majesty," interrupted Fray Ramon, "do you know how much favor you will find in the eyes of the Pope if you go ahead with a public Disputation? We all need to be favorites with the Pope."

The opening debate was scheduled for Shabbat, July 20, 1263 in the royal palace.

🏵 🏵 🏵 🏵 🏵

King James and Queen Yolanda were seated on silk upholstered chairs on a raised platform. Two podiums had been erected facing them, one for Pablo Christiani, one for Rabbi Moses ben Nachman. Behind the disputants, throngs of people, Jewish and Christian, filled the royal chambers. The nobility, bishops and priests, lords, stood side by side and peered down at the scene from the balcony that had been erected for them.

King James raised his hand for silence. "We need to establish some rules of procedure. What subjects will be discussed? What books will be allowed for use as proof texts?

And I warn the disputants: I will not permit undue pressure, there will be no threats, no bullying. The disputants must act respectfully to each other. If Pablo Christiani is victorious, and he convinces the Jews to convert in order to save themselves from the power of the devil, in order to prepare themselves for His coming, all and good. If however, Rabbi Moses is victorious, then I guarantee that this Disputation will not end in suffering for any of my Jewish subjects. I give my word that they will be safe after the Disputation as they are now.

Rabbi Moses stepped forward. "Your Majesty, I agree that we need rules of procedure. This august audience must be made aware that if I am to defend Judaism adequately, it might appear that some of my proofs would be blasphemous, but that is not my intention."

Fray Ramon interjected: "These rules should be established. There should not be any words of blasphemy uttered against our Lord Jesus or his virgin Mother Mary. Further, we should deal only with these questions:

- Has the Messiah come as Christians say, or has he yet to come as Jews say?
- Is the Messiah prophesied in scriptures as a man or as a divine being?
- Do the Jews practice the true law or do the Christians?

Also, we want to use the Talmud as well as the Bible for our proof texts."

※ ※ ※ ※ ※

Pablo Christiani began. "Once Jews were a mighty, independent people. Now, they are a despised people. Just look at their plight; they are cursed, they are scattered throughout the world. This proves that the Church is superior. Jews turned against the Messiah, now the Church has turned against them. And isn't it written in your Talmud that the Messiah was born on the day that the Second Temple was destroyed?"[1] The people standing in the balcony applauded.

Rabbi Moses ben Nachman slowly ascended to his podium. Breathing slowly and deeply, he began his rebuttal: "The source you quoted mentions that the Messiah was born, it does not say that the Messiah has come. Let me give you a clearer example. Moses did not come before Pharaoh on the day he was born, nor was he the redeemer at that time."

Angry outbursts erupted from the balcony. King James held up his hand. "I promised this man complete freedom of speech. We will adjourn this session until Monday when we will reconvene in the monastery."

※ ※ ※ ※ ※

Rabbi Moses ben Nachman stepped forward. "Your Majesty, please allow me to start the second session. Let me explain my opinion about the Messiah, and then Pablo Christiani will be able to respond."

"You have my permission."

"The prophet Isaiah prophesied:

> *It shall come to pass in the end of days ...*
> *And they shall beat their swords into plowshares*
> *And their spears into pruning hooks,*
> *Nation shall not lift sword against nation,*
> *Neither shall they learn war anymore.*"[2]

"From the days of the Nazarene until now, the entire world has been full of violence and robbery. Indeed, the Christians spill more blood than the rest of the nations, and they also lead immoral lives. How difficult it would be for you, My Lord King, and these your knights if they would "neither learn war any more!" Since this world is still in a state of war, since there is still bloodshed, and hate, not love, since there is no brotherhood, no equality, no justice, I maintain that the Messiah has still not come."

Pablo Christiani interrupted: "Do you always deliver such

long speeches?" He cited one source after another, trying to prove his own point of view. Rabbi Moses ben Nachman successfully refuted each point.

The crowd grew restless and unruly. King James left the scene after he set the third session for Thursday in the royal palace.

▧ ▧ ▧ ▧ ▧

Pablo Christiani introduced proofs from Maimonides, which were totally refuted by Rabbi Moses ben Nachman. "The Nazerene was not the Messiah. We believe that the Messiah will gather the dispersed of the Jewish people; the Nazerene gathered no one. The Messiah will be empowered to rebuild the Holy Temple; the Nazerene neither built nor destroyed the Holy Temple. The Messiah will rule over all people; but the Nazerene did not rule over anyone. Besides," continued Rabbi Moses, "the central issue that we are debating is whether or not Jesus was divine."

King James dismissed the disputants with the warning that their arguments had to be completed on the next day. Guards dispersed the tumultuous crowds.

▧ ▧ ▧ ▧ ▧

Rabbi Moses ben Nachman stepped forward. "Please, your Majesty, I beseech you to call a halt to this Disputation. My people have pleaded with me to withdraw, for they see no real victory for either side. They are terrorized by the Dominicans and they fear the wrath of the preachers. They will use every means in their power to distort the results of this debate for their own ulterior motives."

"Rabbi Moses," replied King James, "I gave you my word that you would have complete freedom of speech. The refutations that you cite stimulate my mind. I have not been so mentally stimulated for many years. I want you to continue!"

Pablo Christiani demanded: "Do you Jews believe that the Messiah is divine, as we Christians do?"

"The Messiah, in whom we believe," responded Rabbi Moses, "will be a man, born out of the union of a man and a woman, even as I was, even as you were. Judaism does not believe in the divinity of any man."

The nobles, bishops and priest, lords were deeply agitated at the turn the debate had taken. It seemed clear to them that Pablo Christiani was no match for Rabbi Moses.

King James rose and publicly congratulated Rabbi Moses. "Please accept this gift of 300 solidos for your trouble in preparing for this Disputation." The bishops and priests exchanged wrathful glances.

᠎᠎᠎᠎᠎ ❈ ❈ ❈ ❈ ❈

Rabbi Moses ben Nachman recorded the entire Disputation. Within two years, the Bishop of Gerona obtained the record and presented it to King James as proof that Rabbi Moses had blashphemed Jesus.

"I promised him free speech," the king persisted.

"But you did not guarantee his safety if he recorded his arguments! If you persist in not using this record against him, I will call upon the Pope to implicate him, and your soul will be in danger of damnation."

King James received Rabbi Moses warmly when he arrived at the palace to say goodbye. "You know, my esteemed friend, you should never have recorded the Disputation. The Pope does not like to have written records of anything. He threatened to excommunicate me. This is why I suggested that you leave this country. Where will you go?"

"I will return to my ancestral homeland, to Eretz Yisrael (The Holy Land). I will follow in the footsteps of Rabbi Yehuda HaLayve and Rabbi Yechiel of Paris.

[Ed. Rabbi Yehuda HaLayve (1075-1141) was known as the poet laureate of the Golden Age. He dreamed of living in Eretz Yisrael and emigrated when he was sixty years old. Rabbi Yechiel (d. 1268) and his students emigrated following a Disputation in Paris in 1240-2 after they watched twenty four cart loads of holy manuscripts being burned.]

I hear that many Jews do not live there now, because of the devastation caused by the Crusades. But, I am confident that I will find a place to settle in my old age. Please, do me one favor. Try, to the best of your ability, to see to it, that none of my people are hurt as a result of the Disputation."

Well Known, Recorded Disputations

880 C.E.	Constantinople
1240-2 C.E.	Paris
1263 C.E.	Barcelona
1413 C.E.	Tortosa
1450 C.E.	Rome
1500 C.E.	Cologne
1700 C.E.	Hanover

Martin Gilbert, *Atlas of Jewish History*

A Sacred Trust
— Commentary —
Women Show the Way

What is it in this story that strikes a chord in my heart?

First, the heroine of this story is named Miriam which makes it all the more meaningful to me. But there's more.

That the heroine had her every wish fulfilled—to live in *Eretz Yisrael* in relative security after escaping persecution; working as a midwife delivering Jewish babies which she loved to do, and see her husband find work. Yet one thing she felt was lacking was the opportunity to go to *Meurat Hamachpeyla*—The Caves of Machpeyla—to connect with the history of our matriarchs and patriarchs to feel herself as a link in the chain.

I was touched that the heroine Miriam named after Moses' older sister, was saved in her dilemma in the cave by our matriarchs Sarah, Rebekkah and Leah. On Shabbat, when I bless my daughter to be like the matriarchs, this story will come to mind.

I pray that in her life the memory and stories of the matriarchs and the long line of Jewish women who showed courage in the face of hardship, will guide her and give her strength when she needs a light to show the way.

Miriam Brunn Ruberg,
Director of Jewish Educati,
United Jewish Federation of Tidewater,
Norfolk, VA

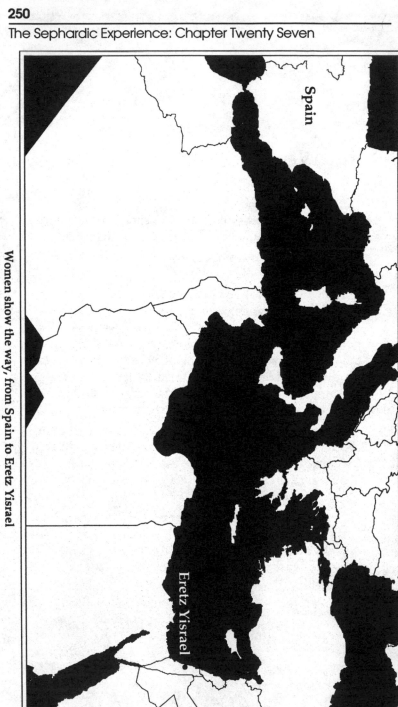

Women show the way, from Spain to Eretz Yisrael

Chapter Twenty Seven
WOMEN SHOW THE WAY

Time Line

| 70 c.e. | 600 c.e. | 1000 c.e. | 1400 c.e. | 1600 c.e. | 1800 c.e. | 2000 c.e. |

— **Location: Spain** —

"Listen, Judah, the past is past. It's true that you are the son of a once powerful Jewish courtier, that your family had status, wealth, and education, that you were brought up familiar with all the happenings in the royal palace. But the situation is different today. And I won't permit you to remain blind to recent developments.

"King Ferdinand has already confiscated most of our wealth to increase his personal treasure. He is yielding to the hate fostered by the Inquisition, and he is determined to exploit the Jews. How long do you think he will permit you to live in Spain now that you can't contribute anything to the financial welfare of this country? He only has to concoct some sort of a pretext, and your life will be in real danger.

"The Inquisitors gain more power every day. They will arrest you, torture you, and burn you at the stake. We must leave this country immediately." Dona Miriam's voice reached a high pitch. Fear resounded in her every word."

"You are right, of course, my dear," responded Judah, "Where will we go? How will we start all over again? I heard that Sultan Muhammad II, known as the Conqueror,[1] leader of the Ottoman Turks, issued a proclamation inviting Jews who were fleeing from persecution in Germany, France, and Spain to settle in Constantinople, or in any other of the lands that he ruled, including *Eretz Yisrael*.

[Ed. The Sultan's proclmation read, "Who among you of all my people that is with me, may his God be with him, let him ascend to Constantinople, the site of my royal throne. Let him dwell in the best of the land, each beneath his vine and beneath his fig tree, with silver and with gold, with wealth and with cattle. Let him dwell in the land, trade in it, and take possession of it."][2]

He thought that the Jews would help him develop his country economically. And I have heard that his successor, Sultan Bayazid[3] said of Ferdinand: Can you call such a king wise and intelligent? He is impoverishing his country and enriching my kingdom.[4]

I've been dreaming of living out the rest of my life in Eretz Yisrael. Yet, I don't know how we will find the money even to pay for passage on a boat. Don Samuel offered to help me. I promised I would meet him at noon. He has an idea for a business. If his idea is successful, I will be able to earn some money. Then, if we decide to emigrate, I'll have something with which to re-settle. Let's not make any hasty decisions. Let's wait a while."

"I know all the problems of resettlement. But your life is more important than position and wealth. I beg you to at least begin thinking about emigrating."

❊ ❊ ❊ ❊ ❊

Dona Miriam paced sadly back and forth in the near empty rooms of their villa. Some of their possessions had been confiscated; some had been sold for sustenance. She wondered what it would be like to live in Eretz Yisrael where she would not be afraid to work as a midwife, to deliver Jewish babies into a world that welcomed them. She repeated her name over and over: "Miriam, Miriam ... just like the Miriam in our Torah, who delivered Jewish babies during the Egyptian slavery."

[**Ed.** The Jewish midwives were named Shifra and Puah. According to the commentary of Rashi, Shifra was *Yocheved* (the mother of Moses) and Puah was *Miriam* (the sister of Moses.)[5]

An insistent pounding at the door interrupted her reverie. Opening it, she found a tall man, dressed as Spanish nobleman on her doorstep.

"I am Jewish," he whispered. "Do not fear to let me in."

She beckoned him to enter, and invited him to sit down in one of the few remaining chairs. "How can I help you?"

"I am wearing this clothing because I do not want to be found out. This disguise has served me well in recent years. I have a great deal of money on me, ten thousand maravedis to be exact, for I just collected the taxes from some farm land that I had leased out to various farmers. The taxes must be turned over to the owners of the land. I know who you are, even though I shall not reveal my identity to you.

"I want to leave this money with you for safekeeping, while I collect the rest that is due me. I plan to return shortly. If, however, I do not return within a year—you know as well as I do how dangerous it is out there—the crown is so anti-Jewish. If I do not return—then you will know that something terrible happened to me—use the money for your own escape." He handed her a mesh bag, excused himself, and disappeared.

Miriam placed the money under her bed and returned to her reverie. She did not mention the incident to Judah when he returned home.

※ ※ ※ ※ ※

Judah and Samuel worked together for almost a year. They knew that some Jews, living as *Conversos*, still occupied positions in the kingdom's financial and administrative services. Judah knew that they served King Ferdinand's purpose to exploit their talent. He knew that they fooled themselves into believing that he would not expel them, as he did the Jews of Andalusia in 1483, when they were no longer useful to him.

[**Ed.** *Conversos* is Latin for having been forcibly converted to another faith. Two other terms have the same connotation: *Marranos* is Spanish for "he who mars true faith," or "pigs," and *Anusim* is Hebrew for forced conversion.]

Because loyal Christians generally hesitated to do business with him, Judah barely made ends meet. As the year passed, he leaned more and more toward emigrating, still not knowing where he would find the money for resettlement.

Pesach (Passover) was approaching. "Time for spring housecleaning," thought Dona Miriam. "Even though this might be our last *Pesach* in Spain, I will do what I have to do." She prepared her house for the holiday. She scrubbed, washed and swept, moving each piece of remaining furniture.

"Look what I found," she ran out of the bedroom, searching for Judah who was sitting in his study. She was holding the mesh bag filled with ten thousand maravedis.

"What's in the bag? Where did you find it?" he queried, trying to calm her.

"I never told you what happened, and after I put the mesh bag under my bed, I forgot about it. Remember the day, last year, when you left to meet Samuel in the market? I must have been daydreaming, or something, when this man, dressed as a Spanish nobleman knocked at the door. He told me he was a tax-farmer, that he had collected ten thousand maravedis from farmers that he had to turn over to the owner's of the land. He was afraid to carry around so much money and wanted to leave it here for safekeeping. He told me that he would be back shortly, but, if he didn't return within a year, we would know that something terrible happened to him and we would be free to use the money for our own escape."

Judah's hands shook, as he counted the money. "I don't know who the Spanish nobleman was. You don't know who he was either. Yet, the year has passed and I think this money must be a sign, pointing us in the direction of fulfilling our dreams. Let us leave for *Eretz Yisrael* right after *Pesach.*"

❊ ❊ ❊ ❊ ❊

Judah and Miriam resettled in *Yerushalayim* in a house overlooking the Temple Mount (the area on which the Holy Temple once stood). There were about two hundred Jewish families earning their livelihood as merchants or craftsmen, and they had to pay taxes to the Sultan. Although many of their Moslem neighbors were intolerant of the Jews who resettled in the Holy City as refugees from Spanish oppression, their situation was much improved over their lot in their native land.

Miriam was solicitous for the welfare of the pregnant women. She visited them, attended to their needs, and assured them that she would be present when they delivered their babies. As time went on, the mothers-to-be trusted Miriam more and more, for it seemed that as soon as she made the delivering mother comfortable, the baby would be born without any undue stress. Her reputation as a midwife spread throughout *Yerushalayim* and beyond.

It happened that the daughter of Murad Bey, the governor and deputy of Sultan Bayazid, was about to deliver his first grandchild. She was having a difficult labor. "Call Miriam, the Jewish midwife. She will be able to help my daughter. "

Miriam made the mother-to-be comfortable. In no time, the baby was born. The governor was overwhelmed. He held the infant, rocked it in his arms, danced with it. Tears of joy flowed from his sparkling eyes.

"You have brought a new life into this world. You have helped my daughter so much. You have saved her life. Name your reward!"

Miriam never expected any reward. She pondered: "What do I want? My dream to live in the Holy Land has been fulfilled. Blessed be God, Judah has been able to find work. We have a roof over our heads and are living in relative security. I am delivering babies, as I used to do. What reward could I ask of the governor? Now that we are here in the Holy Land, I think I would like to visit Meorat Hamachpayla, the gravesite of our matriarchs and patriarchs in Hebron."

[**Ed.** Abraham and Sarah, Isaac and Rebecca, Jacob and Leah are buried in Meorat Hamachpayla.]

I would like to visit the gravesites of my ancestors she replied, "but I have to prepare myself for such a privilege."

"When you are ready, please let me know," said the governor. "I shall send my soldiers to accompany you."

Every day for the next three months, Miriam recited all 150 chapters of *Tehillim*, (Psalms). She fasted every Monday and Thursday. Then she let the governor know that she was ready for her reward.

The governor sent two soldiers to accompany her to Hebron. As they approached Meorat Hamachpayla, Miriam felt more excited, more energetic than she had ever felt before. Her heart palpitated, her entire body flushed with a sense of awe and expectation. Tears of joy spilled from her eyes as she contemplated the privilege of praying at this holy site. They helped her descend to the underground caverns where the actual gravesites were located.

"When you have finished, signal to us by pulling this rope, and we will help you ascend."

Miriam moved from gravesite to gravesite, praying intently. "*Rib-bo-no shel o-lam*, Master of the Universe, God of Sarah, Rebecca, Rachel, and Leah, bestow Your gracious blessings upon me and my family; grant me, and all Your children a good life, blessed with fulfilled years. Remember my meritorious deeds kindly, and may Your Presence hover over my house. Grant me the privilege to bring into this world children who will emulate Your ways, who cling to the paths of Your Torah, whose lives our guided by compassionate deeds. May the light of Jewish life never be extinguished. Please, hear my prayer, in the merit of my holy mothers, Amen."

When she finished praying, she moved to the wall and stood contemplating the privilege she had just experienced. A sense of total calm and peace engulfed her. Then she walked over to the rope, pulled it to signal the soldiers that she was ready to ascend. There was no response. She pulled again and again, but there was no response.

Miriam realized that she was utterly alone. She did not know that the soldiers had obeyed Murad Bey by safely accompanying her to Meorat Hamachpayla. Since he had not ordered them to bring her back to *Yerushalayim* safely, they left her alone in the gravesite, hoping that she would starve to death. They did not like Jews; they feared economic competition from the refugees who flocked to the Holy Land each day.

"How will I ascend from this cavern? And if I do, how will I find my way back to *Yerushalayim* and to my husband? Will I ever deliver another baby, help another widow, feed another orphan? This is not the way this privilege must end."

She closed her eyes, blinking back the tears that now tasted bitter as they spilled from her eyes and brushed her lips. Suddenly, she saw three lights coming toward her.

It must be the tears that are making me see this vision, she thought, and rubbed her eyes dry. But the lights drew closer and closer. She recognized Sarah baking *matzot* for the three angels,[6] Rebecca, covered with a veil as she stepped into Sarah's tent to light the Shabbat candles,[7] and Leah, listening to Rachel teach her the secrets she had learned from Jacob.[8]

The lights moved up and down over the rope that dangled from the top of the cavern to the height of Miriam's shoulders. Miriam grabbed the rope, propelled upward by the lights, and pulled herself higher and higher until she stood on the ground outside the cavern. The lights moved forward; Miriam followed them, running through the Judean hills northward the nineteen miles to her home in *Yerushalayim*. When she stood safely in front of her house, the lights dimmed and disappeared. Miriam understood that her "mothers" had guided her home.

A Sacred Trust
— Commentary —
Kol Nidrei

❦

A group of melodies common to all synagogues of Ashkenazic tradition has been given the name *Misinai* tunes (from Sinai). The melodies found primarily in the High Holiday service are no more than 400 years old, yet tradition "sanctifies" them as if they were given to Israel by Moses on Mount Sinai.

All Ashkenazic synagogues use the same basic motifs albeit with variations as is common with all longstanding melodies that have been transmitted orally. The best-known *Misinai* tune is *Kol Nidrei*.

According to Abraham Zvi Idelsohn, the pre-eminent Jewish musicologist of the 20th century, the melody for *Kol Nidrei* is an amalgam of motifs found in the liturgy and cantillations.

Sephardic Jewry do s not incorporate this melody with the *Kol Nidrei* text.

Velvel Pasternack,
Musicologist,
Tara Publications

❦

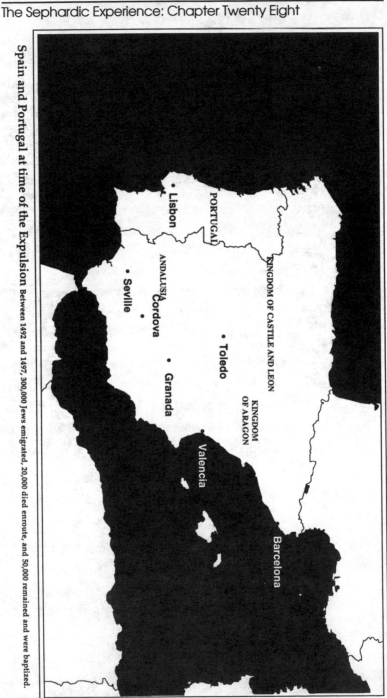

Spain and Portugal at time of the Expulsion Between 1492 and 1497, 300,000 Jews emigrated, 20,000 died enroute, and 50,000 remained and were baptized.

KOL NIDREI

Time Line

| 70 c.e. | 600 c.e. | 1000 c.e. | 1400 c.e. | 1600 c.e. | 1800 c.e. | 2000 c.e. |

— **Location: Spain** —

[**Ed.** The custom of reciting the words of Kol Nidrei, the nullification of communal vows, was instituted by the Babylonian Gaonim around the eighth century. By the year 1,000, during the time of Chai Gaon, the recitation of the words was accepted as the invocation of Divine "pardon, forgiveness, atonement," for the sin of failing to keep a solemn vow. The source of the melody is still subject to investigation, although some researchers have concluded that the melody of Kol Nidrei was composed by one of the Conversos of Spain. It expresses the terror and the pain of the persecutions that they suffered.[1]

The melody for Kol Nidrei is one of the most famous and exalted in Jewish history. Who was its talented composer, who captured the emotions of a historical period through somber music, which still reverberates some five hundred years later? According to one source, the melody is ascribed to a Converso named Da Castilla who witnessed the torture of one of his brothers at the hands of the Inquisition at an *auto-da-fe*.]

His name was Da Silva, one of Queen Isabella's secretaries of the treasury. He chose to remain in Spain after the decree of expulsion was announced, on March 31, 1492. He and his family converted to Christianity, hoping this would guarantee their safety. In the privacy of his home, he observed Jewish rituals. He knew his masquerade was dangerous, yet, he believed that the Inquisition was just a passing phase. Eventually, normal relations between Spanish Catholics and Jews would be restored.

The Inquisition, however, grew more powerful every day. It set up a spy system to ferret out the heretics, and its network reached into every possible corner of Spain.

reached into every possible corner of Spain.

Because the Da Silva's were so prominent, they were placed under careful scrutiny; every move was suspect. Yet, twice each year, on the night of the Seder and on Kol Nidrei night, Da Silva, and hundreds of other *Conversos*, risked their lives and gathered secretly in underground cellars to pray to God.

Because they wore crosses as a sign of their conversion, they first had to annul the vows of Christianity that they had accepted, so their prayers began with the words of Kol Nidrei. Afterward, they prayed for protection from the hands of the Inquisition for another year.

The Inquisition knew about these hidden Jews and waited for an appropriate opportunity to arrest them, try them, torture them, and burn them at the stake.

Five years after the expulsion, on Yom Kippur eve, [[5258/ 1497] the *Conversos*, who were all high ranking officers and advisors, scientists, doctors, philosophers, gathered in Da Silva's underground cellar for Kol Nidrei. In the midst of the Yom Kippur Amida prayer, which includes the confessional, Inquisition soldiers stormed into the room, from every direction at once. They were all masked, wore white flowing surplices over their cassocks, and carried candles. Quickly, they cordoned off the cellar so that no one could escape. One by one, they shackled the *Conversos*, and dragged them from the underground cellar.

The next day, Queen Isabella watched from the viewing stand the spectacle of Da Silva being dragged in chains through the streets toward the pyre. "I was the one who gave the Inquisition totalitarian power over my subjects," she thought. "Da Silva was the best of all my treasurers and I will truly miss him. I don't think there is any possible way to save his life, for he has been judged a heretic. I can, however, show some compassion for him who served me so well by lessening his suffering. I will ask my chief Inquisitor, Thomas de Torquemada[2] to have him choked to death before he sets fire to the pyre." She commanded a servant to ask Torquemada to stop at the viewing stand before proceeding to the pyre.

"I will agree only to the Queen's request if he swears loyalty to the Church," he exclaimed.

Da Silva refused to consider the demands of the Inquisitor. "Yes, I have lived as a hidden Jew for many years, but now I want to die openly as a Jew!"

Queen Isabella rose from her seat in the viewing stand and followed the condemned man as he was dragged closer and closer to the pyre. "Please confess! Swear by the cross that you will become a true Christian. I promise I will find a way to reinstate you to your honored job as my Secretary of the Treasury!"

"Your Majesty! My fathers died to sanctify the Name of God, and now I am ready to die to sanctify His Name also."

As he reached the pyre, he raised his head heavenward and called out: "*Sh'ma Yisrael Adonay Elohaynu Adonay Echad!*" Hear O Israel! The Lord our God, the Lord is One.[3]

[**Ed.** Da Castilla, who had not been present in that underground cellar, witnessed the tragic death of Da Silva, and was inspired to write the composition which became the melody to Kol Nidrei. His soul stirring music has two sections: the first, describes the *Conversos* as they prayed in that cellar, the second describes the Queen's efforts to convince Da Silva to change his mind. The melody was combined with the words of Kol Nidrei and spread quickly through all the lands of the Diaspora in memory of the *Conversos* of Spain.]

A SACRED TRUST
— COMMENTARY —
TALES OF CONVERSOS

❧

These two stories have both common and separate themes.

The common theme is the struggle of *Conversos* to tenaciously hold on to their beliefs under the most difficult circumstances, struggling with the danger of discovery, hoping all the while for the possibility of being restored the privilege of observing their religion openly.

In the first tale, the diverse theme focuses on the circumstance of a child that had been kidnapped and baptized, but miraculously was returned to his family and faith. It is a lesson of hope for all generations; never to despair that our children, who have, for whatever reason, abandoned Judaism, might one day find their way home.

In the second tale, the theme focuses on Jews being "their brothers' keepers." Dona Gracia, a wealthy Jew, instructs future generations by her example, that saving her brothers and sisters and supporting them with her own personal resources is a *Mitzvah* of paramount importance.

Authors

❧

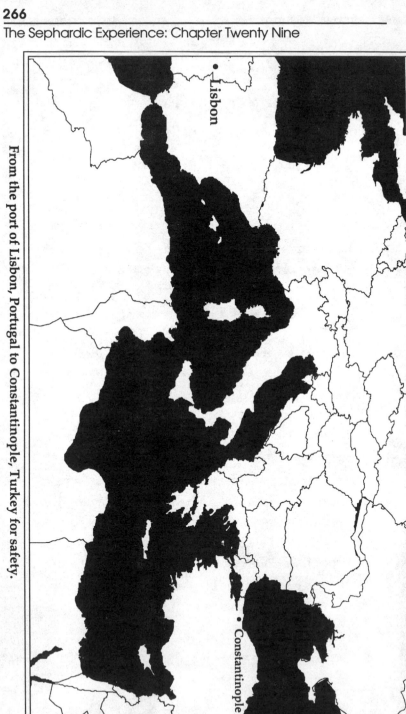

From the port of Lisbon, Portugal to Constantinople, Turkey for safety.

Chapter Twenty Nine

TALES OF CONVERSOS

Time Line

70 c.e.	600 c.e.	1000 c.e.	1400 c.e.	1600 c.e.	1800 c.e.	2000 c.e.

— **Location: Lisbon, Portugal and Constantinople, Turkey** —

[**Ed.** From a letter that was passed down from generation to generation, it is possible to determine the terror under which the Jews, in
general, and the Gracia family, in particular, lived during the Inquisition, that awesome period of time, when they were not permitted to
live in the Iberian peninsula (Spain and Portugal).]

My name is Yosef, the son of Avigdor, the grandson of
Menachem. I am writing this letter as an ethical will with the
instructions that you read it every year on Rosh Hashana. I
want you to thank God for our family being miraculously
delivered from suffering and torment at the hands of the
Inquisition. I worked as a servant in one of the cloisters. On
the eve of Rosh Hashana, the Bishop called me and said:

"Listen to me, my child, you are undoubtedly true to the
Church. I want you to perform a secret mission in order to
prove just how faithful you really are. It is imperative that we
true Christians weed out the heretics from the faithful; you
know, from the Jews that pretend to be Christians but profess
their Judaism in the privacy of their homes. I want you to spy
on the family of Don Gabriel Gracia and watch their every
move. After you have been in his house a while, you will
return to me and tell me everything that you saw there.

"You must be very careful not to divulge the reason for
your being in his house, for after all, he is a very important
and distinguished person in this country. If he should suspect that you are spying, he will report you to the king. The

king will be furious that one of his courtiers is suspect, and he will turn the slanderer over to the Inquisition. If you are tortured, you might implicate me in your confession, so I warn you to be very careful! The reason that I am asking you to do this is because I suspect Don Gabriel is a heretic and I need evidence."

I could not refuse to do the bidding of the Bishop. I also knew that suspected heretics were tortured until they confessed, and then burned at an *auto-de-fe* (publicly, at the stake). I prayed that I would find nothing in the house of Don Gabriel to tell the Bishop.

That evening, I headed for his mansion. It was located in that section of Lisbon where the very wealthy lived. With great trepidation, I approached the gate. The gatekeeper recognized me and admitted me to the study.

"Please wait here," he said. "I will go upstairs and inform my master that you are here."

About an hour later, Don Gabriel descended the long winding staircase, graciously extended his hand to welcome me and said, "Please forgive me for keeping you waiting. I wanted to welcome you to my home in person."

I examined his face carefully. On the surface, he was poised and cheerful, but he bore the wrinkles of a person who had been challenged over and over throughout his lifetime. I wondered why.

He put his arm around me, guided me up the staircase, and we entered a dining room whose table was set elegantly with gold and silver vessels, as if for a very important banquet. He responded to my quizzical expression, "This party is being celebrated in honor of my Father. Of course, you will join us."

I compared the ascetic life I led in the monastery with the luxury in this house. Throughout the meal, my thoughts were in turmoil. I had been sent to spy on this family, to find out if they were heretics, but I didn't want to turn anyone over to the Inquisition.

When the meal ended, and everyone was satiated with the best food and drink, I excused myself. I wanted to find a place to hide on the premises, hoping that I would have nothing to report. I hid near a corner of the big mansion on the outside, in order to have a clear view of their comings and goings. It did not take very long for me to notice a servant prepare the carriage, and Don Gabriel, his father and his son climbed into it. I ran behind the carriage for a while through the very crowded streets. Their progress was very slow. Not wanting to lose sight of them, I finally found an empty carriage that I hired to follow them. They never noticed me behind them.

They drove to the outskirts of the city, instructed the servant to wait for them, and alighted. Slowly, they followed a path, deeper and deeper and deeper into the woods. I was right behind them. When they stopped, I sought refuge behind a broad branched tree with a thick trunk. I was curious. Why had these people feasted and then come to the forest?

I waited patiently, my pulse beating faster and faster. What were they doing? What would I tell the Bishop? Would I be able to relate their suspicious actions in order that suspicion not fall upon me?

Within the hour, the group of people had grown. I thought, that from the distance, I even recognized one of them to be Don Pedro, the treasurer to General Benedict. The people sat on small piles of twigs and tree branches. They removed small books from their pockets, and began to mumble and shake fervently. After a while, Don Gabriel Gracia stood, removed the horn of a ram, the type that shepherds use, from a package he had been carrying under his arm. Don Pedro signalled to him.

My eyes opened wide. I could not believe what they were about to do! Suddenly, Don Gabriel started to blow the horn. I started to shake, I screamed, and then, I must have fainted, for the next thing I knew, I opened my eyes while lying on a bed in Don Gabriel Gracia's mansion. Doctors hovered over me. Don Gabriel touched my shoulder compassionately. I lowered my eyes, embarrassed, for I recognized how much kindness he had shown me. Ironically, I had been ordered by the bishop to find evidence that would implicate him in the eyes of the Inquisition.

Finally, Don Gabriel spoke. "Last night we went out into the forest, as far away as possible from the eyes and ears of the Inquisition. We went in order to sound the *shofar* (ram's horn) in honor of Rosh Hashana, in honor of our Father, Creator of the world. Even though we act as Christians, we are observant of as much of Judaism as possible under these conditions. We did not know that we had been followed until we heard your screams. We were frightened, but decided to continue sounding the *shofar* the required number of times, knowing that we might be arrested, understanding that if we were to die, we wanted to die performing a *mitzvah*. So we finished sounding the *shofar*, turned to go, and tripped over your fallen body.

"Don Pedro recognized you as the Bishop's servant from the cloister. He was convinced that we should kill you in order to save ourselves. I restrained him because there was something about you that was very familiar. I suspected from the anguish I detected on your face that you were not in the cloister on your own free will, but perhaps you had been kidnapped.

"We carried you back to the carriage and to my house, and I called my personal physician, Don Luis, to attend to you. When he removed your clothes, it was my turn to scream. I had a son who had been kidnapped by the Church. He was very young at the time, and I never thought I would see him again. Besides being obvious that you are a Jewish man, you have a birthmark on your chest that I recognized. You are my son Yoseph."

Tears streamed down my cheeks as we embraced. For a long time, neither one of us could speak, but our eyes revealed the intensity of our pain. That night, we decided to flee from the lands of the Inquisition.

❊ ❊ ❊ ❊ ❊

[**Ed.** We cannot positively ascertain if the family in the next story is the same Gracia family. However, the circumstances of their escape and the saga of how they rebuilt their lives are similar.]

Her Hebrew name was Channa, and she was born in Lisbon, Portugal, fourteen years after the expulsion of the Jews from that country. Her family was wealthy and distinguished; her elder brother was a physician at the royal court and he taught medicine at the university.

The family was *Converso*, secret Jews who publicly professed Christianity.

[**Ed.** *Converso* is Latin for having been forcibly converted to another faith. Two other terms have the same connotation: *Marranos* is Spanish for "he who mars true faith," or "pigs," and *Anusim*, which is Hebrew for forced conversion.]

Eventually, the family fled and returned to Judaism, becoming ardent supporters of Jewish life in Moslem ruled lands and in *Eretz Yisrael* (The Holy Land). But when we first meet the family of *"La Senora"* as she was known, they are hiding in Lisbon from the Inquisition.

While still living in Lisbon, Beatrice de Luna[1] (Channa, Dona Gracia), daughter of the Nasi family, married Francisco (Tzemach) Mendez, son of the aristocratic, wealthy Benveniste family, also *conversos*, who were renown international bankers and gem merchants. Their only child was Reyna (Malka). Dona Gracia raised two nephews, Joao Micas (Joseph) and Samuel and adopted them. Joseph later became her son-in-law and the public figure for the family business which she controlled from behind the scenes.

Widowed at the age of twenty-six, Dona Gracia plotted the family's escape from Portugal via England to Antwerp, succeeding in taking her wealth with her. Because there were many other *conversos* living there, she thought that she would be able to return openly to the observance of Judaism, which she loved and longed for with all her heart. But she was still not able to remove her Christian disguise, and resume her life as a Jew, because Emperor Charles V was envious of her great fortune. He plotted to confiscate all her property and accuse her of being a heretic. It took her two years to satisfy the Emperor through bribes and loans, and then she fled, with her family, to Venice where they thought they would be safe, but this was not the case.

Meanwhile, nephew Joseph appealed to Sultan Suleimein, ruler of the Ottoman/Turkish Empire, to become involved in liberating the family from Christian Europe, and welcome them to his country. After eleven years of flight, Dona Gracia Mendez reached Constantinople, removed her Christian disguise, and returned to the religion into which she was born.

She acquired a palace called Belvedere, located on the Bosphorus, (Constantinople) and from there she directed her family's financial affairs. As difficult and dangerous her disguise during her early life, so was her total commitment to Judaism once she reached safety.

Belvedere became the center of Jewish affairs. She daily served dinner to eighty poor Jews. She organized and supported the *yeshiva* of Rabbi Joseph ibn Levy as well as synagogues and other charitable institutions both in Constantinople and in Salonika. Through her connection with the good offices of the Sultan, she aided the redemption of many other *Conversos,* helping them resettle in countries not hostile to Jews so that they, too, could return to their faith. She was so successful in this endeavor, that many of the Jews she helped were able to transfer their wealth to their new countries.

When news reached her that Pope Paul IV had arrested the *conversos* who had been hiding in the Italian city of Ancona, with the purpose of turning them over to the Inquisition to be burned at the stake, she asked the Sultan to put pressure on the Pope to release the Jews. The Sultan hinted to the Pope that reprisals against Christians living in Constantinople would be made unless he ordered the release of the Jews he held prisoners. Dona Gracia organized a boycott of the port of Ancona, and shifted much business to the port of Pesaro. Eventually, the Pope freed only those Jews who were Turkish citizens who had been in Italy on business matters.

Her most important project was leasing the city of Tiberias in *Eretz Yisrael*, from the Sultan for 1,000 ducats a year for the purpose of rebuilding it as a home for the *conversos* who settled there after their escape. Plans were laid for a new defensive wall, for a new bath at the hot springs, for the creation of a textile center which would use the silk spun by silkworms and the wool of sheep grazing in the surrounding field, and a printing press. These industries provided a livelihood for the many refugees who returned "home."

By our standards, she was very young when she died, only 59 years old. The news of *La Senora's* death was received all over the Jewish world with a sense of the profoundest grief, for she was truly a role model of kindness and love. The poet Samuel Usque compared her attributes to the illustrious women who preceded her; she had the compassion and piety of Miriam, the wisdom and governing ability of Devorah, the holiness and virtue of Esther: [2]

> "The noble princess, the glory of Israel, the wise woman who built her house in holiness and purity, with her hand sustains the poor and needy ... many are they whom she has rescued from languishing in a dungeon ready for death ... and led them into safe places ... she has founded houses where all may learn the law of God..."

A Sacred Trust
— Commentary —
Sailing with Columbus

۶ۢ

Judaism is a portable faith. For thousands of years, though deprived of a land of their own, Jews managed to establish and develop Judaism in the midst of their wandering.

This remarkable diary tells of a Jew who sailed with Columbus. In the middle of the journey his Judaism finds expression. As he spots land, uppermost in his mind is that this at last might be a place where one can be freely and fully Jewish.

As the plaintive notes of his Kol Nidre prayer rise up, we can hear the remarkable song of the Jewish spirit over the centuries, a spirit that would sing in every land of our exile; for while Jewish hearts were turned towards Zion, until they could return they held fast to a faith that would comfort and uplift them wherever they might be.

Rabbi David J. Wolpe,
Author of "The Healer of Shattered Hearts"
and "Teaching Your Children About God"

۶ۢ

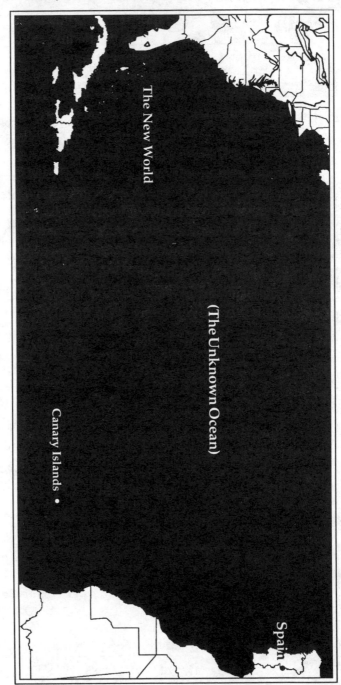

The New World

(The Unknown Ocean)

Canary Islands •

Spain

Conversos sailed with Columbus on the final day of the Expusion Decree in 1492.

Chapter Thirty
SAILING WITH COLUMBUS

Time Line

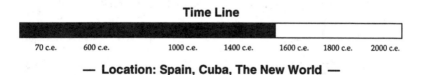

| 70 c.e. | 600 c.e. | 1000 c.e. | 1400 c.e. | 1600 c.e. | 1800 c.e. | 2000 c.e. |

— **Location: Spain, Cuba, The New World** —

[**Ed.** This is an entry in the diary of Yosef ben HaLayve Haivri, (the Jew) known as Luis de Torres, written in Cuba, in the New World, on the land awarded to him by His Majesty, thirty-one years after Christopher Columbus discovered the Indies, (1523), on the occasion of his seventy-first birthday.]

I was born in Cordova, Andalusia, Spain. The details of how my people lived have already been recorded, both their illustrious contributions to this country during the Golden Age, and the tremendous suffering imposed upon them after the Christian reconquest and the Inquisition. My father was a scribe who was privileged to write a Torah scroll during his lifetime. I was also educated to be a scribe, always surrounded by Hebrew books, manuscripts, and Torah commentaries.

I was fluent in the Hebrew language and therefore, I was invited to accompany Christopher Columbus on his voyage of discovery as an interpreter. He thought, that when he would reach China and the Far East, he would locate the exiled Jews from the Ten Lost Tribes, and he wanted me to be able to communicate with them.

The three ships, the Santa Maria, the Nina, and the Pinta sailed many days and nights until we sighted dry land. According to my calculations, we arrived on Friday afternoon, two hours after mid-day, which, on the Jewish calendar was Hoshana Raba, twenty-one days in the month of Tishrei, in the year 5253 after Creation.

[**Ed.** Hoshana Raba is the additional name given to the seventh day of Succot. On this day, worshippers solemnly circle the synagogue seven times, in procession with the *etrog* and *lulav*, for it marks the day when the final verdict of forgiveness is sealed following Yom Kippur. After the seventh procession, a bundle of willow branches is beaten on the ground five times.]

Because the memory is so vivid, I am completely recording every detail as a chronicle for all future generations.

That fateful day, the day of our expulsion from Spain was *Tisha B'Av* on the Jewish calendar in the year 5252.[1] That day marked the tragedy of the destruction of both Holy Temples many centuries before, and now, one more tragic event was added to that mournful day. Three hundred thousand people, descended to the Mediterranean Shore, searching for passage to a new land where they could openly practice Judaism.

I was among them. However, I was not a refugee. I had been commissioned to join Christopher Columbus' voyage of discovery. I hoped that if we found Jewish brethren, I would be able to live my life in peace and in freedom. Don Rodriguez, his uncle Don Gabriel Sanchez, Alonso de Loquir, Rodrigo de Triana, Chon Kabrera, Doctor Birenal, and Doctor Marko all agreed with me and joined. Except for Rodrigo, they sailed on the other ships. We were *Conversos*, living in perpetual fear of the Inquisition, hoping that we would find a way out of our precarious situation.

We sailed for seventy-two days Most of of the time the ocean was serene and the trade winds blew gently from east to west. Usually, Columbus pored over the navigational diagrams prepared by Rabbi Avraham Zacuto, an astronomer and historian, who fled from Spain to Portugal when the Jews were expelled. Some of the time, the ocean churned, heavy with storm and waves. We feared we would capsize, and drown in the depths. On those frightful nights, Columbus stood on deck, his eyes searching for the stars that darted in between the cumulonimbus clouds, watching for the appearance of the North Star to measure navigational latitude. He was determined to sail until he reached land, and his rallying call was, "*Adelante!* (sail on!)"

We sailed through the month of September, marking the Holy Days of Rosh Hashana among ourselves. On the eve of Yom Kippur, which occurred on Sunday night that year, we sighted a magnificent sight; covered with lush, rich foliage, a sandbank floated in the middle of the ocean. It was our last sighting of land; we had a backwards glimpse of the Canary Islands.

The ocean was calm. Toward nightfall, I wrapped myself in my *tallit*, went up on the deck, and chanted the "*Kol Nidrei.*" Voices from the Pinta and the Nina echoed across the water and joined me in prayer. It seemed that the waves responded in rhythm to the sound of our voices.

When I finished, Columbus called me over to his side. "Isn't the dove one of the symbols of the Jewish people?" he queried, "You know that my family name, Colombo, also means dove. There must be a reason for this voyage. We are not sailing on this ship in vain! Let me read to you what I wrote here:

> And it came to pass on the day that the Jewish people were expelled from Spain at the hands of his majesty King Ferdinand ... on that day the power was given to me to go forth to search new paths across this dark and fearsome ocean to a new world.

We sat quietly, side by side, until the rays of the eastern light silvered the horizon.

Eleven days later, we noticed the first signs that land was not far distant. Sea swallows, long pointed wings and forked tails, swooped gracefully overhead, plunging headlong into the water to catch small fish.

I noticed that slender branches with leaves that were narrow, oval shaped, tapering to a point floated in the water, and washing up to our ship. I was able to reach one, and when I pulled it from the water, I discovered that I was holding a willow branch. I was overcome with joy.

"It's a miracle, it's a miracle," I shouted. "In this new place, God had provided me with the willow branch so that I might fulfill the *mitzvah* of *Hoshana Raba*." I waved it enthusiastically toward the Pinta. Alonso de Loquir responded by waving his own willow branch back.

That night, the night of *Hoshana Raba,* all the sailors slept peacefully. The crescent of the moon sparkled gloriously on the water while I sat all night with Rodrigo de Triana reciting *Tehillim* (Psalms), from a Spanish translation, as is our custom. We read together by the light of the moon:

O give thanks unto the Lord, for He is good,

For His mercy endureth for ever.

So let the redeemed of the Lord say,

Whom He has redeemed from the hand of the adversary ...

Then were they glad because they were quiet,

And He led them unto their desired haven.[2]

We beseech You, O Lord, save (us) now, Hoshana![3]

With the first flickering light, we who had been awake all night, were the first ones to see land. It was not a dream! It was not a vision! Rodrigo ran to alert Columbus. The excitement and the hysterical screams awakened all the sailors on our ship and on the other two ships. They began to sing and dance to a new song: "Land! Land! Land!"

We disembarked on the beach at Fernandez Bay, San Salvador, and took possession of a New World for Spain. Columbus always believed that this island, and the other ones he sighted later on this voyage of discovery were the Indies, near Japan or China.

And I, Yosef ben HaLayve Haivri, sang with my friends, with Alonso de Loquir, Chon Kabrera, Rodrigo de Triana, Don Rodriguez, Don Gabirel Sanchez, Doctor Birenal, and Doctor Marko a different song, a song of thanksgiving to God for leading us to a place where we might publicly acknowledge our Judasim.

A Sacred Trust
— Commentary —
The Question of "Why?"

This story is meant to provide consolation to the bereaved who ask the eternal question, "Why?" But in me it provokes an entirely different reaction. First, with regard to grief, can women like Rachel move from the agony of a husband's or a child's death to acceptance in the space of a year or two? Is it proper to circumscribe a person's need to express grief or mourning? Does the tendency of the story to demand of Rachel that she suppress honest feelings with simplistic notions of happiness and balance not present a serious problem?

Second, does the concept that everything in the world happens by divine plan render human beings powerless to change their fate? When Job spoke his outrage to God, that the just and the wicked were subject to the same fate, I was offended that God answered Job with a series of questions: What do you know of My secrets, to dare to question My means? My ends? What do you do you know about justice and the way I choose to dispense it? Much as I admired Job's rebellion, I was deeply troubled by his hasty abdication. Like Rachel, Job appeared to me more dignified when he was grief-stricken than after he rebuilt his life under the guise of his newly-found faith in divine mercy.

Third, would a Jewish feminist resent Avraham's injunction to Rachel that, now that he has answered her questions, she must rejoice with her children and with the pleasures of life in the physical world? What pleasures? How, exactly, was Rachel to rejoice when Avraham left her alone to feed a family on almost nonexistent means? Our story reminded me of Y.L. Peretz's critique of women's inferior position in the hierarchy of the 19th-century Eastern European shtetl, wherein she was a prime repository of social injustice. While our story has earlier kabbalistic undertones, such as the husband's mission to return to heaven to head the Yeshiva of the Eternal World, shtetl husbands had real-life opportunities for study, participation in religious affairs and synagogue life. Though it is true that men had to work long and hard to bring in what little sustenance they could, yet, unlike their wives, they could find respite from their toil in loftier outlets. Do the answers to Rachel's "Whys" provide the consolation that is intended? For me, personally, the story elicited more questions than answers.

Carol Diament, Ph.D,
Director, National Jewish Education Department of Hadassah
Author of "Jewish Marital Status

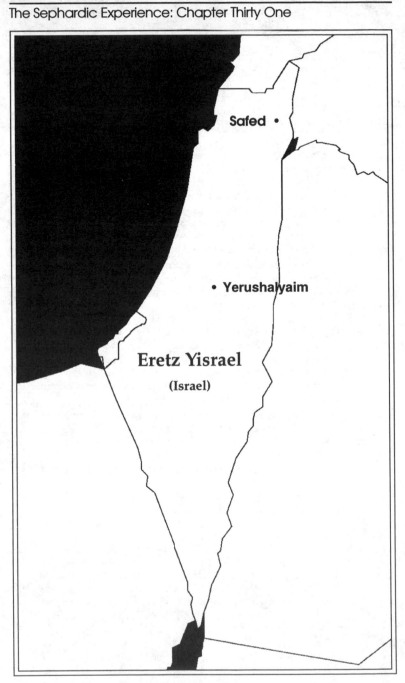

Safed in Eretz Yisrael

Chapter Thirty One
THE QUESTION OF "WHY?"

Time Line

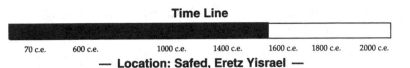

| 70 c.e. | 600 c.e. | 1000 c.e. | 1400 c.e. | 1600 c.e. | 1800 c.e. | 2000 c.e. |

— Location: Safed, Eretz Yisrael —

[**Ed.** According to our tradition, the *Zohar*, the book of mysticism describing the secrets of Torah, was written by Rabbi Shimon bar Yochai while he hid in a cave for thirteen years. He fled from the Romans, who had sentenced him to death, and remained hidden until a new, more kindly disposed emperor replaced Hadrian and revoked the death decree. We can not accurately trace the transmission of the *Zohar* for the next thousand years, until it reappeared again in Spain in the writings of Rabbi Moshe de Leon. Then, due to social tension, anxiety, insecurity and the horrors of the expulsion, Jews began looking for answers. The development of Lurianic[1] *Kabbalah* (Jewish mysticism) flourished in Safed (a town in *Eretz Yisrael)* in the middle of the sixteenth century and illustrated that we only know part of the answers.]

Yosef walked briskly from the synagogue toward his mother's house. He stopped there each week to wish her Shabbat Shalom before joining his own family.

Her house sparkled radiantly and peacefully; candlelight glowed, spreading its warmth and hauntingly beautiful shadows throughout. The reflection of the little flames cast their shadow on the side wall and slowly ascended.

The empty chair at the head of the table indicated his father's passing two years before. Only his mother Rachel's sobs shattered the calm. Her tears dropped unto the pages of the *Tehillim* (Psalms) she held lovingly in her hands, soaking the pages. She smiled wanly amidst her pain, responding to his greeting with but a nod of her head and a mumbling sound, unable to control her sobs. *"Shabbat Shalom,"* she choked, as the words blurted out.

"You have to stop, mother! You cannot continue to cry. It's two years already! You know that you are not permitted to cry on Shabbat."

"I know you are right, but today is the second anniversary of his death, so how can I refrain from crying?"

"I can understand your intense grief tonight, but how do you explain your crying yesterday, and the day before, and the day before that? Forgive me, please, for speaking to you so harshly, but you must know, you must believe that father is resting peacefully in the Eternal World. He certainly cannot be pleased that you have not stopped mourning for him. *There is a time to cry, and a time to stop, a time to mourn, and a time to dance...*[2] By not stopping, you are declaring that you do not agree with God's plan for the world!"

"You are right, Yosef," whispered his mother, "I will try harder to control my thoughts and my tears."

Instantaneously, the sobbing resumed, the younger children watching silently as Yosef left the house with 'Shabbat Shalom' on his lips.

David, the second oldest recited the *kiddush* and valiantly attempted to add cheer to the Shabbat meal. Rachel breathed deeply, slowly, involved herself in eating the meal she had prepared and the songs and Torah study which her children shared. By the time they went to sleep, she felt calmer.

She thought about other young widows that had readjusted their lives. Then she recalled how her parents had arranged for her to marry Avraham; she trembled as the memories of their life together flashed before her. Finally, she fell into a deep sleep and dreamed ....

Throngs of people were running, beckoning her to follow them. She pulled herself up from the bed, ran towards the people. "I must follow them, I must follow them!" she mumbled. "Look, their destination seems to be the outskirts of the city. What a wonderful sight! I have never seen anything so majestic!"

Rays of sunlight sparkled across the horizon, revealing the crowns of lush verdant trees against a creamy blue sky. Fluffy clouds hovered overhead, suspended, moving gently. The wind whispered through her hair. Covering the ground, bright flowers lifted their petals to drink the sunlight; she deeply inhaled the sweet fragrance in the air that surrounded her like exotic perfume. Underground geysers shot forcefully skyward.

Suddenly, an old man, dressed in a loosely fitted white linen garment, with a long flowing white beard darted into her view. He approached her and spoke softly: "Do you want to see Avraham?"

Without waiting for a reply, he said: "Follow me!"

The old man led her to a clearing in the garden. Trembling, she focused her eyes on an amazing sight in the distance, on the teacher who stood in front of his students. Everything was hazy.

She perceived the students sitting in a semi-circle, in rows like the spokes of half a wheel, in order that each one could see his neighbor. Two scribes stood in front of them, one on the right side and one on the left side, to transcribe the lesson.[3]

"Those students are sitting the same way students sat in the ancient Sanhedrin," she choked. "That teacher seems too young to instruct such a scholarly looking group," she thought. She peered more intently at the teacher. Recognizing Avraham, she screamed his name and fainted.

When she came to, the old man interrupted her reverie. "Wait a few minutes. He will be finished teaching his class shortly, and then you will be able to talk to him. You can sit here on the ground."

The students rose and disappeared. Avraham walked toward her and when he reached her side, he sat down beside her. "I have so many questions to ask you," she began. "First, tell me why you left me alone at such a young age?"

"I want you to know," he responded slowly, "that in the world in which you live, people fulfill their mission, the reason for their creation. The world in which I live now is the Eternal World, the World of Truth. Many years before I met you, I was a great scholar, but I never took time from my studies and communal responsibilities to marry, to raise children and to support a family. When I died, I was appointed to head this yeshiva of the Eternal World. I held this position until the Heavenly Court investigated my background. When it found out that I had never married, I was returned to the physical world until I fulfilled my mission. In order to support my family, I became a businessman. After the birth of our seventh child, it was judged that I could return to the World of Truth."

"I never knew that you were such a great scholar," Rachel whispered.

Avraham replied: "In the physical world, I had other priorities, the sustenance of my family was of paramount importance. You mentioned that you had many questions. What else would you like to know?"

"Our son Yosef works so hard to earn a meager livelihood from the successful business that you left him. Why must he work so hard?"

"Do you remember the *Din Torah* (a disputation adjudicated by a religious court) between Yosef and another Jew? Even though the court found in his favor, his opponent suffered much mental pain, unnecessarily, because the matter should have been resolved between the two of them. It should never have been brought into the court. Yosef is working off the pain he caused a fellow Jew. The sentence was imposed upon him for a period of four years. He has one more year before he completes his sentence and then he will become successful."

"And our son David is already past marriageable age. He is twenty-four and the matchmakers don't even bring me appropriate proposals. And even if they did, I don't have enough money to provide a wedding for him!"

Avraham smiled. "The reason for you not receiving proposals of marriage for our son David is because his soulmate is still too young for marriage. Besides she lives in another country. In five more years, she will arrive in your city and bring with her a substantial dowry. The newlyweds will have everything they need to set up a home."

Rachel trembled. She hesitated to ask her last question for the memory of that incident still filled her with grief. "Why was our youngest murdered by a drunk?"

"I think you understand by now, that everything that happens in the world happens by Divine Plan. Man, living in the physical world, can not understand, nor does he seek to understand.

"Our youngest son was originally born into a distinguished and noble family. During an uprising, most of the Jews of the particular city where he lived were murdered. Only a few babies were hidden and saved. A gentile woman cared for them for six months, until she found surviving relatives to whom to turn them over. He became a leader of his generation and when he died, the Heavenly Court decreed that he should be reborn and live with a Jewish mother to make up for the time he spent with the righteous gentile who saved his life. When a short time passed, he opted to be the sacrificial offering in order to save his entire city, for the Jews once again had become scapegoats.

"Now, I think I've answered all your questions. I want you to remember that the Creator creates only good. Humans look with thwarted vision; they cannot comprehend nor envision the complete picture. Before I leave you, I want you to promise me that you will stop mourning for me. Rejoice with our children and with the pleasures of life in the physical world!"

He disappeared from her dream.

Startled, she awoke, rubbed her eyes, looked around at all the familiar sites in her bedroom, and, still laying in her bed, realized that she had been dreaming. She rose, washed her hands, walked over to her chair and sat quietly, thinking over what she had dreamed. She watched the rays of dawn dissipate the darkness of the night.

Her children awakened to find her still sitting in her chair, much calmer and more peaceful than they had seen her during the past two years. She spoke softly, tenderly: "I dreamed about your father, of blessed memory. He told me that it was time to stop mourning, that it was time to rejoice with you, that it was time to enjoy the pleasures of the physical world." She hesitated before she said: "And to show him that I heard him, I will go to the synagogue this morning instead of staying home by myself and mourning."

❖ ❖ ❖ ❖ ❖

Sources,
Further Readings
and Footnootes

— The Talmudic and —
— Post-Talmudic Period —

Introduction to Part One

1 Talmud Bavli, Baba Kamma 113b.
2 Talmud Bavli, Gittin 62a.

Chapter One: R. Yochanan
Source: Talmud Bavli , Gittin 56a.

Chapter Two: Rachel & Akiva

Source: Talmud Bavli, Nedarim 50a.
1 Talmud Yerushalmi, Shabbat 6:1
2 Talmud Bavli, Yevamot, 62b.
3 Talmud Bavli, Shabbat 59b.

Chapter Three: Beruriah

Source: Talmud
1 Talmud Bavli, Pesachim 62b.
2 Tehillim, Psalms 104:35
3 Talmud Bavli, Berachot 6a.
4 Avot 1:5
5 Talmud Bavli, Eruvin 53a.
6 II Shmuel, Samuel 23:5
7 Talmud Bavli, Eruvin 53b-54a.
8 Tosefta Kelim, Talmud Bavli, Baba Kama 4:9, found at the end of Tractate Nida.
9 Talmud Bavli, Kiddushin 80b.
10 Job 1:21
11 Mishlei, Proverbs 31:10, and Midrash Agaddah.

Chapter Four

Source: Midrash Ayleh Ezkerah,
Bamberger & Wahrmann,
Yerushalayim., 1938.
1 Hadrian ruled 117-138 C.E.
2 Yaakov Katz, Yisroel V'Ha-a-mim, Volume I, Tel Aviv, Dvir Publishing Co., 1962.
3 The Roman governors were Lulianus and Turnus Rufus. ArtScroll Machzor, Yom Kippur.
4 Sh'mot, Exodus 21:6
5 Devarim, Deuteronomy 6:5
6 Talmud Bavli, Berachot 61b.
7 Talmud Bavli, Avodah Zarah 18a.
8 The name of Rabbi Chutzpit is mentioned in Talmud Bavli Berachot 27b.
9 Talmud Bavli, Pesachim 50a: "They occupy such an exalted position in the next world ... (commentary)."
10 Tehillim, Psalms 95:1
11 B'rayshit, Genesis 2:3
12 Tehillim, Psalms 31:20
13 Talmud Bavli, Sanhedrin 14a.

Chapter Five: Yeuda & Antonius

Sources: Talmud Bavli, Avodah Zarah 10b, Tosefot
Yaakov Katz, Yisrael V'Haamin, Vol. I, Tel Aviv, D'vir Publishing Co., 1962.
1 Kohelet, Ecclesiastes 1:5, Talmud Bavli, Kiddushin 72b.
2 Talmud Bavli, Pesachim 37b, Yevamot 48a, Menachot 32b.
3 Talmud Bavli, Gitin 59a.
4 Marcus Aurelius Antoninus, 121-180 C.E.

Chapter Six: Rav

Sources: Seder Hadorot Hashalem, Rabbi Yerucham Mayer Layner, editor, Warsaw, Poland, 1901. Reprinted by his grandson, New York, 1985.

Rav Sherira Gaon, The Iggeret of Rav Sherira Gaon, Rabbi Natan Dovid Rabinowich, editor, Yerushalayim,

Moznaim Press, 1988.

1   Talmud Bavli, Niddah 24b.

2   Talmud Bavli, Berachot 47a, Yevamot 57b (Rashi), Shabbat 53a and many other Talmudic sources.

3   Talmud Bavli, Chulin 137b.

4   Talmud Bavli, Megilah 29a.

5   Mishlei, Proverbs 2:20

6   Devarim, Deuteronomy 6:18; Talmud Bavli, Bava Metzia 83a.

7   Vayikra, Leviticus 19:15

8   Talmud Bavli, Avodah Zara 10b.

9   I Shmuel, Samuel 2:7

10   Talmud Bavli, Berachot 20a, Taanit 24b.

11   Talmud Bavli, Berachot 16b.

12   Talmud Yerushalmi

13   Talmud Bavli, Baytzah 32b.

14   Talmud Bavli, Kiddushin 41a.

Chapter Seven: Bustenai

Sources: Rabbi Yehuda Layb HaKohen Fishman, Saray Hamayah, Volume V, Yerushalayim, Mossad HaRav Kook, 1947.

S.D. Goiten, Jews and Arabs: Their Contacts through the Ages, New York, Schocken Books, 1955.

Dr. Marcus Lehman, Five Novelettes, New York, Merkos L'Inyonei Chinuch, 1964.

1   Rabbi Benjamin Tudela. The Itinerary of Benjamin of Tudela, edited by Signer, Adler, and Asher, Joseph Simon Publishers.

Chapter Eight: Wheel of Fortune

Sources: For Biography

Rav Sherira Gaon, The Iggeret of Rav Sherira Gaon, Rabbi Natan Dovid Rabinowich, editor, Brooklyn and Yerushalayim, Moznaim Press, 1988.

Rabbi Mattis Kantor, The Jewish Time Line Encyclopedia, Northvale, N.J., Jason Aronson, Inc., 1989.

Source: For Story

Aharon Swirsky, Zuto Shel Nahar, Yerushalayim, Mashavim Press, 1983.

1   Tehillim, Psalms 75:8

Chapter Nine: Four Captives

Sources: Yitzchak Isaac HaLevi, Dorot HaRishonim, Vol. VI, Pressberg, 1897. Reprinted in Israel.

Abraham ben David HaLayvi ibn Daud, The Book of Tradition: An Authoritative History of Spanish Jewry.

Franz Kobler, Letters of the Jews Through the Ages: a Self Portrait, Two Volumes. New York, East and West Library (Subsidiary of Hebrew Publishing Co.), 1952.

— The Medieval Period —

Chapter Ten: Rabaynu Gershom

Source: Dr. Marcus Lehman, Meor Hagolah, Five Novelletes, Brooklyn, New York, Merkos L'Inyonei Chinuch, Inc., 1964.

1   B'rayshit, Genesis 16:2

2   Do not pretend to consult with witches or wizards, Vayikra, Leviticus 19:31

Chapter Eleven: The Jewish Pope

Sources: Y.L. Baruch, Sayfer Hamoadim: Rosh Hashana V'Yom Kippur, Vol. I, The Oneg Shabbat (Ohel Shem) Society, Tel Aviv, Dvir Publishing Co., 1952.

Avraham Grossman, Chachmei Ashkenaz Harishonim, Yerushalayim, Magnes Library Press of Hebrew University, 1981.

Raphael Halpern, Etz Chaim, Tel Aviv, Hakodash Ruach Yaakov Press, 1978.

Ahron Jellinek, Bayt Hamidrash,

Yerushalayim, Bamberger & Wahrman Publishing Co., 1938.

Yisroel Klapholtz, Hachozrim B'Teshuvah, Bnai Brak, Hotzaat Pa'er Hasayfer, 1981.

Dr. Marcus Lehman, (Ben Zion Tabak, Editor), Elchanan, The Jewish Pope, New York, The Board of Jewish Education, 1953.

David Lerner, The Enduring Legend of The Jewish Pope. (From a senior honors thesis written for a class in Jewish folklore at Harvard University.) Subsequently published in Judaism Quarterly.

AUTHOR'S NOTE

From a compilation of all the above sources, four versions of this story are extant:

a) Rabbi Shimon Hagadol discovers his son by his completing the verse of the piyyut.

b) Elchanan had a peculiar birthmark which his father recognized.

c) Rabbi Shimon had taught Elchanan a special chess move. They studied together before they recognized each other. They relaxed over a chess board. When Elchanan moved his chess piece in that special way, his father realized that it was only his son who could have known that move.

d) Elchanan, Rachel, and their many children lived thereafter together in Mainz. Elchanan followed in his father's footsteps as a Torah scholar and leader of his generation.

Chapter Twelve: I Will Die a Jew

Sources: Elyahu Ki Tov, Sayfer Hatodaah, Yerushalayim: Yeshurun Publishers, 1966.

Avraham Grossman, Chachmei Ashkenaz Hareshonim, Yerushalayim, Hebrew University Press (Y.L. Magnes), 1981.

Rafael Halperin, Atlas Etz Chaim, Tel Aviv, Hakadush Ruach Yaakov, 1978.

This version of the story was published in Labovitz and Labovitz, A Touch of Heaven, New Jersey, Jason Aronson, 1990.

[1] "Relatively secure" means that the fate of Jewish communities during the Middle Ages depended upon the whim of either the feudal lord or the bishop.

[2] During the Middle Ages, leaders of the Catholic church preached that Christianity is the true religion. Priests and feudal masters, seeking to attain salvation for their Jewish subjects, tortured and forcefully converted them to Christianity.

[3] Machzor: High Holiday Prayer Book.

Chapter Thirteen: Tales of Rashi

Sources: Rabbi Zechariah Fendel, Challenge at Sinai, New York, Rabbi Jacob Joseph School Press, 1978.

N.Z. Safrai, Rashi U'Baaley Tosafot, Yerushalayim, Hozaat Hemesorah, 1990.

Chumash Bayt Yehuda Hashalem: B'Rayshit, "Toldot Rashi," New York, Hozaat Orah, 1954 This book is a collection of Yiddish commentaries on the Torah. There is no single author.

The commentaries of RASHI (RABBI SHLOMO BEN YITZCHAK, 1040-1105) were distributed quickly throughout the diaspora. It was the first printed book that was published by Rabbi Avraham ben Gershon, in Reggio, Kalbreya, Italy, in Adar (February/March, 1475). In order to tell the difference between the letters of the Torah and the letters of Rashi's commentaries, the printers used a variation that is thinner.

[1] II Melachim, II Kings 1:8

[2] B'rayshit, Genesis 29:26. Laban promised his younger daughter Rachel to Jacob, but he substituted Leah, his eldest. Jacob had to work another seven years for Rachel.

[3] Avot 4:27

Chapter Fifteen: York

Source: Z. Ariel, Geborim U'Kedoshim

Press, 1961, Tel Aviv, Yosef Shreberk.
1   March 17, 1190.
2   Tehillim, Psalms 20:8

Chapter Sixteen: Rabbi Mayer's Letter

Sources: Dr. Irving A. Agus, Rabbi
    Mayer of Rothenburg (Two Volumes):
    His Life and His Works as Sources for
    the Religious, Legal, and Social History
    of the Jews of Germany in the
    Thirteenth Century, Philadelphia, The
    Dropsie College for Hebrew and
    Cognate Learning, (Press of the Jewish
    Publication Society), 1947.
Rabbi Mattis Kantor, The Jewish Time
    Line Encyclopedia, Northvale, New
    Jersey, Jason Aronson, Inc., 1989.
Dr. Marcus Lehman. Five Novelettes.
    Brooklyn, New York. Merkos L'Inyonei
    Chinuch.1964.
Ephraim A. Orbach, Baaley Tosafot (Two
    Volumes), Yerushalayim, Bialik
    Institute, 1980.
MAHARAM, Rabbi Mayer ben Baruch
    (Rothenburg)
In a letter that the Maharam wrote to
the Rosh (Rabbi Asher ben Yechiel,
his foremost disciple) from Ensisheim
Fortress where he was imprisoned,
dated 1290, in answer to a responsum:
"... In this place of wilderness I do not
possess Tosafot to (Tractate) Gittin
(supplements to Rashi's commentary
on the Talmudic tractate dealing with
the laws of divorce) nor works on
ritual, and, therefore I am putting
down all these words just as I have
been inspired by Heaven.... For what
can a man know who dwells under
the shadow of death, and has lacked
all the amenities of life for three years
and six months, who has been for-
saken in affliction by all good men, a
trodden threshold which was once
called Mayer son of Baruch?"

Quoted in Franz Kobler, Letters of Jews
    Through the Ages (Two Volumes): A
    Self-Portrait of the Jewish People, New
    York, East and West Library
    (Subsidiary of Hebrew Publishing Co.)
    1952.

1   Between 1283 and 1286.
2   Hapsburg, 1218-1291.
3   June 28, 1286.
4   Talmud Bavli, Gitin 45a. Other Tal-
    mudic opinions conflict with the
    proof text that Rabbi Mayer chose
    to discourage the Jewish commu-
    nity from ransoming him, because
    he knew that the appetite of Em-
    peror Rudolf was without bounds.
    Another Talmudic statement
    teaches: "Rabbi Eleazar ben
    Azaryah says, the saving of life su-
    persedes the Shabbat." Talmud
    Bavli 132a.
5   April 27, 1293.

Chapter Seventeen: The Blood Libel

Sources: Menachem Mendel, Otzar
HaChag: Pesach, Yerushalayim, 1984.
1   Even before the formation of com-
    pulsory ghettos in Venice, 1516, Jews
    voluntarily lived in secluded quar-
    ters, for security. The Jewish com-
    munity of Offenbach, near
    Bachrach, is mentioned in the list of
    communities whose members were
    martyred at the time of the Black
    Death persecutions in 1348.
2   Raphael Halpern, Atlas Etz Chaim,
    Tel Aviv, Ruach Yaakov Press, 1978
3   Avot 1:4
4   Talmud Bavli, Shabbat 132a.

Chapter Eighteen: Number Seven

Sources: Menachem Mendel, Sepuray
HaChag: Chanukah, Yerushalayim,
Defus HaNachal, 1983.
1   Torah u'gedulah b'makom echad:
    Torah and greatness in one place."
    Talmud Bavli, Gitin 59a.
2   Judaica Encyclopedia.
3   Philip Ziegler, The Black Death,
    London, William Collins Sons &
    Co. Ltd., 1969, Wolfeboro Falls, New
    Hampshire, Alan Sutton Publish-
    ing, Inc., 1991.
4   Will Durant, The Story of Civiliza-
    tion: Part VI, N.Y., Simon & Schuster,

1957, and Ziegler, op. cit. I.

5   Ziegler, op. cit., and Durant op. cit.

Chapter Nineteen: Netilat Yadayim

Source: According to our tradition, Rebbe Shalom Rokeach, the first Belzer Rebbe, saw the "Diary of the City of Cracow." He told this story to his disciples and they to theirs, until it has come down to us today.

1   Pope Sixtus IV, 1474-1484.

2   Sh'mot, Exodus 20:17-21. The subtopics under the laws of sacrifices include the laws of the holy days, for different types of sacrifices were prescribed for each holy day, and each festival is celebrated with particular customs and rituals; Devarim, Deuteronomy 16:1-17. The laws of sacrifices are connected to the laws of prayer, since prayer substituted for sacrifice after the destruction of the Holy Temple; Hoshea 14:3 *'u'ne-shalma pa-rim sefa-tay-nu,* we shall offer prayers rather than sacrifices, Metzudat David Commentary. Prayer means to love the Lord your God and to serve Him with all your heart and all your soul; Devarim, Deuteronomy 11:14.

3   "Be just as heedful of a seemingly simple mitzva as a seemingly stringent one." Sifre, Rashi, Devarim, Deuteronomy 12:28.

Chapter Twenty: Shimon the Silent

Source: Sippurim Prager Sammlung: Judisher Legenden, R. Lowit Verlag, Wien und Leipzig, 1921.

1   Rashi, B'rayshit Genesis 23:2

Chapter Twenty One: Joselman

Sources: Dr. Marcus Lehman, Rabbi Joselman of Rosheim, Great Britain, L. Honig Sons, 1974. Reprinted, Yerushalayim/New York, Feldheim Publishers, 1982.
Eric W. Gritsch and Marc H.

Tanenbaum, Luther and the Jews, New York, Lutheran Council in the USA, 1983.
Jaroslav Pelikan, The Enduring Relevance of Martin Luther: 500 Years After His Birth, New York, The New York Times Magazine, September 18, 1983.

1   Rosemary Radford Ruether. Faith and Fratricide : The Theological Roots of Anti-Semitism. New York. Seabury Press. 1974.

2   Johann Pfefferkorn,1469-1521.

3   "Judenspiegel," "Osterbuch," and "Judenfeind."

4   Johann Reuchlin, 1455-1522.

5   Rabbi Ovadiah Sforno, 1470-1550.

6   See Chapters 10, 11, 12 for their stories.

7   written 1523.

8   written 1543.

Chapter Twenty Two: The Golem

Source: Yisrael Klapholtz, Hachozrim B'Teshuvah, Bnai Brak, Hotzaat Pa'er Hasayfer, 1981.
M.Z. Porush, HaGolem MePrague, Tel Aviv. Pa'er Publishing Company, 1955.
R. Lowit Verlag, Sippurim Prager Sammlung: Judisher Legenden, Wien und Leipzig, 1921. (This book is an anthology of stories about the Prague ghetto.)

1   Rabbi Zechariah Fendel, Challenge of Sinai, New York, Rabbi Jacob Joseph School Press, 1978.

2   Reuben Alcalay, The Complete Hebrew English Dictionary, Tel Aviv. Massadah Publishing Co, 1965.

3   Tehillim, Psalms 128:6

Chapter Twenty Three: Diary

Source: Marvin Lowenthal, trans, The Memoirs of Gluckel of Hameln, New York. Schocken Books, 1977.

1   Thirty Years' War, 1618-1648.

2   Talmud Bavli, Shabbat 127a.

3   The olive plant is a metaphor for the

blessings of children. Tehillim, Psalms 128:3

[4] Medlar is a small tree in the rose family. It grows in Europe and Asia, and bears brown fruit, shaped like small apples. The fruit is edible only after it begins to decay.

[5] The Jerusalem Post, International Edition, Week Ending February 29, 1992, describing the exhibit devoted to 1,000 years of Jewish communal life in the Alsace region of Germany, at the Israel Museum, Yerushalayim.

[6] Vayikra, Leviticus 19:18

[7] Quoted in the name of Shammai, Pirkei Avot 1:15

[8] January 11, 1689.

— The Sephardic Experience —

Introduction
[1] I Melachim, I Kings 10:22
[2] Yonah, Jonah 1:3

Chapter Twenty Four: Connections

Sources: Eliyahu Ashtor, The Jews of Moslem Spain, Vol. I, Philadelphia, The Jewish Publication Society, 1973.

Norman A. Stillman, The Jews of Arab Lands: A History and Source Book, Philadelphia, The Jewish Publication Society, 1979.

[1] Because of the various translations of the correspondence that was preserved, many versions of this story exist. Nevertheless, the details are basically the same and serve as an important information document. Rabbi Yehuda HaLayvi (1075-1141) spent twenty years writing the Kuzari, a philosophic work using the literary framework of the Khazar king discussing religious differences with the Christian cleric and the Moslem theologian. The Kuzari attempts to prove the superiority of Judaism in a dialogue between the king and the Jew, whom he invites to teach him.

Chapter Twenty Five: Reminiscence

Sources: Franz Kobler, Letters of the Jews Through the Ages, Two Volumes, A Self Portrait of the Jewish People, East and West Library (Subsidiary of the Hebrew Publishing Co.), 1952.

Nathaniel Kravitz, Three Thousand Years of Hebrew Literature, Chicago, The Swallow Press, 1972.

Norman A. Stillman, The Jews of Arab Lands: A History and Source Book, Philadelphia, The Jewish Publication Society, 1979.

[1] See Chapter Ten: A Tale of Two Wives.

[2] See Chapter Nine: The Journey of the Four Captive Rabbis.

Chapter Twenty Six: Disputation

Sources: Aviezer Burstein, Gedolay Dayah, Tel Aviv. Zioni Publishing House, 1963.

Rabbi Charles B. Chavel, translator, Ramban (Nachmadies): The Disputation at Barcelona, New York, Shilo Publishing House, 1983.

Rabbi Charles B. Chavel, commentator, Ramban: Commentary on the Torah, , B'rayshit, Genesis, New York, Shilo Publishing House, 1971.

Rabbi Joseph Telushkin, Jewish Literacy, New York, William Morrow & Co., 1991.

Video, The Disputation at Barcelona: A Theological Debate Between Christians and Jews, Written by Hyam Macoby, Produced by Jenny Reeds for B.B.C.

[1] The reference is from a Midrashic work, not the Talmud. The source is Aycha Rabba (Lamentations Rabba) 1:51.

[2] Yeshayahu, Isaiah 2:4

Chapter Twenty Seven: Women

Sources: B. Netanyahu, Don Isaac Abravanel: Statesman and Philosopher, Philadelphia, The Jewish Publication Society, 1953.

Sh'moneh Seforim, Bayt Pinchas, Bul-

garia 1913, Reprinted in New York, 1983.

[1] Sultan Muhammad II, 1451-1481.

[2] Quoted in Judaica from M. Lattes. Likkutim de-Vei Eliyahu.

[3] Sultan Bayazid II, 1481-1512.

[4] Quoted in Judaica from Aboab, Nomologia, 195.

[5] Sh'mot, Exodus 1:15

[6] B'rayshit, Genesis 18:6

[7] B'rayshit, Genesis 24: 65, 67, commentary of Rashi.

[8] B'rayshit, Genesis 29:25, in his commentary, Rashi explains "When Rachel saw that Laban was about to bring Leah to Jacob for the marriage ceremony, she taught her sister all of Jacob's secrets, so that she would not be shamed."

Chapter Twenty Eight: Kol Nidrei

Source: Menachem Mendel, Otzar Hachag: Yom Kippur, Yerushalyaim, 1985.

[1] Otzar Yisrael

[2] Thomas de Torquemada, d.1498.

[3] Devarim, Deuteronomy 6:4

Chapter Twenty Nine: Conversos

Sources: Brayer, Menachem, The Jewish Woman in Rabbinic Literature, Hoboken, New Jersey, Ktav Publishing House, 1986.

Mendel, Menachem, Sepuray HaChag: Rosh Hashana, Yerushalayim, Defus Hanachal, 1983.

This story was printed in Our Story: The Jews of Sepharad, Annette Labovitz and Eugene Labovitz, New York, CAJE special Publication, 1991.

[1] Beatrice de Luna, Channa, Dona Gracia, 1510-1569.

[2] Miriam, Devorah and Esther were three of the seven prophetesses. The other four were Sara, Channa, Avigail and Chulda.

Chapter Thirty: Columbus

Sources: Menachem Mendel, Otzar HaChag, Succot, Yerusahlayim, Defus Hanachal, 1984.

This story was printed in Our Story: The Jews of Sepharad, Annette Labovitz and Eugene Labovitz, New York, CAJE Special Publication, 1991.

[1] August 1, 1492.

[2] Tehillim, Psalms 130:1,2,30

[3] Tehillim, Psalms 118:29

Chapter Thirty One: Why?

Sources: Yaakov Yisrael HaKohen Byfus, Kuntres Zeh Yenachamenu, Sayfer Yalkut Lekach Tov, Kefar Chassidim, Israel, Tashber HaRav, 1990.

This story was printed in Our Story: The Jews of Sepharad, Annette Labovitz and Eugene Labovitz, New York, CAJE Special Publication, 1991.

[1] Rabbi Yitzchak ben Shlomo Luria (1534-1572), father of Lurianic Kabbalah, taught that man on earth is the counterpart of the creative processes on high.

Lurianic Kabbalah is permeated with the Jewish national and Messianic mission, and the doctrine of fixing the world through mitzvot and prayer. The "fixing" leads to perfection which will then be followed by redemption.

[2] Kohelet, Ecclesiastes 3:4

[3] Sanhedrin 4:3

Complete index is in Volume Two

Volume I

of

A SACRED TRUST

Stories of Jewish Heritage and History

is our way of contributing to

Jewish Cultural Literacy

Volume II

(Publication Date: Pasach/Passover, 1995)

will complete this portrait
of our precious heritage.

We will have followed the stories
of our ancestors, beginning
with our exile from *Eretz Yisrael*
through our experiences in the Diaspora,
to our return to *Eretz Yisrael*
and the modern State of Israel.

Order today from the publisher for $18.
Offer includes Postage and Handling!

Send your name and address to the:
Isaac Nathan Publishing Co., Inc.
22711 Cass Avenue, Woodland Hills, CA 91364

Be sure to send your name, address, and ZIP.
Indicate how many copies you want and
whether they are Volume I or Volume II.

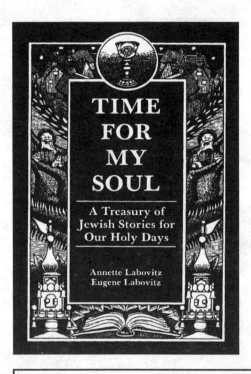